THE Squadron Boating Course

Fundamental Boating Education
for the Power and Sail Boater

**The United States
Power Squadrons®**

Printed in the United States of America
United States Power Squadrons
1504 Blue Ridge Road
PO Box 30423
Raleigh NC 27622-0423
919-821-9281
Fax: 919-836-0813
1-888-FOR-USPS (367-8777)
www.usps.org

This publication is designed to provide general information on boating safety, piloting, and navigation. It was prepared by United States Power Squadrons and its members, and is sold with the understanding that professional nautical services are not being provided. Do not use this publication as a substitute for original sources of nautical information, including government publications, rules, regulations, laws, and manufacturers' recommendations, where appropriate. The subject matter of this publication is likely to become outdated over time, and may have changed since our last publication date. Consequently, you must research original sources of authority to update this material and ensure accuracy when dealing with specific "on the water" conditions or boating problems.

040415E119965

Contents

Illustrations

Tables

Acknowledgements

United States Power Squadrons acknowledges and thanks the following organizations for their assistance in checking facts and providing technical information and advice throughout the project resulting in this text

American Red Cross
American Water Ski Association
Charters West, Gonder's Rules of the Road, Budd E. Gonder
Connecticut Department of Environmental Protection, Boating Division
E.S. Ritchie & Sons, Marine Compasses
Maptech, Inc.
National Marine Manufacturers Association
National Oceanic & Atmospheric Administration,
National Ocean Service, Charting & Mapping Division
Nautical Software, Inc.
Personal Watercraft Industry Association
Underwriter's laboratories, Marine Department
United States Army Corps of Engineers

United States Coast Guard Infoline
United States Coast Guard, Survival Systems Branch

The contents of this text, including Section 16, Personal Watercraft Operation, have been approved by the National Association of State Boating Law Administrators and recognized by the United States Coast Guard as acceptable to the national Recreational Boating Safety Program.

1

You Are the Skipper!
What Would You Do?

1 This introductory section provides brief examples of just a few of the important topics relating to boating safety that we will study in this course.

2 We invite you to join a classroom discussion of how to handle these safety-related situations. Draw on your own boating experiences or just plain common sense.

Situation 1:
Falling Overboard

3 Have you ever been onboard a boat when someone accidentally fell overboard? What happened?

**Figure 1
Falling Overboard Without a PFD**

4 You are skippering a boat when one of your passengers falls overboard.

5 What would you do?

6 Why do people fall overboard?

7 How can falling overboard be prevented?

Situation 2:
Fire Onboard

8 Have you ever seen or read about a boat catching fire or blowing up? This is an all-too-common occurrence, resulting in personal injury and property damage.

**Figure 2   Fire Onboard With the
Extinguisher in a Bad Location**

9 What would you do if you had a fire on your boat?

10 What do you think are the main causes of boat fires?

11 How can fires on a boat be prevented?

Figure 3   Restricted Visibility

Situation 3:
Restricted Visibility

12 Have you ever been out on the water when a thick fog rolls in, completely encompassing your boat, as shown above?

13 You are out cruising when a dense fog overtakes you.

14 What should you do?

15 What should you not do?

Figure 4   Same View as Figure 3, Unrestricted Visibility

Situation 4:
Vessel Priority

16 Have you ever been in close proximity to other boats and wonder what you're supposed to do?

17 You are operating your sailboat under sail only (no engine running) in a narrow channel. You appear to be on a collision course with a large ferryboat coming toward you.

18 What do the Navigation Rules require of each boat?

Situation 5:
Adequate Boat Equipment

19 Having the right equipment onboard is a part of operating your boat safely.

20 You've just purchased an 18-foot runabout.

21 What equipment do you think you should have on board? Name the items.

2

Boat Terms and Types

1 Boating has developed its own special language. It may sound strange to you, but it is practical and part of the fun of learning about boating. Terms described in this chapter and throughout the course should become a part of your boating vocabulary. Sooner or later, every boater tells about another boat: one in distress, one for sale, one operated recklessly, or just a pretty boat. The ability to recognize and describe basic types and styles of boats is an important part of your boating knowledge.

2 Upon completion of this chapter, you should:
- be able to use and understand the special language associated with boats and boating
- be familiar with the materials used in constructing boats
- recognize the various types of boat hulls and styles available in recreational boats
- be acquainted with types of power systems that move boats through the water
- understand the factors in boat design that make a boat seaworthy
- know what to look for when selecting a boat

Figure 5   Parts of a Boat

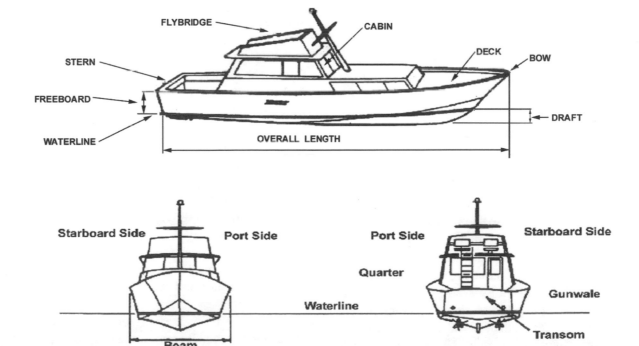

Boat Terms

3 Special terms describe the size and dimensions of boats, their parts and equipment, and directions when you are on board.

Boat Parts and Features

4 The *hull* is the basic structure and shell of a boat. The main lower centerline structural part of a hull is the *keel*. The forward end of a boat is the *bow*, while the after end is the *stern*. The after part of the side of a boat is the *quarter*. A *transom* is the stern portion of the hull. The upper edge or rail of a boat is the *gunwale* (pronounced "gun'l"), derived from the "gun walls" of ancient ships.

5 The floor of a boat is the *sole*. The *deck* of a boat is the portion that covers the hull. The *bilge* is the lowest part of the inside of a boat. A *cabin* is an enclosed living space on a boat. A *flying bridge* is a raised steering position on a powerboat, usually above the regular steering station. *Cockpits* are sunken spaces below the gunwale line, usually towards the stern portion of the boat. Beds on a boat are called *berths*. A *head* is a marine toilet. A *galley* is a nautical kitchen.

6 A *rudder* is a moveable board under the boat, used to steer the boat. It is attached to a *rudder post*. A *tiller* is attached to the upper end of the rudder post and used to turn the rudder. The *helm* is a steering wheel or tiller with its related gear.

Dimensions of a Boat

7 *Length overall* (LOA) is the most common term used to describe the size of a boat. It is measured from the forward part of the bow to the after part of the stern. It does not include attachments that are not part of the hull, although bow pulpits and swim platforms that are molded into the hull become part of the overall length of a boat. *Beam* is the maximum width of the boat. *Draft* is the depth of the boat underwater. *Freeboard* describes the distance from the water's surface to the lowest part of the gunwale or transom.

Direction on a Boat

8 *Forward* is the direction toward the bow; *aft* is toward the stern. Facing the bow, the right side of the boat is *starboard*; the left side is *port*.

Sailboat Terms

9 Most of the terms defined above refer to all boats. However, sailboats have special equipment. We will describe some of it here.

10 Sailboats differ from powerboats in two ways:
1) the basic power to move sailboats comes from sails and the wind
2) sailboats usually have a large underwater extension of the hull called a keel or centerboard

11 **Spars** are poles that support the sails. The *mast* is an upright spar on which sails are set. A *boom* is a horizontal spar used to hold the bottom of a sail.

12 **Sails.** The *mainsail* (pronounced "mains'l") is the boat's principal sail. It is set aft of the *mainmast*. Sails flown forward of the mainmast are *headsails*. (A *jib sail* is a typical headsail.)

13 **Standing Rigging.** *Stays* are wire lines that support a mast fore and aft. There are *forestays* and *backstays*. (Some sailboats have only a forestay.) *Shrouds* are wire lines that support a mast from side to side. A *chainplate* is a metal strap fastened to a boat to which shrouds and stays are attached.

14 Stays and shrouds are collectively called *standing rigging*. Tension-adjusting devices

called *turnbuckles* are used to tighten standing rigging.

15 **Running Rigging.** The lines used to raise, set, and trim sails are called *running rigging*.

16 **Sailboat Hulls.** The keel on a sailboat is a downward extension of its hull. It helps to keep the boat more stable relative to the forces of the wind and water. It reduces the boat's tendency to heel (lean to one side) and drift sideways.

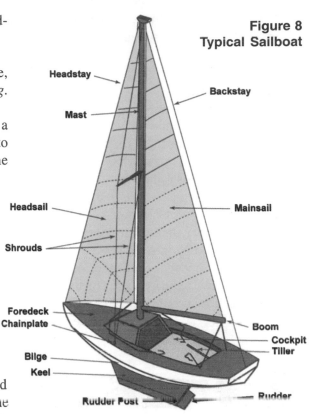

**Figure 8
Typical Sailboat**

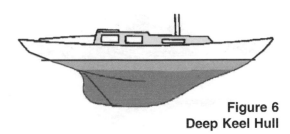

**Figure 6
Deep Keel Hull**

17 A *centerboard* is a hinged board lowered through a slot in the hull that performs the same functions as a keel. If not hinged, it is called a *daggerboard*.

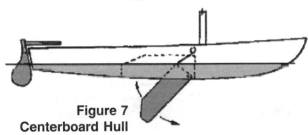

**Figure 7
Centerboard Hull**

18   There are sailboats that have combination centerboards and keels. A centerboard that extends through the keel (often referred to as a *swing* keel) can be raised when in shallow water.

Types of Watercraft

19 Boat builders use a variety of materials. The number of styles, designs, models, and sizes can be bewildering to a person shopping for a first boat. Choosing the right boat is the first step in enjoying boating.

Construction Materials

20 There is probably no such thing as an ideal material for boatbuilding. Wood was used in building boats for hundreds of years; it was easy to work with, plentiful, and inexpensive. Unfortunately, wooden boats require a large amount of maintenance. There are still many wooden boats, and some boaters will own nothing else.

21 Most recreational boats today are built of *fiberglass*. Fiberglass is a mixture of plastic resin and glass fibers. It makes strong and relatively lightweight boats that are reasonable in cost and require little maintenance. The availability of fiberglass boats is one reason for the great popularity of boating today.

22 Other materials used in boat construction include aluminum, steel, and neoprene-coated

fabrics. Inflatable boats made from the latter are quite resistant to tears and punctures.

Powerboats

23 There are many types of powerboats, from small utility boats and inflatables to seagoing cruisers. Jet-propelled personal watercraft and runabouts are very popular recreational boats today.

24 **Utility Boats** are those originally designed for rowing. They include dinghies, flat-bottomed, and rowboats, low-freeboard jon boats (square-ended on both ends) and skiffs (pointed one end, square-ended on the other). These boats are often powered by small outboard motors, and even sails. Due to their

Figure 9   Typical Utility Boat

small size and light weight—take extreme care when using them; they can be unstable in the water. Never install an outboard engine with greater horsepower than the *Capacity Plate* limit. Doing so can cause the vessel to become very difficult to control, and be a danger to you and others around you.

25 **Inflatables** can also be used as utility boats, especially as *dinghies* (service boats for larger craft). They are stable in the water, and often powered by small outboard motors.

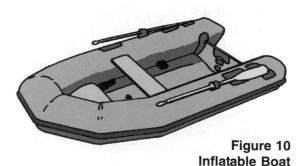

Figure 10
Inflatable Boat

26 **Runabouts** range from small, outboard-powered boats to large ocean racers capable of great speeds. They are often sporty boats with shiny surfaces, upholstered seats, and carpeting. Smaller versions usually lack cooking, sleeping, and head facilities. *Open Fishermen* are small runabouts made for fishing. Relatively easy to clean, they often have a center steering station called a *center console.*

Figure 11
Runabout

27 **Cruisers** are quite seaworthy and offer more accommodations. They range from 20-foot weekenders to yachts over 100 feet in length.

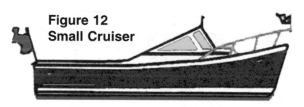

Figure 12
Small Cruiser

Cruisers usually have berths, heads, and galleys, and many rival luxury homes.

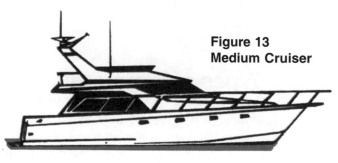

Figure 13
Medium Cruiser

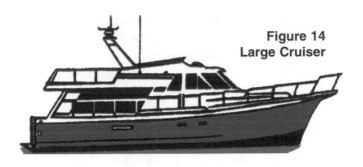

**Figure 14
Large Cruiser**

28 **Sportfishermen** are fast, high-powered small and medium cruisers that have open aft cockpits.

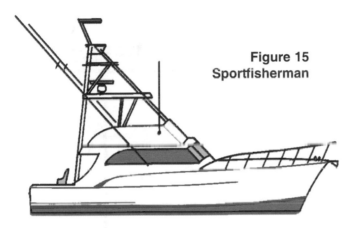

**Figure 15
Sportfisherman**

29 **Trawlers** are cruisers that emphasize comfort and convenience rather than speed. They are designed for long-range cruising.

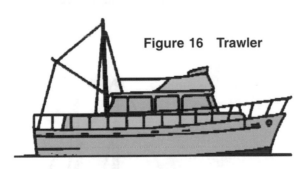

Figure 16   Trawler

30 **Houseboats** offer spacious living quarters at deck level and may have a flying bridge and sun deck above the cabin. The hull is usually shallow, broad, and flat, but sometimes has a V-bottom (explained below) or

a pontoon hull. Only use houseboats in protected waters where tall waves and strong winds will not be encountered.

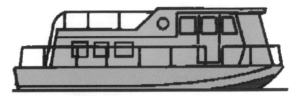

Figure 17   Houseboat

31 **Pontoon Boats** are shallow-hulled boats with a platform built on pontoons. The original pontoon boat was a wooden raft built over two rows of steel drums. Now these boats are fancy and fast, and made of fiberglass, aluminum, or steel. They are used for parties, swim platforms, and fishing on inland waters.

**Figure 18
Pontoon Boat**

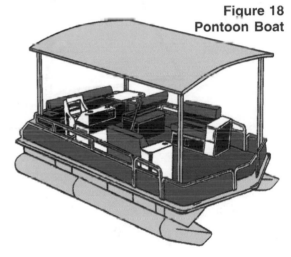

32 **Personal Watercraft and Jet Boats** use inboard engines to power a water-jet pump as the primary source of propulsion.

**Figure 19
Personal Watercraft**

33 Passengers are positioned on, rather than within, the hull of personal watercraft (sometimes called jet skis), but usually sit inside a jet boat. At high speeds, jet-drive boats are more difficult to control than other types of boats.

Sailboats

34 Sailboats come in a variety of sizes and styles. They range from small daysailers to large cruising sailboats with engines and very comfortable accommodations.

35 **Catboats** carry a single sail on a single mast. The mast is placed far forward in the boat. Catboats were used over a century ago as working fishing boats.

**Figure 20
Catboat**

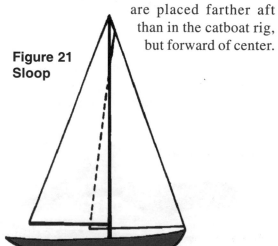

36 **Sloops** are the most popular type of sailboat. They are rigged with one mast and two sails—mainsail and headsail. Their masts are placed farther aft than in the catboat rig, but forward of center.

**Figure 21
Sloop**

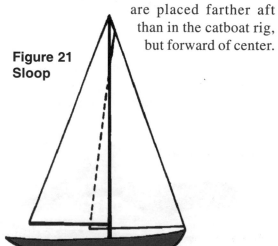

37 **Ketches and Yawls** have two masts, a mainmast and a *mizzenmast*. The latter is a shorter mast aft of the mainmast.

38 The mizzenmast on a ketch is about two-thirds the height of the mainmast and located forward of the rudder post.

**Figure 22
Ketch**

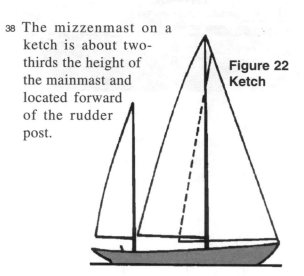

39 The mizzenmast on a yawl is approximately one-half the height of the mainmast and is located aft of the rudder post.

**Figure 23
Yawl**

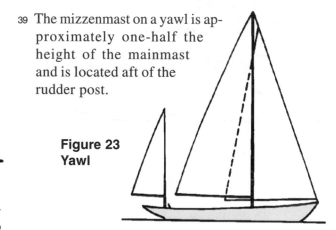

40 **Schooners** have two or more masts. The forward mast is the same height or shorter than the mainmast. Schooners are almost always medium-to-large vessels.

**Figure 24
Schooner**

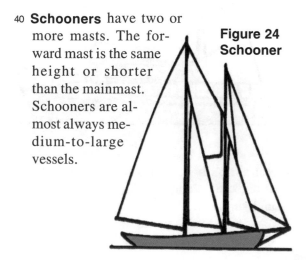

41 **Motorsailers** are combination sailboats and powerboats, with features of both. They have larger engines and smaller sails than a sailboat. They also have larger and more comfortable cabins. In motorsailers, sailing ability is often sacrificed for roominess.

42 **Multi-Hulls** have more than one hull. *Catamarans* have two narrow hulls connected by crossbeams or a deck. *Trimarans* have three hulls. Multi-hulls have a wide beam that usually provides good stability. (*Stability* is the ability of a boat to resist tipping and overturning.)

Figure 25 Catamaran

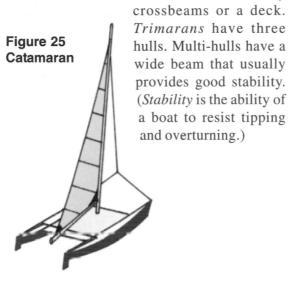

43 **Canoes and Kayaks** are very popular on inland waters. Canoes are sometimes equipped with small outboards. Relative to larger boats, both of these craft are unstable, especially in rough water. Knowledge, skill, and experience are necessary to use them safely.

Types of Hulls

44 There are two general types of hulls: *displacement* and *planing*. They are significantly different.

Displacement Hulls

45 If you lower a boat into the water, some of the water must move out of the way to make room for the boat. If you could weigh that displaced water, you would find it equals the weight of the boat. That weight is the boat's *displacement*.

Figure 26 Displacement Hull

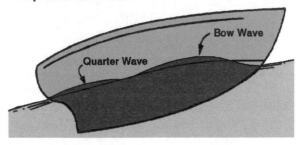

46 A *displacement hull* is one that maintains its full displacement of water whether sitting still or moving. A displacement hull pushes water aside as it moves. It will never climb onto the surface of the water.

47 Vessels with displacement hulls are limited to slower speeds. However, the longer the length of a displacement boat, the faster it will go. Many cruisers, including trawlers, and most sailboats are displacement boats.

Planing Hulls

48 *Planing hulls* climb and ride on the surface of the water when sufficient power is applied. They can skim along at high speed, riding on top of the water, rather than pushing it aside. Their displacement becomes less as their speed increases.

49 At rest, however, a planing hull sits in the water as a displacement hull. Boats with planing hulls can be rough riding, depending on hull design. Some are less stable when

Figure 27 Planing Hull

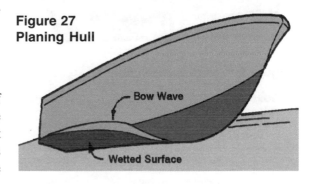

riding on top of the water. Runabouts, sportfishermen, personal watercraft, jet boats, and a few small sailboats are examples of planing vessels.

50 Many boats today combine the best features of the two basic types of hulls. They perform well at low speed as a displacement hull, and at high speed as a planing hull. These are often referred to as *semi-displacement hulls.*

Bottom Shapes

51 The bottom of a boat may be *round, flat,* or V-*shaped.* Round-bottom boats are displacement hulls, offering a slow but comfortable ride through the water. However, they tend to roll and can be unstable.

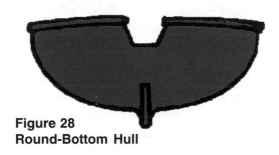

**Figure 28
Round-Bottom Hull**

52

Flat-bottom boats are the basic planing hull. They ride roughly in choppy water but are inexpensive to build.

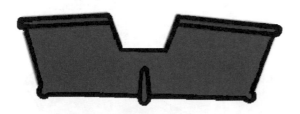

Figure 29   Flat-Bottom Hull

53 Boats with V-bottoms are variations of planing hulls that offer good stability and less pounding at high speed in rough water.

**Figure 30
Vee-Bottom Hull**

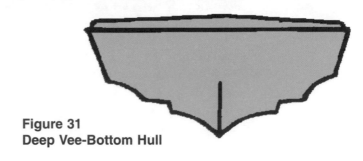

**Figure 31
Deep Vee-Bottom Hull**

54 There are boat bottoms that are combinations of two types; one type forward, gradually changing to another type toward the stern.

Drive Mechanisms

55 Most powerboats move through the water by the turning of a *propeller,* sometimes called a *screw.* Propellers are multi-bladed wheels that turn, drawing in water from ahead and pushing it out astern. *Twin-screw* boats have two engines and two propellers.

56 **Jet Drives** have no external propeller. An inboard engine powers a water pump. The pump exhausts large quantities of water under high pressure through an external jet. The force of the water pushes the boat through the water. You steer the boat by moving the jet from side to side.

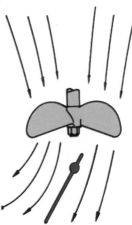

**Figure 32
Typical Propeller
and Rudder**

Figure 33   Jet Drive

Power Plants

57 There are two basic types of boat power plants: outboard motors and inboard engines.

58 **Outboard Motors** are mounted on the transom, or on special brackets on the transom. They move the boat with a propeller. The

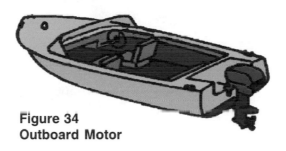

**Figure 34
Outboard Motor**

motor and its lower unit turn to steer the boat. Outboard motors usually weigh less than inboard engines, and do not take up space inside the boat; this is important in small craft. Outboards are relatively easy to detach from the boat. This makes servicing and replacement easy and less expensive.

59 Another convenience is they may be tilted up in shallow water.

60 **Inboard Engines** are installed inside the boat. They require a *shaft* (a cylindrical rod)

Figure 35   Inboard Engine

to transmit power from the engine to a propeller or water jet pump. The shaft passes through a special fitting in the hull. The fitting keeps out most of the water, while allowing the shaft to turn the propeller. The small amount of water that does enter serves to lubricate the fitting. However, the fitting should be checked frequently to ensure there is no excess leakage, for this is a major cause of boat sinking.

61 **Stern Drives,** often called *Inboard/Outboards,* or *I/Os,* operate with an inboard engine that is placed inside the boat, up against the transom. The drive shaft exits through a special fitting in the transom. Through a series of gears, shafts, and couplings, the shaft transmits its rotary motion to the propeller. The lower unit is similar to one found on an outboard motor, and may be tilted up. The boat is steered by turning the lower unit.

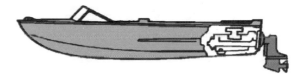

Figure 36   Stern Drive

Factors Influencing Seaworthiness

62 Three important factors affect the seaworthiness and safety of a boat:
1) size
2) design
3) construction materials

Size

63 The length and beam of a boat affect seaworthiness. Generally speaking, the longer and wider the boat, the safer it will be.

Design

64 To a degree, more freeboard increases safety. However, higher sides on a boat expose a larger surface to the wind, which can affect maneuverability.

65 The shape and size of a hull affects buoyancy, which can influence seaworthiness. For maximum stability, the greatest weight of the boat should be concentrated low in the boat.

Construction Materials

66 The stronger the materials used to construct a boat, the safer and more seaworthy it will be.

Selecting the Right Boat

67 Always plan in advance when shopping for a boat. The following are questions you should ask yourself before visiting a showroom or boatyard:

- What type and style will best serve your planned use of the boat?
- Will you be boating on open, coastal waters, or protected lakes and rivers?
- How large a boat do you need for the number of people accompanying you?
- Have you considered the operational, maintenance, and storage expense, as well as the initial expense?

68 Obtain advice from knowledgeable persons about particular brands and types of boats that interest you. Check with the USCG Customer Infoline to determine if there have been consumer complaints or safety recalls on any boat that you are interested in buying.

USCG Customer Infoline

69 Infoline operators provide callers with information on boating safety recalls and take consumer complaints about possible safety defects. They answer questions about such things as safety equipment requirements, boating safety classes, registering a boat, and completing accident reports.

70 Boaters in the United States, including Alaska, Hawaii, Puerto Rico, and the Virgin Islands, may call 1-800-368-5647 to reach Infoline. (1-800-689-0816 for the hearing impaired). Hours are 8:00 A.M. to 4:00 P.M. Eastern Standard Time, Monday through Friday, except federal holidays.

Homework

Name: _____ **Date:** _____ **Group:** _____

1. The lowest part of the inside of a boat is the:
   a. helm.
   b. cuddy.
   c. quarter.
   d. bilge.

2. The maximum width of a boat is known as the:
   a. quarter.
   b. LOA.
   c. beam.
   d. tiller.

3. The depth of water required to float a boat is known as its:
   a. beam.
   b. head.
   c. helm.
   d. draft.

4. Freeboard is the:
   a. right side of a boat when facing the bow.
   b. height of a boat's gunwale measured inside the cockpit.
   c. vertical distance from the water surface to the lowest part of the gunwale or top of the transom.
   d. provision of food and quarters for volunteer crews on ocean races.

5. Extreme care should be taken when using small utility boats such as dinghies, rowboats, jon boats, and skiffs because they:
   a. are difficult to anchor.
   b. are limited in speed.
   c. can be unstable in the water.
   d. are weak in construction, and can spring leaks easily.

6. A boat that usually has a shallow, broad, flat hull and should not be taken into exposed waters is the:
   a. sportfisherman.
   b. sailboat.
   c. cruiser.
   d. houseboat.

7. A type of boat that is more difficult to control at high speeds than other types of boats is the:
   a. jon boat.
   b. sailboard.
   c. jet drive boat.
   d. dinghy.

8. A popular sailboat that is rigged with one mast and two sails is the:
   a. catboat.
   b. schooner.
   c. sloop.
   d. ketch.

9. A displacement hull is one that:
    a. is capable of very high speeds.
    b. skims along the surface of the water.
    c. pushes water aside as it moves.
    d. may easily capsize in heavy seas.

10. The special fitting through which the
    shaft of an inboard engine passes through
    the hull should be checked frequently
    because it could:
    a. wear if it turns the wrong way.
    b. leak excessively and cause the boat
        to sink.
    c. corrode if made of a metal such as
        Monel.
    d. create sparks if made of vinyl and
        tightened too tightly.

11. Three factors affect a vessel's
    seaworthiness and safety—its design,
    material of construction, and:
    a. propulsion system.
    b. type of head.
    c. size.
    d. cockpit.

3

Marine Radiotelephone

1 The best radiotelephone system for recreational boats is the VHF radio. VHF stands for very high frequency, the part of the radio spectrum in which the system operates. Although not required equipment, a marine VHF radio can be as vital a piece of safety equipment as a life jacket or fire extinguisher. It provides 24-hour contact with the Coast Guard, communication with other boats and shore facilities for the exchange of information, and is a ready source for weather information. Future improvements will make VHF radio as useful as a home telephone.

2 VHF radios have a range of only 20–30 miles, but usually provide clear, static-free messages. Vessels cruising beyond this range will need long-range SSB (single-sideband) radiotelephone equipment.

3 Upon completion of this chapter, you should know how to:
- use a marine radio properly under routine circumstances
- use your marine radio correctly and expeditiously in an emergency
- recognize the advantages and limitations of other radio services for marine use; such as, citizens' band (CB), amateur radio, and cellular telephones

Licensing Requirements

4 You do not need a license to operate a VHF radio, radar, or EPIRB (Emergency Position Indicating Radio Beacon) on your recreational boat in U.S. waters.

5 A ship's station license issued by the Federal Communications Commission (FCC) is required if you:
- operate a boat over 65 feet (20 meters) long
- travel to foreign ports or talk to foreign stations
- use an SSB radio or International Maritime Satellite Organization (INMARSAT) equipment

6 A restricted radiotelephone operator's permit may also be necessary if you visit a foreign country. If you are required to have a license, it must be on board and available for inspection whenever you are underway. For information about licenses and fees, contact the FCC Customer Assistance Hotline, 1-888-225-5322.

Operating Procedures

7 Marine radiotelephone regulations change often due to new technologies and the ever-increasing use of VHF radio. The FCC constantly updates regulations in an effort to make better use of the frequencies. The Radio/Technical Chairman of your local USPS squadron will be aware of the latest developments in FCC rules.

8 You may legally use a marine radio for only four types of communication:
   1) distress
   2) safety
   3) operational
   4) public correspondence

9 **Distress Communications** include calls relating to danger to life and property.

10 **Safety Communications** include safety bulletins, weather warnings, and talking with other boaters to avoid collision.

11 **Operational Communications** include calls relating to navigational information, and to arrange for such things as supplies, accommodations, repairs, and meeting other vessels.

12 **Public Correspondence Communications** are calls made through a marine radiotelephone operator that connect a boat's radio to the shore public telephone network. As of June 2003, this service is no longer available on VHF radio; see page 19, Public Correspondence Channels, for further details. However, high seas Public Correspondence on SSB radio continues to be available.

Listen to Channel 16

13 The Navigation Rules state that if you have your radio on when underway, you must tune it to Channel 16, the international distress, safety, calling channel. In some Coast Guard districts, Channel 09 has been designated as the recreational boating calling channel. Check with local boaters, marina operators, launch ramp supervisors, or boating law enforcement officials in the area where you plan to operate your boat to learn what channel to use for calling and monitoring for urgent marine information.

14 Your safety and that of fellow boaters depends on someone hearing a call for assistance. Listening to this channel ensures that a large number of boats will hear an emergency call.

Special Words

15 The use of special *procedural words* makes messages clearer and shorter. However, both the sender and listener must learn to use them properly. Examples are:

> *Affirmative:* You are correct

> *Negative:* No

> *Out:* I am through talking, and I do not expect you to reply

> *Over:* I am through talking, and I expect you to reply

> *Roger:* I received your last call OK

16 Never use "10" Codes on VHF radio. These are codes sometimes used by police departments and CB radio operators.

Emergency Calls

17 There are three emergency signals that have priority on any VHF channel (especially Channel 16).

18 **The Distress Signal: Mayday.** This is a call to ask for assistance if there is immediate danger to life or property. It has priority over all other radio calls. Use a Mayday call for life-threatening medical emergencies or if your boat is sinking or on fire.

19 A Mayday situation can be hectic. A partially completed Distress Communication Form will be of great help in making an organized distress call in a time such as this. A copy of this form is on page 22.

Choosing the Correct Channel

20 Recreational boaters may legally use only a few of the many channels available. The following channels are those designated for recreational boating use:

Communication Purpose	Channel Numbers	Description
Distress, Safety, and Calling	16	A required channel on all VHF radios. For ship-to-ship and ship-to-coast communications. Used for distress calls and for initial contact with other vessels or shore stations. Channel 16 is monitored by the Coast Guard as well as harbormasters, marinas, fuel docks, and other shore stations. After contact on this channel, you must switch to a working channel for your communication.
Coast Guard Liaison and Maritime Safety Information	22A	Used for contact with Coast Guard ship, coast, and aircraft stations after first establishing communications on Channel 16.
Ship to Coast & Ship to Ship "Calling Channel"	09	For communications with marinas and public docks and for contacting commercial vessels about matters of common concern. Channel 9 is also a nationwide alternative calling channel for non-commercial vessels, supplementing Channel 16.
Ship to Ship and Ship to Coast "Working Channels"	68, 69, 71, 72, 78	For use after initial contact on a calling channel. Channel 72 is a ship-to-ship working channel only. (In the Great Lakes area, channels 79 and 80 are also working channels for recreational boats, but share these with commercial traffic. In Puget Sound and the Straits of Juan de Fuca, recreational vessels may also use Channel 67 as a working channel, sharing this channel with commercial vessels.)
Intership Safety	06	Required on all VHF radios. Used only for safety-oriented communications such as the avoidance of collision, and for search and rescue.
Port Operations	12, 14, 20, 66, 73, 74	For use by facilities directing the movement of vessels in or near ports, locks, and waterways.
Bridge to Bridge Navigation Safety	13	For contacting other vessels about meeting and passing situations and talking with locks and bridges. You must use low power except in an emergency.
Distress, Safety, General Purpose	70	For boats equipped with Digital Selective Calling (DSC) equipment. Voice communications are illegal. (When fully implemented, all VHF radios will be DSC compatible. A DSC transceiver can send information to other DSC receivers with the sender's ID, position, nature of distress, and contact channel.)

Table 1   Radiotelephone Channels For Recreational Boaters

21 You will need the following information if you make a Mayday call:
   1) an accurate location of your boat
   2) a good description of your boat
   3) the number of people on board
   4) a description of the problem

22 **The Urgency Signal: Pan-Pan** (pronounced *pahn-pahn*) is used when there is a threat to the safety of a person or boat, but the threat is not as serious as in a Mayday call. Examples are:
   • loss of a person overboard
   • running out of fuel
   • losing your way in a fog
   • getting entangled in fishing gear
   • unable to control or operate your vessel

23 Prepare a Distress Communication Form in advance to help you with this type of call.

24 **Safety Signal: Security.** (Pronounce this *say-cure-it-tay*.) Use this signal for navigation safety messages. You'll hear it used with:
   • weather alerts
   • operational signals (such as when a boat is backing out of a slip or approaching a blind bend)
   • reports of navigational hazards; for example, a partially sunken object in a busy channel

25 The necessary information needed when calling the Coast Guard is listed on a Vessel Information Sheet. Copy the form shown on page 22. Prepare it in advance and post it and a Distress Communication Form near your radio.

26 **Responding to an Emergency Call.** Unless you are in a position to help, do not use your radio on a channel being used for an emergency until you hear a Silence Fini (pronounced *see-lawnce feenee*) all-clear announcement.

27 If you do not hear the Coast Guard reply to an emergency call, and you feel you are close to the vessel in distress, call the distressed vessel. Give your vessel name three times, and speak the words Received Mayday. Then allow a short time for other stations to acknowledge receipt of the message.

28 If you are in a position to assist, and are certain you will not interfere with other distress-related calls, contact the vessel in distress and explain what help you can offer. Meanwhile, make every effort to contact the Coast Guard.

Routine Calls

29 A VHF radio has a low/high power switch to increase power from 1 watt to 25 watts for longer range transmissions. Low power (1 watt) is enough for most communications. If you use low power, you will be less apt to interfere with the calls of other vessels. To make a routine call to another boat:

30 Listen on the calling channel (Channel 16 or 09) for 30 seconds to be sure you will not interfere with a conversation already in progress. If you do not do this, you can destroy the value of two calls; your own and the message of another boat.

31 If the channel is clear, push down the talk button on your microphone. Hold the microphone one inch from your mouth and slowly call the name of the other boat in a normal tone of voice:

   "Annie this is Queen"

32 Always start a broadcast with the name of the boat you are calling and the name of your boat. Repeat the name of the boat you are calling two or three times if necessary. This first call should not exceed 30 seconds. If you do not make contact, wait at least two minutes before repeating the call. Repeat this procedure no more than three times. If you do not make contact during this period, wait 15 minutes before making your next try.

"Queen this is Annie, Reply 68"

33 Annie has responded with instructions to switch to Channel 68, one of the working channels.

Queen responds: "68" or "Roger"

34 Roger means "I received your last call OK." Both vessels then switch to Channel 68.

Queen on 68: "Annie"

Annie on 68: "Queen"

35 Continue with your message. Think before you speak and make your message simple. It must be about your boat's business and no longer than three minutes in length. Chit-chat is not permitted.

36 Each boat then acknowledges completion of the call and returns to the calling frequency:

"Queen Out"

"Annie Out"

Radio Checks

37 The best way to obtain a check on the operation of your radio is to call another boat. After contact, shift to a working channel and ask how they hear you. Only ask for a radio check from the Coast Guard as a last resort.

NOAA Weather Radio Channels

38 **WX ChannelFrequencies(MHz)**

WX Channel	Frequencies (MHz)
WX–1	162.550
WX–2	162.400
WX–3	162.475
WX–4	162.425
WX–5	162.450
WX–6	162.500
WX–7	162.525

39 Channels WX–1, WX–2, WX–3, WX–4, WX–5, WX–6, and WX–7 offer around-the-clock broadcasts of the latest weather information. Taped weather messages are repeated every 4–6 minutes and updated several times a day; more often when unusual weather develops. The Environment Canada Weather Department uses WX–1, WX–2, and WX–3. Canada also provides continuous marine weather coverage on channels 21B or 83B (put radio in international mode) which also shows up on WX–8 (161.650 MHz) or WX–9 (161.775 MHz) on many newer marine VHF radios.

Public Correspondence Channels

40 VHF Channels 24, 25, 26, 27, 28, 84, 85, 86, 87, and 88 were originally set aside by the FCC for boaters to contact public correspondence stations. Through these stations, the VHF radio became a part of the commercial telephone system and boaters could make telephone calls to or from any telephone on shore or to another boat. However, with the recent increase in the use of cellular telephones by boaters, the use of public correspondence stations has become so light that the operation of this system is no longer commercially feasible. As of 6 June 2003, all of the VHF public correspondence stations have ceased operation; and the operating company, MariTEL Marine Communications, is seeking other uses for the channels, which have been set aside for that function.

Prohibited Communications

41 Boat owners are responsible for the proper use of their radios. Improper use can result in substantial penalties.

42 It is a criminal offense to use profane or indecent words, language, or meaning on a radio.

43 Do not allow children to use your marine radio: it is not a plaything.

44 Making a false Mayday or any phony call to the Coast Guard is a felony. These calls cost time and money and have tied up emergency channels resulting in the loss of life. Special equipment is now being used to put an end to these abuses.

Handheld VHF Radios

45 Boaters often use handheld VHF radios on small craft such as runabouts and daysailers. However, it is illegal for a recreational boater to use a marine VHF radio on shore. This includes handheld radios and radios installed in trailerable boats. Use radiotelephones only on the water.

Other Radio Services

46 CB radio, amateur radio, and cellular telephones may all be used on a boat, but do not replace a VHF radio.

CB Radio

47 A CB radio is inexpensive and useful in relieving the VHF band. For example, use a CB radio for casual communications between boats traveling together on a cruise. Do not use a CB radio in an emergency unless there is no operable marine radio aboard. The Coast Guard does not monitor CB radio calls and a CB radio has very limited use as a safety radio.

Amateur Radio

48 An Amateur Radio Operator's License is needed to use an amateur radio. You can use it in addition to regular VHF radio in an emergency and in long-range communications. The Coast Guard does not monitor amateur radio channels. Never consider amateur radio a replacement for marine radio.

Cellular Telephones

49 Cellular telephones are popular for land communications. Even on small lakes and rivers, they may be useful for contacting local law authorities. However, their value at sea is severely limited. They cannot provide direct contact with Coast Guard vessels or aircraft, eliminating your ability to communicate directly with rescue craft.

50 There are other factors that also reduce the value of a cellular telephone. Other boats that may be in a position to help you cannot hear emergency telephone calls. Cellular phones don't produce radio signals upon which Coast Guard radio-directional-finding equipment can "home in" or determine your boat's position. A cellular phone transmits with 3 watts of power, versus 25 watts for VHF radios. This further limits their usefulness in emergencies.

51 Thus, depending upon a cellphone rather than a VHF radio to relay information may be catastrophic in a severe emergency.

VHF Radio is Best

52 A boater's best method of communication with the Coast Guard is VHF radio. The Coast Guard monitors Channel 16 twenty-four hours a day. In a distress situation, using Channel 16 for a Mayday not only alerts emergency dispatchers, such as marine police and the Coast Guard, but all other vessels within range. Quite often the boat nearest an emergency is another recreational vessel; police and Coast Guard units may be miles away.

53 In addition to hearing your call, rescue services can "home in" on your VHF signal. These services are not available when you substitute a CB, amateur radio, or cellular telephone for a VHF radio.

Marine Radiotelephone Information

54 Advanced courses in marine electronics, such as the USPS Marine Electronics course, address the use of marine radiotelephone in detail. The Radio Technical Commission for Maritime Services (RTCM) publishes a Marine Radiotelephone User's Handbook. Copies are available from the RTCM at PO Box 19087, Washington, DC 20036.

Emergency Position Indicating Radio Beacon (EPIRB)

55 There are two types of EPIRB systems currently in use on recreational boats today. The older units transmit an analog signal on 121.5 MHz. The newer type transmits a digital identification code on 406 MHz and a low-power "homing" signal on 121.5 MHz. Once activated, either automatically or manually, the 406 MHz EPIRB signal is instantly detected by geostationary satellites which cover most of the earth.

56 The latest 406 MHz EPIRBs incorporate a GPS receiver to provide position information. The alert is transmitted to Mission Control Centers which alert search and rescue resources nearest to the EPIRB. Those EPIRBs without the GPS feature require that low-orbiting satellites receive and localize the general region of the distress. This can take up to two hours. Once the alert is received, aircraft then "home in" on the EPIRB signal to effect the rescue. Note: the older 121.5 MHz system is being phased out over the next several years.

57 The newest technology is the INMARSAT E 1646 MHz float-free, automatically activated EPIRB, detectable by INMARSAT geostationary satellites. This system is recognized by the Global Maritime Distress and Safety System (GMDSS), but these units currently are not sold in the U.S.; however, the FCC is considering recognizing these devices.

58 **Note:** Prior to being used to summon help, the 406 MHz EPIRB must be registered with the National Oceanic and Atmospheric Administration (NOAA); the 1.6 GHz EPIRB must be registered with INMARSAT.

Vessel Information Data Sheet

When asking for assistance from the Coast Guard, you may be asked to furnish the following details. Fill out this list as completely as possible; post it alongside your transmitter with the Distress Communications Form.

1. **Identification**

   Boat Name: _____

   State Reg. No. or Documentation No.: _____

2. **Description of Vessel Requiring Assistance**

   Power or Sail: _____; Inboard _____; Outboard _____; I/O: _____

   Type of boat: (ketch, sloop, trawler, sportfisher, row boat, etc.) _____

   _____. Manufacturer/Class: _____

   Length: _____; Draft: _____; Home Port: _____

   Hull Markings (color, trim, etc.): _____

3. **Survival Gear Aboard**

   PFDs _____
   Flares _____
   Flashlight _____
   Raft _____
   Dingy or Tender _____
   Anchor _____
   Spotlight _____
   Auxiliary Power _____
   Horn _____

4. **Electronic Equipment**

   Radio(s)   VHF   MF   HF
   Channels/Freq. Available _____
   VHF Channel 22A _____
   MF–2670 kHz _____
   Radar _____
   Depth Finder _____
   Loran _____
   Direction Finder _____
   EPRIB (121.5/243 MHz) _____
   EPIRB (156.8/156.75 MHz) _____
   EPIRB (406 MHz) _____

5. **Vessel Owner/Operator**

   Name: _____

   Address: _____

   Telephone: _____ – _____ – _____

   Is owner an experienced boater?   Yes: _____; No: _____

6. Miscellaneous
   Be prepared to describe weather conditions, water depth, etc.

Distress Communications Form

Instructions: Complete this form now (except for items 6 through 9) and post near your VHF radio.

Speak *Slowly—Clearly—Calmly*

1. Make sure your radio is on.

2. Select either *VHF Channel 16 (156.8 MHz)* or *2182 kHz.*

3. Press the microphone button and say **Mayday—Mayday—Mayday.**

4. Say *This is* _____ , _____ , _____ .
   (your boat name)   (your boat name)   (your boat name)

5. Say *Mayday:* _____
   (your boat name)

6. *Tell where you are:*
   (What navigational aids or landmarks are nearby?)

7. *State the nature of your distress.*

8. *State the number of adults and children aboard, and the condition of anyone injured.*

9. *Estimate the present seaworthiness of your boat.*

10. *Briefly describe your boat:* _____ ;

    State Registration Number: _____

    Type of Boat: _____; Length: _____ feet;

    Draft: _____ feet; No. of Masts: _____; Hull Color: _____;

    Trim Color: _____; Hull Material: _____ ;

    No. Engine(s): _____
    _____
    (Anything else you think will help rescuers find you)

11. Say: *I will listen on Channel 16/2182.* (*Cross out number that does not apply.*)

12. End message by saying: *This is* _____ (boat name), *Over.*

13. Release microphone button and listen. Someone should answer.
    If they do not, repeat call, beginning at item 3. If there is still no answer, switch to another channel and begin at item 3 again.

Homework

Name: _____ **Date:** _____ **Group:** _____

1. The basic radiotelephone system for recreational boats is:
   a. cellular telephone.
   b. citizen's band.
   c. amateur radio.
   d. VHF radio.

2. The use of a VHF marine radiotelephone on a recreational boat in U.S. waters requires:
   a. an operator's examination.
   b. a FCC operator's license.
   c. no license of any kind.
   d. a FCC station license.

3. The use of a marine VHF radiotelephone on a recreational boat is restricted to:
   a. distress, safety, and operational communications on permitted channels.
   b. trivial chatter on channels 68, 69, 70, 71, 72, 78.
   c. calling the Coast Guard on channel 68 for a radio check.
   d. obtaining weather broadcasts on channels 24, 25, 26, 27, 28, 84, 85, 86, 87, 88.

4. The international distress, safety, and calling channel is:
   a. 19
   b. 16
   c. 13
   d. 9

5. Calling channels for recreational vessels to contact other vessels or shore stations are:
   a. 8 and 7
   b. 11 and 9
   c. 16 and 9
   d. 17 and 14

6. The emergency distress signal on channel 16 that requests urgent assistance for a vessel threatened with immediate danger to life or property is:
   a. Security.
   b. Mayday.
   c. Help.
   d. Pan-Pan.

7. A Distress Communication form:
   a. is required on all boats over 26 feet.
   b. should be filed with the Coast Guard before leaving on a cruise.
   c. can only be filled out by a licensed operator.
   d. will be of great help when making an organized distress call.

8. You would expect to hear _____ on channels WX–1, WX–2, WX–3, WX–4, WX–5, WX–6, WX–7:
   a. distress calls
   b. weather forecasts
   c. ship-to-ship communications
   d. time signals

9. Which of the following communications is permitted on a working channel?
   a. casual chit-chat between skippers.
   b. arranging to meet another vessel.
   c. first mates arranging the menu for an evening cocktail party
   d. children amusing themselves by calling their friends

10. You may use a hand-held VHF radio:
    a. on high power only.
    b. from shore to "mother ship".
    c. only when on the water.
    d. on low power only.

11. The following type of call is a felony and incurs stiff penalties:
    a. Security call.
    b. request for a radio check.
    c. hoax Mayday call.
    d. Pan-Pan call.

4

Knots and Lines

1 Knot tying is part of the practice of marline-spike seamanship-the general knowledge of knots and the care of rope. The term originates from a pointed metal tool, a marlinespike, used in working with rope. Every skipper needs to know how to tie at least a few basic knots.

2 Upon completion of this chapter, you should be able to:
- recognize the advantages and disadvantages of three basic types of rope
- tie four fundamental knots that should be adequate for a student's first boating needs
- coil a line properly

Definitions

3 Rope is purchased as *rope*. When you put a rope aboard a vessel it becomes a *line*. However, there are a few exceptions such as "lanyard ropes" on bells, "bolt ropes" on sails, and "tiller ropes" on tillers.

4 A line, rope, or cable has three parts:
- a *bitter end*—the inboard end made fast to the vessel
- a *working end*—the outboard end that is fastened to things
- a *standing part*—the section between the bitter end and the working end

5 A knot is a general term for securing a line to an object, another line, or to itself. A good knot is easy to tie, easy to untie, and will not slip under tension.

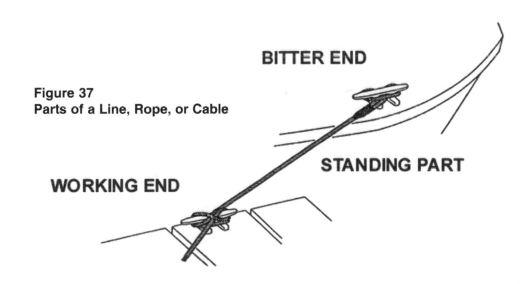

Figure 37
Parts of a Line, Rope, or Cable

BITTER END

STANDING PART

WORKING END

The Squadron Boating Course

Types of Rope

6 For many years, rope was made from natural fibers such as manila. Natural fiber rope is now obsolete for marine use. Rope made of synthetic fibers has far superior qualities. The three most common types of synthetic rope used today are nylon, polyester, and polypropylene. It is important to buy the correct rope for the use intended.

Nylon

7 Nylon rope is strong, with good resistance to chafing and rubbing. It can stretch considerably without damage to its fibers. This shock-absorbing quality makes it ideal for anchor, mooring, and dock lines.

Polyester

8 Polyester rope is sold under brand names such as Dacron® or Terylene®. It is about 10% weaker than nylon rope. However, it stretches very little and for this reason is commonly used for sailboat rigging.

Polypropylene

9 Polypropylene rope is the least costly of the synthetic ropes. It lacks the strength of nylon or polyester and is slippery, which increases the chance that a knot will not hold. Compared to the other types of rope, polypropylene deteriorates more rapidly in sunlight. A useful characteristic of polypropylene is that it floats. This reduces the risk of getting the line wrapped around a propeller, making it ideal for towing dinghies and water-skiers.

Types of Weave

10 Rope is woven in two forms:
- *laid*—the fibers are twisted into strands with three strands twisted around each other, most often in a clockwise direction

Figure 38   Three-Strand Laid Rope

- *braided*—the fibers are interwoven in a clockwise and counterclockwise fashion along the length of the rope. Braided rope generally has two parts, a hard strong core, and a softer cover

Figure 39   Two-Part Braided Rope

11 While braided rope is smoother and easier on the hands, it is more expensive and has a tendency to snag on pilings and other objects.

Figure 40   The Figure-Eight Knot

The Figure-Eight Knot

12 The figure-eight is a stopper knot.

Use This Knot to:

- tie in the end of a line to temporarily keep the line from unraveling
- keep a line from running through openings such as in grommets or blocks (grommets are metal or plastic reinforcing rings fitted into holes in cloth, canvas, etc.; blocks are nautical pulley.)

13 When the figure-eight knot is used for this purpose, it is far superior to an overhand knot because it makes a sizable knot that is easy to untie.

To Tie the Figure-Eight Knot

1) Add one more turn to an overhand knot
2) Form a loop with the working end of the line
3) Pass the small end around the standing part of the line before pulling it through the loop; when you are through, the knot will look like a figure eight

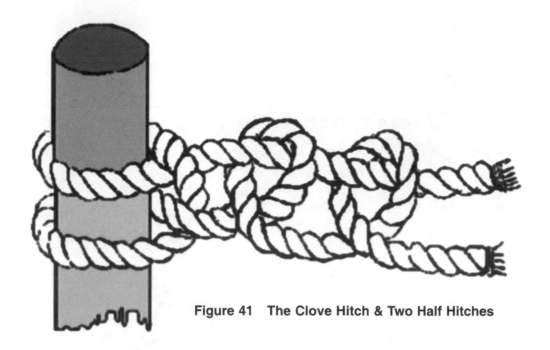

Figure 41   The Clove Hitch & Two Half Hitches

The Clove Hitch and Two Half-Hitches

14 The clove hitch and two half-hitches are easy to tie and untie. They are easily adjustable and will not slip or come undone if tied properly. The clove hitch without the half-hitches is not reliable; it can slip if not under constant tension.

Use This Knot to:

- tie a line to a post or piling
- tie a fender to a railing-it allows easy adjustment
- tie a line to a loop, grommet, or ring

To Tie the Clove Hitch and Two Half-Hitches

1) Loop the working end of the line around the object twice, in the same direction, once below the standing part of the line; once above it
2) Finish the clove hitch by passing the working end of the line between the second loop and the standing part of the line
3) Form a half-hitch by passing the free end of the line around the standing part of the line, and under itself

15 Do this once more for the second half-hitch. Always remember to secure a clove hitch with two half-hitches.

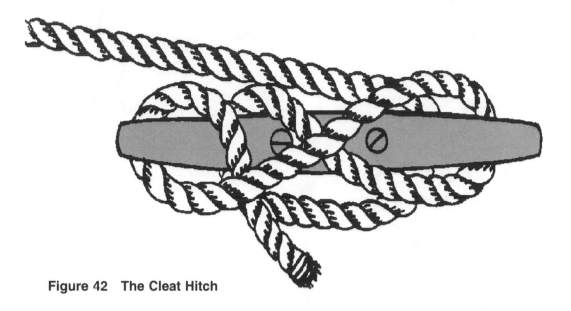

Figure 42   The Cleat Hitch

The Cleat Hitch

16 This is the simplest but most important hitch used on a boat, and involves nothing more than making a few turns of the line around the horns of a cleat. (A cleat is a fitting with two projecting horns to which lines are made fast.) You must tie it correctly or it will be hard to untie under tension. Tied correctly, the knot is easy to tie, untie, and release under load. It will not slip or come undone.

17 The following are some of the lines often fastened to a cleat with a cleat hitch:
- anchor lines
- dock lines
- mooring lines
- tow lines
- sailboat halyards

To Tie a Cleat Hitch
1) Lead the working end of the line under the horn of the cleat that is farthest from the object being fastened
2) Lead the line around the base of the cleat, so that it passes under each horn once
3) Form a figure eight around the horns of the cleat, being careful to keep the line on top of the previous turns around the horns; there is no added strength or security gained by using more than a single figure eight
4) Secure the working end with a half-hitch over the horn opposite the strain
5) When tied correctly, the working end will lead off the cleat on the opposite side from the standing part and in an opposite direction

18 When tied properly, it will be easy to release under load. Under normal circumstances it is sufficient to hold a boat to a dock. You can finish off with two half-hitches when tying off in exposed areas or where strong winds, currents, or surges are likely.

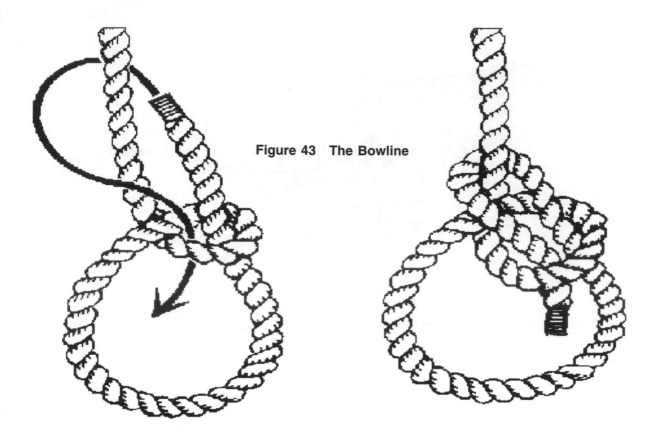

Figure 43   The Bowline

The Bowline

19 The bowline is a versatile knot that forms a secure loop in the end of a line. It has many uses on a boat. With practice it is easy to tie and untie and will not slip or jam-all of the characteristics of a good knot.

Use This Knot to:

- form a secure loop on a mooring line to place over a cleat or post
- tie a line to a fitting, such as an anchor or mooring ring
- tie together lines equal and unequal in diameter, using a bowline at the end of each line
- form a free-running noose by passing a portion of the line through a bowline loop

To Tie a Bowline

1) Make a small overhand loop, with the working end on top of the standing part of the line
2) Pass the working end up through the loop from the back, counterclockwise around behind the standing part, and back down through the loop
3) Grasp the working end and the standing part, pulling in opposite directions to tighten the bowline

20 The story of the rabbit, the hole, and the tree may help you remember the method of tying this knot. The standing part of the line is the tree. The small loop you make is the hole. The working end of the line is the rabbit. The rabbit comes up out of the hole, goes around the tree, and then goes back down into the hole.

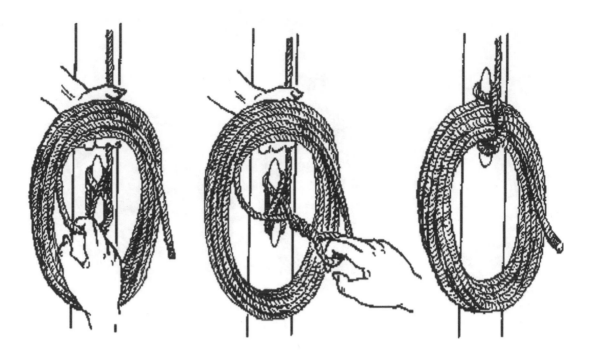

Figure 44   Coiling a Halyard After Fastening It to a Cleat

Coiling a Line

21 The lines on your boat, whether sailboat or powerboat, should be properly coiled and neatly stowed when underway.

To Coil Halyards After Fastening Them to a Cleat

22 Coil laid line with the lay. Most laid line is twisted left to right, which means coiling in that direction:
   1) Holding the line in your left hand, make equal diameter loops about two feet long with your right hand

   2) As each loop is made into the open palm of the left hand, make a quarter turn to the right with your right hand (if left-handed, reverse the hands)
   3) Hang the coil on a cleat; reach inside and pull out some slack
   4) Twist this slack line and place the twist over the cleat; this forms a sort of spring that will hold the coil in place

23 You may coil braided line without the quarter-turn twist. Since no twist is woven into the line, there is none to be removed.

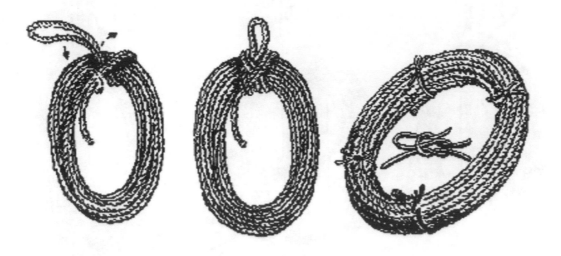

Figure 45   Coiling Spare Lines

To Coil Spare Line

24 The first two illustrations shown in Figure 45 show a good method of coiling spare line that may be needed in a moment's notice. The third illustration shows a method for longer-term storage.

Homework

Name: _____ **Date:** _____ **Group:** _____

1. When you put rope aboard a vessel it becomes:
    a. twine.
    b. cordage.
    c. line.
    d. small stuff.

2. The section of a rope, line, or cable between the bitter end and the working end is called the:
    a. loop.
    b. standing part.
    c. free end.
    d. knot.

3. A good knot is easy to tie, easy to untie, and will:
    a. look shipshape when tied.
    b. easily run through a grommet or ship's block.
    c. not slip under tension.
    d. resist chafing.

4. Nylon rope can:
    a. withstand tension without stretching.
    b. rot and deteriorate if stored wet.
    c. float on the surface of the water.
    d. stretch considerably without damage to its fibers.

5. A type of line commonly used for sailboat running rigging is:
    a. polypropylene.
    b. polyester.
    c. nylon.
    d. manila.

6. Polypropylene line is ideal for towing dinghies and water-skiers because:
    a. its dull color can't be seen.
    b. it is stronger than other types of rope.
    c. it floats on the surface of the water.
    d. it is easy on the hands.

7. A good stopper knot is the:
    a. square knot.
    b. figure eight knot.
    c. bowline.
    d. anchor hitch.

8. A good knot to use with two half-hitches to secure a line to a piling is the:
    a. cleat hitch.
    b. figure eight.
    c. stopper knot.
    d. clove hitch.

9. Tied correctly the cleat hitch is easy to tie, untie, and:
    a. release easily under load.
    b. fasten easily to a piling.
    c. tie two lines together easily.
    d. make a free-running noose.

10. A versatile knot that may be used to form a secure loop in the end of a line is the:
    a. clove hitch.
    b. figure eight knot.
    c. cleat hitch.
    d. bowline.

11. Adding two half-hitches to finish off a
    clove hitch is important because without
    them it will:
    a.   not fit over most pilings.
    b.   be difficult to untie.
    c.   not go around a cleat.
    d.   slip if not under constant tension.

5

Charts

1 Charts are exactly the opposite of road maps. Maps show you where you *can* go, but charts show you where you *cannot* go.

2 As a boater, you must always know where you are and the best way to reach your destination safely. Charts are pictures of parts of the earth's surface. They provide a variety of information to aid you in the operation of your boat. They are vital to your safe boating.

What Charts Show

3 References in this section (such as A, B, C, etc.) match the references on the Typical Chart, Figure 47.

Chart Symbols

4 Charts use symbols to show natural and man-made features of the earth's surface. *Nautical Chart No.1* is a booklet that explains the nautical terms and symbols used on National Ocean Service (NOS) charts.

Chart Colors

5 Nautical charts use four colors to describe the makeup of the earth's surface:
- *white* for deep, safe water
- *blue* for shallow water
- *green* for tidal areas covered at high water
- *gold* for dry land

Direction

6 Direction is measured in degrees from 000° to 360°, clockwise from geographic north. (Geographic north is 000° or 360°.) *Compass roses* on charts have circles marked in degrees like those on a compass. Note the compass rose on the Practice Chart in the appendix of your student manual. (The ☆ indicates geographic north.)

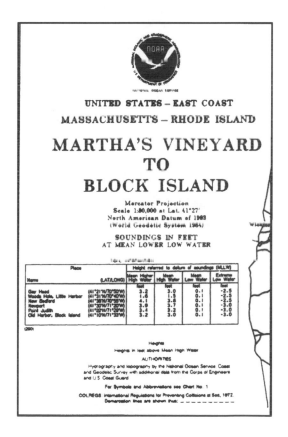

Figure 46   A Chart Title Block

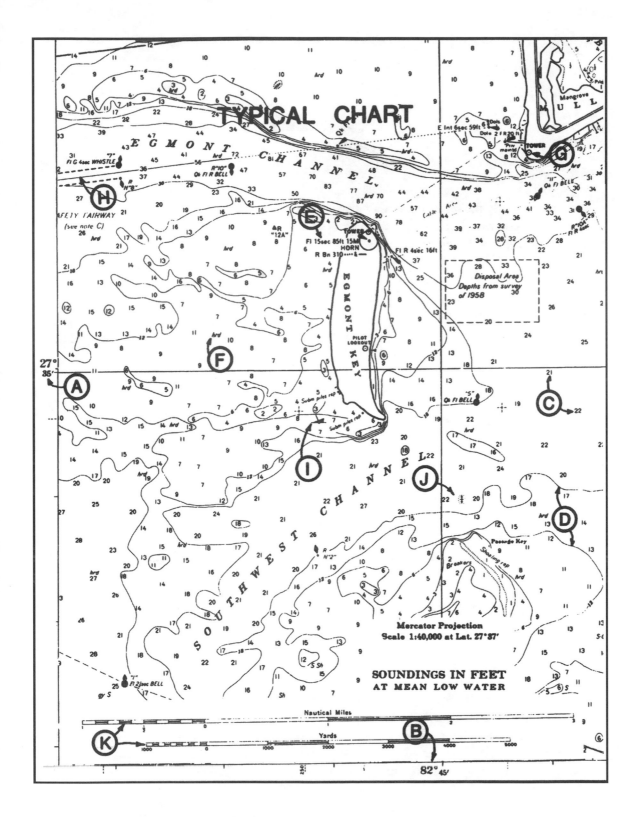

Figure 47 A Typical Chart

Depths

7   Numbers that show the depth of the water are important features of a chart. (See C, Figure 47.) Depths on charts may be in feet, meters, or fathoms. (A meter is approximately 3.3 feet; a fathom is 6 feet.) Always look in the *chart title block* for the measurement scale used. (See Figure 46.)

8   Some charts show depths at *Mean Low Water* (MLW). However, since in most locations there are two low waters each day, and one is usually lower than the other, newer charts give depths at *Mean Lower Low Water* (MLLW). The depths are an average of the lowest daily water levels over a period of time. Keep in mind that since charted depths are *averages,* there will be times when the *water depth will be even less* than that indicated.

Variation

9   The angle between the directions of geographic north and magnetic north is called *variation.* Variation changes, depending on your location. We will study variation in Chapter 9, The Mariner's Compass. You will find the angle of variation in the center of each chart's compass rose. Note the variation (15° 15′ W) in the compass rose on the Practice Chart in the appendix of this manual.

Depth Contours

10   The solid, dashed, or dotted lines connecting points of equal depth are known as *depth contours.* (See D.)

Heights of Objects

11   The heights of objects, such as lighthouses, are listed in feet above *Mean High Water* (MHW). (See E.)

Nature of the Bottom

12   When anchoring, know the type of bottom under your boat. Check *Nautical Chart No. 1* for explanations of abbreviations used to describe bottom characteristics. Hard, soft, rocky, sand, mud, clay, silt, gravel, stones, coral, shells, and seaweed are examples of types of sea beds. (See F.)

Prominent Landmarks

13   These are valuable reference points. If there is a circle around a position dot, it is an exactly located landmark and may be used for navigation purposes. A label will describe the landmark. It may be a tower, spire, church, chimney, flagpole, etc. (See G.)

Dredged Channels

14   Dredged channels appear as parallel dashed black lines. (See H.)

Marine Hazards

15   Marine hazards have a variety of symbols and abbreviations. For instance, there are different types of rocks and wrecks. Visible wrecks (See I) have a different symbol than those of sunken wrecks (See J). Asterisks (*) indicate rocks that cover and uncover with each change of tide; crosses (+) indicate rocks covered at low water.

Distance Scales

16   Distance scales are printed on many charts. (See K.) Ocean charts use nautical mile scales; Inland water and Great Lakes charts use statute mile scales. A *nautical mile* is approximately 6,076 feet: 1,852 meters: 1.15 statute miles. A *statute mile,* or land mile, is 5,280 feet or 1,609 meters. You may also find chart scales in yards and kilometers.

Vertical Clearances

17 You will frequently want to know the clearance under shore objects such as bridges and utility lines. The clearance under a bridge may determine if it is necessary to ask for an opening. Sail-boaters must always be careful to keep masts away from overhead power lines.

18 In areas where water rises and falls with tidal action, charts show vertical clearances in feet above MHW. *MHW* is the average of the highest water levels over a period of time. Keep in mind that, since these are average water heights, there will be times when the vertical clearance will be even less than that shown.

Latitude and Longitude Grid System

19 This system makes it possible to locate any point on the earth. It consists of two sets of imaginary lines on the earth's surface:

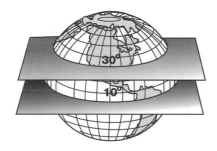

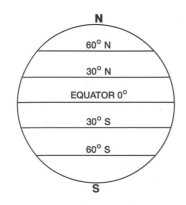

Figure 48   Parallels of Latitude

20 **Parallels of Latitude (L)** run east and west and are parallel to the equator. They are numbered from L 0° at the equator to L 90° N at the North Pole, and from L 0° at the equator to L 90° S at the South Pole. There are countless numbers of parallels of latitude—not just those at whole degrees. You describe the latitude of any position in degrees and parts of degrees, north (N) or south (S) of the equator. Since the United States is north of the equator, it is entirely in north latitude.

21 **Meridians of Longitude (Lo)** run north and south to the geographic poles. Lo 0° passes through Greenwich, England. Longitude lines are numbered east (E) from Greenwich toward Europe and Asia, or west (W) from Greenwich toward the United States from Lo 0°. There are countless numbers of meridians of longitude—not just those at whole degrees.

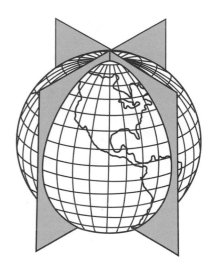

22 You describe the longitude of any position in degrees and parts of degrees, east or west of Greenwich, to a maximum of 180°. East longitude and west longitude meet at 180°, in the Pacific Ocean (the International Date Line). Almost all of the United States is in west longitude because it is west of 0° Lo.

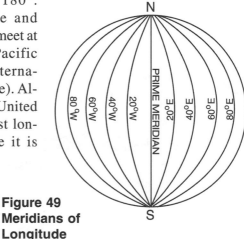

Figure 49 Meridians of Longitude

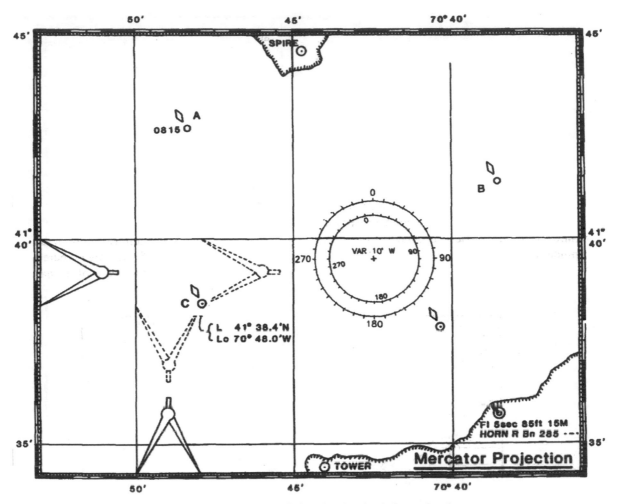

Figure 50   Determining Latitude & Longitude

23 **Latitude and Longitude Scales.** On most conventional charts, geographic north will be at the top of the chart. You will find latitude scales along the left and right margins. See Figure 47 (A) and Figure 50. Longitude scales are along the top and bottom margins. See Figure 47 (B) and Figure 50. For more exact measurement, degrees of latitude and longitude are divided into minutes and tenths of minutes. (There are 60 minutes in 1 degree.)

24 Some charts, including small-craft charts, may not show geographic north at the top of the chart because they are printed to show as much shoreline as possible. On these charts,

scales divide degrees of latitude and longitude into minutes and seconds, rather than minutes and tenths of minutes. There are 60 seconds in 1 minute (no relation to clocks or telling time); 30 seconds = 0.5 minute. You will find latitude and longitude scales near the distance scales or in convenient places along the illustrated parallels of latitude and meridians of longitude. The compass rose will always help you find true north.

Determining Latitude and Longitude

25 Figure 50 shows a method of determining the latitude and longitude of a location on a

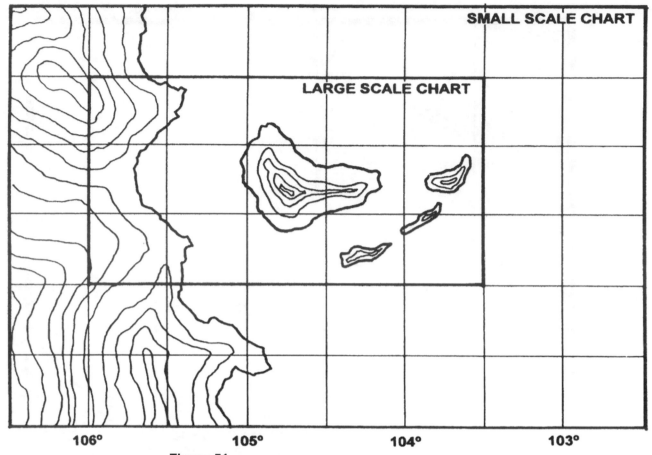

Figure 51
Small Scale Charts Show a Large Area
Large Scale Charts Show a Small Area

chart. The area on this chart is north of the equator (north latitude) and west of Greenwich (west longitude). Parallels of latitude run horizontally through the chart.

26 Note L 41° 35′ N toward the bottom, and L 41° 40′ N near the center. Scales to divide degrees of latitude into minutes and tenths of minutes are in the left and right margins.

27 Meridians of longitude appear as vertical lines in three locations—Lo 70° 40.0′ W, Lo 70° 45′ W, and Lo 70° 50′ W. Scales to divide degrees of longitude into minutes and tenths of minutes are in the top and bottom margins. Between the parallels of latitude and meridians of longitude are five one-minute segments, each divided into ten smaller segments which represent 0.1 minute.

28 Example: To measure latitude at Buoy "C" (Figure 50, left of the compass rose), set one leg of your dividers on the buoy's position circle and the other leg on the L 41° 40′ N line. Move the dividers to the left latitude scale, as shown, and read the value at the bottom leg of the dividers. The latitude is 41° 38.4′ N.

29 You will find longitude using the same procedure, except that you measure to the Lo 70° 50′ W line and move the dividers to the longitude scale. The longitude is 70° 48.0′ W. It is good practice to measure from the closest printed latitude and longitude lines.

30 As a practice exercise, find the latitude and longitude of Buoy "A" (Figure 50, near the top). [L 41° 42.6′ N, Lo 70° 48.4′ W]

Chart Scales

31 NOS classifies charts according to their scale. The size of the area shown on a chart depends upon its scale. Charts can show small areas or large areas. Actual distances on a chart are reduced to fit on a piece of paper. This reduction is the scale of the chart.

32 As an example, a chart with a scale of 1:20,000 will show 20,000 inches of the earth's surface in 1 inch of the chart. A chart with a scale of 1:80,000 will show 80,000 inches of the earth's surface in 1 inch of the chart. A 1:80,000 chart will show a larger area than a 1:20,000 chart, but there will be less detail.

33 Normally, you will want to choose a chart that shows the most detail for the area where you will be boating. Look for the scale of a chart in the chart title block.

Chart Types

34 Many nautical charts are printed on large sheets of heavy paper. Some are as large as 36 × 54 inches and designed for use on a large chart table.

35 Roll your charts to keep them in good condition. If you use them on a small boat, you may have to fold them. Fold the chart horizontally with its face side out. Divide it across the top into five equal parts. Then, starting with the right-hand edge, fold the sections back on themselves, accordion style. You may want to keep your charts in a transparent plastic cover, especially if you use them on an open boat.

36 NOS offers the following types of charts: (Numbers in parentheses are the chart scales.)

37 **Sailing Charts** (1:600,000 and up) are for offshore sailing between distant coastal ports. They show a huge area and little detail.

38 **General Charts** (1:150,000 to 1:600,000) are for courses well offshore but where you may establish position from landmarks and other aids to navigation.

39 **Coast Charts** (1:50,000 to 1:150,000, with most at 1:80,000) are for coastal navigation and show inside shore reefs and shoals. Their primary use is for entering large bays and harbors and for navigating certain inland waters. Coast charts show major hazards to navigation and general information on depths.

40 **Lake Charts** (1:50,000 to 1:500,000) are similar to Coast Charts.

41 **Harbor Charts** (1:5,000 to 1:50,000) are for navigation and anchoring in harbors and small waterways. They show a large amount of detail, including depths and aids to navigation.

42 **Small-Craft Charts** (1:10,000 to 1:40,000) are published for areas that have a lot of small boat traffic. They have convenient, fold-out segments for use in the confined spaces of a small boat. Their covers include useful information such as tidal data and marine facilities in the area.

43 **Marine Facility Charts** (1:10,000 to 1:40,000) are charts that clearly mark repair yards, marina locations, and sources of available services and supplies.

U.S. Coast Pilots

44 NOS publishes nine *United States Coast Pilots* for various parts of the country (including the Great Lakes) that provide detailed information to supplement nautical charts.

45 They include such information as channel descriptions, anchorages, location of fuel piers, location of haul-out and repair facilities, bridge and cable clearances, hours of drawbridge operation, tide and tidal current information, weather conditions, navigational hazards, prominent features, small-craft facilities, and federal regulations applying to the areas.

46 See Appendix D for information on how to obtain NOS publications.

Use Up-to-Date Charts

47 The use of old charts for navigation is not a good practice. Charts are only as good as the information on them, and changes do occur in aids to navigation, shore features, and underwater hazards.

48 NOS publishes *Dates of Latest Editions-Nautical Charts* on a quarterly basis listing the latest charts, their size, and cost. Look in the chart margin for its publication date.

49 Keep your charts up to date by subscribing to the *Local Notice to Mariners* for your area. This is published weekly by each Coast Guard district. You may also obtain *Local Notice to Mariners* by fax and on the Internet. (Check with your local Coast Guard district for the online address.)

50 A sample page of a *Local Notice to Mariners* is shown in Figure 53 on page 43.

Figure 52   Chart Publication Date

Digital Charts

51 Today, charts are available via a number of media. For example, the traditional National Oceanic and Atmospheric Administration (NOAA) paper charts are faithfully reproduced in waterproof format and divided into sections and inserted into paper and waterproof chart books by commercial companies. In addition, there is a growing trend toward charts provided in digital formats for use with computers and specialized devices called chart plotters.

52 The same NOAA charts, and those from other hydrographic offices, are scanned with high precision and distributed on CD-ROMs. These charts, called raster (reflecting the scanning process), are faithful reproductions of the originals with the same colors, features, and information. They are read by specialized computer programs which display selected chart segments on the computer screen. This same software permits reading the coordinates directly at the computer cursor position. It also permits defining points, called waypoints, that define the end points of a course line. These points then can be transferred to a GPS (Global Positioning System) receiver for navigation on the water.

53 Remember that latitude and longitude coordinates provide the language for communicating information between the chart and electronic devices such as your GPS receiver. When using GPS, it is essential that you know how to plot your current position as reported on the device. GPS provides only a

**U.S. Department
of Transportation**

**United States
Coast Guard**

LOCAL NOTICE TO MARINERS
COASTAL WATERS FROM EASTPORT, MAINE TO SHREWSBURY, NEW JERSEY

WEEKLY SUPPLEMENT
** FAX-ON-DEMAND – LOCAL NOTICE TO MARINERS AT (703) 313–5931 or 5932 **
** Electronic Bulletin Board Service: (703) 313–5910 **
300 to 28.8 bps, 8 data bits, no parity, 1 stop bit
** NIS watchstander, 24 hours a day at (703) 313–5900 **

** INTERNET ADDRESS **
HTTP://www.navcen.uscg.mil
OR
FTP://ftp.navcen.uscg.mil

Weekly supplemental editions contain only new information available subsequent to the issue date of the monthly
edition. NOTE: Chart corrections and Light List changes are published only once (the week in which they appear). A
complete listing of current discrepancies and temporary changes appeared in the monthly issue, LNM 36/96. This
publication is issued weekly at no cost to the subscriber. If you have questions about this publication or wish to be
placed on the mailing list, contact the address or phone number listed below.

COMMANDER, FIRST COAST GUARD DISTRICT (oan)
408 Atlantic Avenue, Boston, Massachusetts 02110–3350
Telephone (Day): 1–800–848–3942. To order LNM: Ext. 8335 (After 4:30 p.m. Ext. 7722)   24 Hour FAX: (617) 223–8073
Coast Guard's Customer Infoline (8:00 a.m. – 4:00 p.m.): 1–800–368–5647. Hearing impaired (TDD) 1–800–689–0816

Figure 53   Local Notice to Mariners

three-dimensional position in space, converted to latitude and longitude coordinates. It has no inherent knowledge of what is around you at that location. You must use a chart for that essential information.

54 Another form of a digital chart is called vector. Instead of scanning the chart, the chart maker (either manually or with the help of special software) traces the importang geographical features. Points along that trace are stored in the file by their latitudes and longitudes. This method results in file sizes considerably smaller than raster charts.

These smaller files are more suitable for storage on specialized chart chips. These chips generally are used aboard boats in devices called chart plotters. A chart plotter often incorporates a GPS unit and displays your position directly on the vector chart. This saves you effort and eliminates the possibility of transcription error in manually plotting your position.

55 Appendix A is an introduction to using digital charts along with a GPS unit. This material is optional in this course.

Homework

Name: _____ **Date:** _____ **Group:** _____

1. Blue areas on a chart indicate:
    a. deep, safe water.
    b. tidal areas.
    c. shallow water.
    d. dry land.

2. Depths on a chart may be in feet, meters, or fathoms. You can tell the measurement used from the:
    a. chart compass rose.
    b. chart title block.
    c. special instruction sheet that accompanies the chart.
    d. purplish-red explanatory notes in the center of the chart.

3. Charts of tidal water areas always show vertical clearances of overhead objects at:
    a. mid-tide.
    b. low water.
    c. a reference plane decided by town authorities.
    d. mean high water.

4. In the grid system that makes it possible to identify any point on the earth's surface, imaginary latitude lines or parallels of latitude:
    a. run east and west.
    b. run north and south.
    c. are numbered from 0° to 180°.
    d. run through the geographic poles.

5. On your practice chart in the appendix, what is the latitude and longitude of the lighthouse on Channel Island in the center of the chart?
    a. L 40° 38.5´ N, Lo 71° 34.8´ W
    b. L 41° 41.7´ N, Lo 71° 53.8´ W
    c. L 41° 44.6´ N, Lo 71° 34.8´ W
    d. L 40° 38.5´ W, Lo 71° 34.8´ N

6

Aids to Navigation

1 For boaters, aids to navigation are like street signs and caution signs for drivers. Each gives you information you need to know to locate and move your vehicle (boat or car) safely.

2 An *aid to navigation* is any object that:
   1) warns of danger
   2) helps pilot a boat safely
   3) aids in finding position

3 The U.S. Aids to Navigation System marks the federal waters of the United States. It is maintained by the U.S. Coast Guard. Federal waters include all lakes and waterways that connect with the high seas and are navigable by seagoing boats.

4 The U.S. System is designed for use with nautical charts. You can tell the exact meaning of an aid to navigation by looking at a chart. You can also tell your position relative to a particular aid to navigation shown on a chart. There are many privately maintained aids that conform to the federal system.

5 The Uniform State Waterway Marking System (USWMS) was discontinued 31 December 2003. However, many states continue to use it. It differs in several ways from the U.S. System. Following page 56, you will find four color plates (unnumbered pages 57–60) showing the U.S. Aids to Navigation and USWMS.

6 Upon completion of this chapter, you will be able to:
   • recognize and understand the purpose of the various kinds of navigational aids
   • use these aids intelligently in the safe operation of your boat

Marks

7 In this chapter we will study marks-aids to navigation you see while boating. There are two categories of marks: lateral marks and non-lateral marks.

8 You can identify marks in daylight by their shape, color, markings, and sounds-at night by their light and sound characteristics. U.S. Coast Guard *Light Lists* describe all lights, buoys, and beacons maintained in the navigable waters of the United States. (See pages 50 and 51.)

9 Always identify aids to navigation on your chart. Always use a chart when you are boating; it is a necessary tool for safe navigation. When you see a defective aid, report it to the Coast Guard.

10 Never tie a boat to an aid to navigation. It is illegal and could prevent another boater from seeing the mark, causing an error in navigation, a grounding, or an accident.

Types of Marks

11 There are two general types of marks: buoys and beacons.

12 **Buoys** are floating objects anchored at specific locations. They may range in size from three to thirty-eight feet high. You may identify them by their shape, color, numbers, letters, sound devices, or lights. (See the color plates at the end of this chapter.)

13 Buoys appear on charts as diamonds with small circles that indicate their approximate position. It is difficult to place and maintain buoys in exact locations. Severe storms, ice, and collisions with large vessels often move buoys. In addition, buoys will swing around their moorings with wind and current. The size of the circle depends upon the depth of the water and the length of the mooring chain.

14 Lighted buoys on charts are depicted by a magenta (purplish-red) outline around their position circles.

15 **Beacons** are marks that are permanently fixed (fastened) to the earth's surface, and therefore more reliable. They may be as large as lighthouses and as small as daybeacons. *Daybeacons* are fixed structures such as posts and pilings that are usually found in shallow water or on shore. Daybeacons support *daymarks*-boards of various shapes and colors that identify daybeacons during daylight hours.

16 Unlighted beacons appear on charts as small triangles or squares. Lighted beacons, called lights, appear on charts with magenta exclamation points (!). (See color plates.)

17 *Do not pass close to beacons.* You may collide with their foundations or the very obstruction that they mark!

Red—Right—Returning

18 This is the 3R Rule of the U.S. Aids to Navigation System. The rule states:

When **R**eturning from sea, keep **R**ed side-of-channel marks to your **R**ight— starboard.

19 This means that you will keep green side-of-channel marks to your port. (See color plate 2, page 58.)

20 **Returning** is:
  • entering a harbor or bay from the open ocean
  • traveling up a river from the sea
  • traveling in a clockwise direction around a landmass

21 For example, you are returning when you travel:
  • southerly along the Atlantic Coast
  • southerly down the Intracoastal Waterway
  • northerly and westerly along the Gulf Coast
  • up the Mississippi River from the Gulf of Mexico
  • northerly along the Pacific Coast to Alaska

22 On the Great Lakes, colors and numbering of marks start at the outlet end of each lake and proceed westerly and northerly toward their upper ends. An exception is Lake Michigan, where the direction of marks is southerly.

Shapes and Colors of Marks

23 The shapes and colors of marks make it easy to identify them. (See color plates.)

24 **Conical-Shaped Nun Buoys and Triangular-Shaped Daymarks** show the starboard (right) side of a channel when coming in from sea (see Red-Right-Returning, above). They can be either solid red or painted with red and green bands (with the top band always red).

25 **Cylindrical-Shaped Can Buoys and Square-Shaped Daymarks** show the port (left) side of a channel when coming in from sea. They can be either solid green or painted with green and red bands (with the top band always green).

26 **Spherical (Globe-Shaped) Buoys** are used for special purposes.

Numbers and Letters

27 Numbers and letters identify many marks and help you find them on charts. In the U.S. System, numbers identify solid red and solid green marks. Red marks (on the returning starboard side of a channel) have even numbers; green marks (on the returning port side) have odd numbers. The numbers increase in value as you return from sea.

28 The Coast Guard attempts to keep the numbers on marks in order. However, you may find numbers missing if a mark is not needed, removed, destroyed, or carried off-station. A new mark added into a previously completed grouping may have a letter following the number. For example, mark "7A" will be between marks "7" and "9." Letters also identify special marks, as described below.

Lighted Marks

29 Lighted marks help to guide you at night and during times of restricted visibility. Most lighted buoys are metal floats with a light at the top of a short skeleton tower that supports the lighting mechanism. (See color plates.) Their lights may be red, green, white, or yellow, depending on their meaning.

30 The lights of marks that show the starboard side of a channel when returning from sea are red. Those that show the port side when returning from sea are green. Safe water and isolated danger buoys have white lights. Special-purpose buoys have yellow lights.

31 Lights usually go on at sunset and off at sunrise. They may also be on during periods of limited visibility.

32 Lights on beacons are the same as those on buoys. Charts will tell you the distance they can be seen in clear weather. The height of the light on the beacon, the height of the observer, and conditions such as rain, haze, and fog are factors that affect their visibility.

33 Lights on navigational aids have many patterns. For example, *fixed*-pattern lights show steadily and continuously; *rhythmic*-pattern lights blink on and off with a regular pattern. Lighted aids are not always reliable, for at times their lighting mechanisms may fail. If you find a light not working, report it to the Coast Guard so other boaters may be notified and the light repaired.

Lateral System

34 Color plate 1 (page 57) shows the Lateral System of the U.S. Aids to Navigation System.

35 The lateral system identifies the port and starboard sides of a route. They include side-of-channel marks and preferred-channel marks.

Side-of-Channel Marks

36 Following the Red-Right-Returning rule described above, these marks identify the port and starboard sides of a channel. Coming from sea, starboard-side marks will be red; port-side marks will be green.

Table 2 **Side-of-Channel Marks** **When Returning From Sea**		
	Port	Starboard
Color	Green	Red
Shapes:		
Unlighted	Cylindrical (can)	Conical (nun)
Lighted	Skeleton tower	Skeleton tower
Daymark	Green square	Red triangle
Light (if fitted)		
Color	Green	Red
Rhythm	Varied flashing	Varied flashing
Identification	Odd numbers	Even numbers

Preferred-Channel Marks

37 These marks identify channel junctions and obstructions and have red and green horizontal bands. The color of the top band indicates the preferred or major channel, in reference to the Red-Right-Returning system. Always consult your chart to determine which channel is best for your boat and destination.

38 For example, if you wish to use the preferred channel and it is to port as you come from sea, the preferred channel buoy will have a red top band, and you will keep it to your starboard side. If the preferred channel is to starboard, the buoy will have a green top band, and you will keep it to your port side.

Non-Lateral System

39 Non-lateral marks supplement the lateral marks described above, but have no lateral significance. They include isolated danger marks, safe water marks, special marks, and information and regulatory marks.

Isolated Danger Marks

40 Isolated danger marks are placed on, above, or near a danger which has navigable water all around it. *Approach them cautiously!* (See color plate 1.)

Safe Water Marks

41 These marks have safe water on both sides and identify the centers of navigable channels and off-shore approach points.

Special Marks

42 Special marks call attention to a special feature of an area. Their meanings are described

Table 3 Preferred-Channel Marks When Returning From Sea		
	Preferred Channel to Port	Preferred Channel to Starboard
Color	Red and Green horizontal bands, top band red	Green and Red horizontal bands, top band green
Shapes:		
Unlighted	Conical (nun)	Cylindrical (can)
Lighted	Skeleton tower	Skeleton tower
Topmark (if fitted)	Red cone, point up	Green cylinder
Daymark	Red triangle, lower $\frac{1}{2}$ green	Green square, lower $\frac{1}{2}$ red
Light (if fitted)		
Color	Red	Green
Rhythm	Flashing 2 + 1 (2 short/1 short)	Flashing 2 + 1 (2 short/1 short)
Identifier	Letters	Letters

on charts, or in Light Lists, Coast Pilots, or Local Notices to Mariners. Examples are anchorage areas, fish nets, spoil areas, pipelines, and traffic separation schemes. (See color plates.)

Information and Regulatory Marks

43 Information and regulatory marks alert mariners to various warnings or regulatory matters. The USWMS also uses these marks, as described later in this chapter.

Table 4 — Isolated Danger Marks	
Color	Black and Red horizontal bands, top band black
Shape	Skeleton tower
Topmark/Daymark	Two black spheres
Light (if fitted)	
Color	White
Rhythm	Flashing, groups of 2
Identification	Letters
Safe Water Marks	
Color	Red and White vertically striped
Shapes	
Unlighted	Spherical
Lighted	Skeleton tower
Topmark (if fitted)	Red Sphere
Daymark	Octagonal red and white divided vertically
Light (if fitted)	
Color	White
Rhythm	Morse Code "A" (short flash—long flash)
Identification	Letters
Special Marks	
Color	Yellow
Shapes	
Unlighted	Conical (nun) or Cylindrical (can)
Lighted	Skeleton tower
Daymark	Yellow diamond
Light (if fitted)	
Color	Yellow
Rhythm	Fixed or flashing
Identification	Letters

Ranges

44 Ranges are beacons used to show the centerline of a channel or point a direction for other uses. You will find two beacons placed a suitable distance apart. The front marker is lower than the rear marker, so the two can be seen together in a vertical line when a boater is on a safe course in the marked channel. A horizontal separation of the two beacons alerts a boater to steer back into the center of the channel until the two beacons are in line again. Always refer to a chart to determine what section of a range you may travel safely.

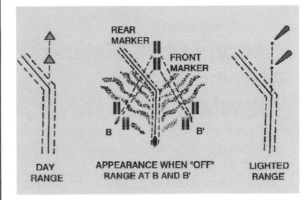

Figure 54
Placement of Beacons in a Range

45 Ranges may vary in shape and color, particularly where one range leads to another. They are almost always lighted. Letter markings often distinguish one range from another. When a range is lighted, the far light has a longer rhythm than the near light. A *front range* is one observed ahead of your boat; a *back range* is one observed astern.

Sound Signals

46 Sound signals on some marks help boaters find them in restricted visibility.

47 **Bells and Gongs** produce irregular sounds from the motion of the waves. Gongs sound a variety of tones, different from bells, which produce only a single tone.

48 **Whistles** create a high-pitched sound produced by the motion of the waves.

49 **Horns** are electrically operated and give off lower-pitched sounds. You will usually find horns in areas where there's little sea motion.

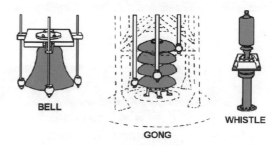

Figure 55   Types of Sound Signals

2) A white buoy with a black top represents an obstruction. Pass to the *north* or *east*. It may have a number.
3) A red and white vertically striped buoy indicates that an obstruction exists *between* the buoy and the nearest shore.

53 (Caution: the red and white vertically striped buoys of the USWMS system have a *totally different meaning* than red and white striped buoys in the U.S. System.)

Uniform State Waterway Marking System (USWMS)

50 USWMS was originally intended for state use on inland lakes and waterways not shown on nautical charts. It is now used on other waters and supplements the federal system. Refer to color plate 4 (page 60) to see that this system varies from the standard U.S. system as follows:

USWMS Lateral System

51 This system outlines the edges of channels. Side-of-channel marks are solid red and black, instead of solid red and green as in the U.S. System.

USWMS Cardinal System

52 You will find this system on lakes where the idea of returning from sea does not apply. Three types of buoys mark safe-passage areas. All *may* have lights and/or reflectors for night navigation.
1) A white buoy with a red top represents an obstruction. Pass to the *south* or *west*. It may have a number.

USWMS Information and Regulatory Marks

54 These marks show controlled areas, areas of danger, and exclusion areas where boats are not allowed.
- *Regulatory* marks are white. You will find orange bands around the edges of daymarks and the tops and bottoms of buoys.
- Orange diamonds are *Dangerous Area* marks with the word *Danger* (or a description of the danger) in black letters within the diamond.
- Orange diamonds with a cross through them are *Exclusion Area* marks. You may find an explanation in black letters outside the diamond. You will find exclusion areas near dams, rapids, swimming areas, etc.
- Orange circles are *Controlled Area* marks with the type of control indicated

in black letters within the circle. Examples are *No Wake, Slow Speed, No Anchoring, Steerage Speed Only,* etc.
* Orange squares or rectangles are *General Information* marks with directions or information in the center.

Mooring Buoys

55 Mooring buoys are for recreational boater use. They are white buoys with a horizontal blue band midway between the waterline and the top of the buoy. If lighted, this buoy will show a slow flashing white light.

Variations to the U.S. System

56 Boaters in certain parts of the United States will encounter special navigational aids systems that differ from the United States Aids to Navigation System described above.

Intracoastal Waterway System

57 This is a variation of the U.S. System that has its own system of markings. Color plate 1 illustrates these aids.

Western River System

58 You will find this on the Mississippi River and its tributaries. It differs slightly from the basic U.S. System as described in Appendix C, Inland Boating, and color plate 4 (page 60).

Electronic Aids to Navigation

59 There are many electronic aids to navigation, but their study is beyond the scope of this basic course. Popular and very effective electronic aids include Radar, Loran, and Global Positioning Systems. A knowledge of basic piloting is always necessary as a backup for these systems. We will study basic piloting in this course.

60 Advanced courses such as the USPS Advanced Piloting and Marine Electronics courses teach principles of modern electronic navigation. You may also obtain USPS Learning Guides for Global Positioning Systems (GPS), Radar, and Loran-C through your nearest USPS squadron or marine products store.

Homework

Name: _____   **Date:** _____   **Group:** _____

1. An accurate way to find out where you are on the water is to:
   a. look at your compass.
   b. find your location in the Local Notice to Mariners for the area.
   c. locate your position relative to a particular aid to navigation on a chart.
   d. ask a passing boater.

2. Daymarks are used to identify:
   a. precise locations of buoys.
   b. approximate positions of floating aids.
   c. isolated danger buoys.
   d. daybeacons in daytime.

3. A can buoy will be _____ in shape and shown on a chart as a small circle and a _____.
   a. spherical; square
   b. round; triangle
   c. conical; diamond
   d. cylindrical; diamond

4. When returning from sea using the U.S. Aids to Navigation System, you always keep:
   a. green side-of-channel marks to starboard.
   b. yellow marks to port.
   c. red side-of-channel marks to starboard.
   d. lighthouses and other beacons towards shore.

5. In U.S. waters, solid red starboard side-of-channel marks will have:
   a. no numbers or letters.
   b. odd numbers.
   c. letters only.
   d. even numbers.

6. As you return from sea, identifying numbers on navigation marks will:
   a. increase in value.
   b. be the same on both sides of the channel.
   c. be in 4-inch block letters.
   d. decrease in value.

7. In the U.S. system, lighted navigation marks that show the port side of a channel when returning from sea have:
   a. green lights.
   b. yellow lights.
   c. red lights.
   d. white lights.

8. Red and green horizontally banded marks identify:
   a. fish traps and weirs during seasonal fish runs.
   b. temporary aids in navigable channels during the holiday season.
   c. safe water in navigable channels and offshore approaches.
   d. preferred channels in locations of channel junctions or obstructions.

9. In the U.S. system, red and white vertically striped marks identify:
    a. controlled areas of slow speed, no wake, etc.
    b. dumping ground locations in open water.
    c. safe water on both sides and the center of navigable channels and offshore approaches.
    d. preferred channels where there are channel junctions or obstructions.

10. Two beacons placed a suitable distance apart to show the centerline of a channel are called:
    a. a fairlead.
    b. a range.
    c. a header.
    d. articulated beacons.

11. Aids to navigation are equipped with sound signals to:
    a. discourage sea birds from building nests.
    b. to help boaters find marks in restricted visibility.
    c. provide a pleasant nautical background atmosphere.
    d. assist boaters in identifying aids in clear visibility.

U.S. AIDS TO NAVIGATION SYSTEM
on navigable waters except Western Rivers

LATERAL SYSTEM AS SEEN ENTERING FROM SEAWARD

PORT SIDE
ODD NUMBERED AIDS

■ GREEN LIGHT ONLY

FLASHING (2)	
FLASHING	
OCCULTING	
QUICK FLASHING	
ISO	

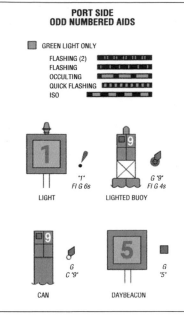

PREFERRED CHANNEL
NO NUMBERS-MAY BE LETTERED

PREFERRED
CHANNEL TO
STARBOARD
TOPMOST BAND
GREEN

■ GREEN LIGHT ONLY

COMPOSITE GROUP FLASHING (2+1)

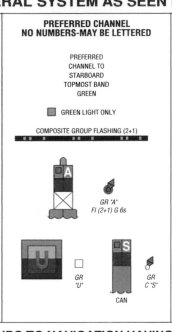

PREFERRED CHANNEL
NO NUMBERS-MAY BE LETTERED

PREFERRED
CHANNEL TO
PORT
TOPMOST BAND
RED

■ RED LIGHT ONLY

COMPOSITE GROUP FLASHING (2+1)

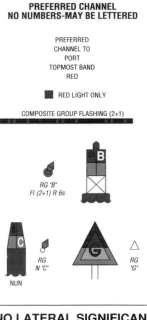

STARBOARD SIDE
EVEN NUMBERED AIDS

■ RED LIGHT ONLY

FLASHING (2)	
FLASHING	
OCCULTING	
QUICK FLASHING	
ISO	

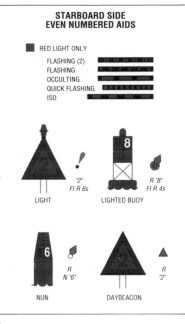

AIDS TO NAVIGATION HAVING NO LATERAL SIGNIFICANCE

ISOLATED DANGER
NO NUMBERS--MAY BE LETTERED

□ WHITE LIGHT ONLY

Fl (2) 5s

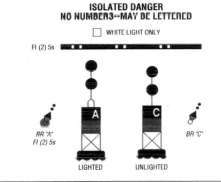

SAFE WATER
NO NUMBERS - MAY BE LETTERED

□ WHITE LIGHT ONLY   MORSE CODE

Mo (A)

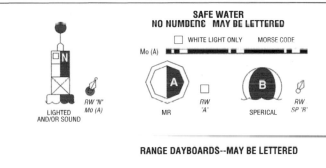

RANGE DAYBOARDS--MAY BE LETTERED

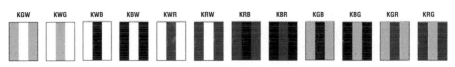

KGW	KWG	KWB	KBW	KWR	KRW	KRB	KBR	KGB	KBG	KGR	KRG

DAYBOARDS--MAY BE LETTERED

□ WHITE LIGHT ONLY

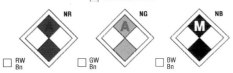

□ RW Bn	□ GW Bn	□ BW Bn

TYPICAL INFORMATION AND REGULATORY MARKS

INFORMATION AND REGULATORY MARKERS

WHEN LIGHTED, INFORMATION AND REGULATORY
MARKS MAY DISPLAY ANY LIGHT
RHYTHM EXCEPT QUICK FLASHING
AND FLASHING (2)

□ WHITE LIGHT ONLY

NW
□ W Bn   ◆DANGER◆

EXCLUSION AREA   RESTRICTED OPERATIONS   DANGER

SPECIAL MARKS--MAY BE LETTERED

□ YELLOW LIGHT ONLY

FIXED
FLASHING

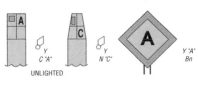

SHAPE OPTIONAL--BUT SELECTED TO BE APPROPRIATE
FOR THE POSITION OF THE MARK IN RELATION TO THE
NAVIGABLE WATERWAY AND THE DIRECTION
OF BUOYAGE.

Aids to navigation marking the Intracoastal Waterway (ICW) display unique yellow symbols to distinguish them from aids marking other waters. Yellow triangles △ indicate aids should be passed by keeping them on the starboard (right) hand of the vessel. Yellow squares □ indicate aids should be passed by keeping them on the port (left) hand of the vessel. A yellow horizontal band provides no lateral information, but simply identifies aids as marking the ICW.

Plate 1

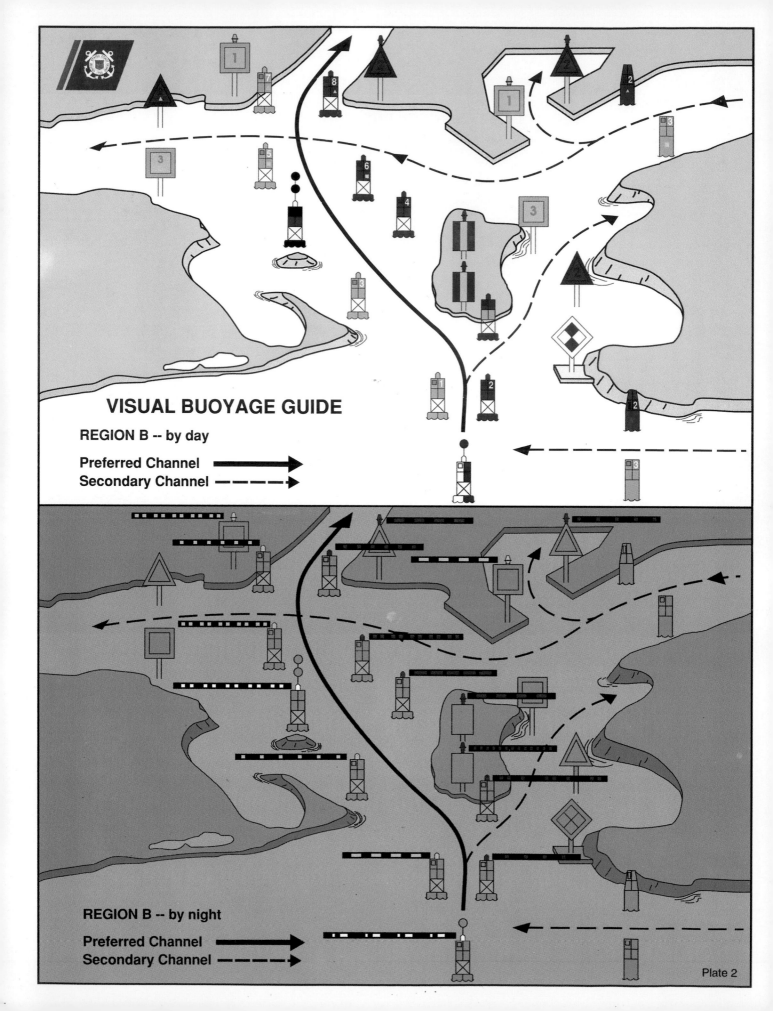

VISUAL BUOYAGE GUIDE

REGION B -- by day

Preferred Channel

Secondary Channel

REGION B -- by night

Preferred Channel

Secondary Channel

Plate 2

FICTITIOUS NAUTICAL CHART

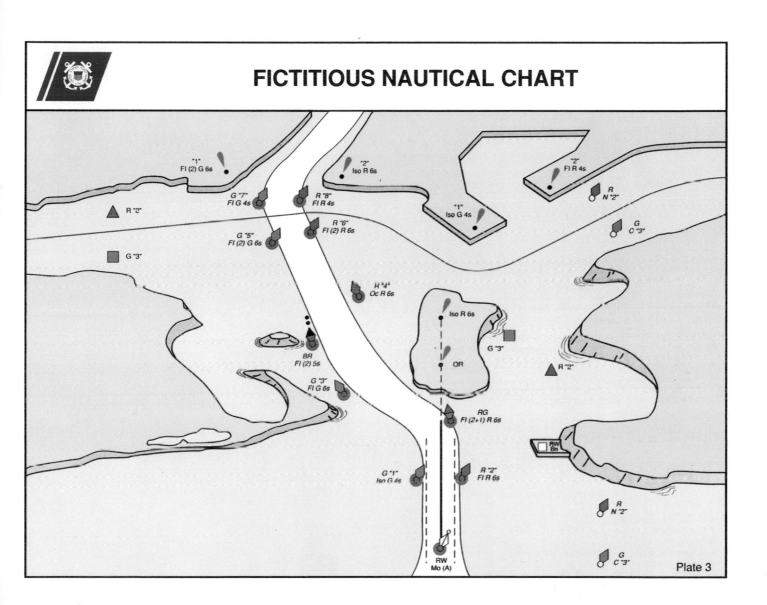

"1"
Fl (2) G 6s

"2"
Iso R 6s

"2"
Fl R 4s

G "7"
Fl G 4s

R "8"
Fl R 4s

R
N "2"

R "2"

"1"
Iso G 4s

G
C "3"

R "6"
Fl (2) R 6s

G "5"
Fl (2) G 6s

G "3"

H "4"
Oc R 6s

Iso R 6s

G "3"

BR
Fl (2) 5s

QR

R "2"

G "3"
Fl G 6s

RG
Fl (2+1) R 6s

RW
Bn

G "1"
Iso G 4s

R "2"
Fl R 6s

R
N "2"

RW
Mo (A)

G
C "3"

Plate 3

U.S. AIDS TO NAVIGATION SYSTEM
on the Western River System

AS SEEN ENTERING FROM SEAWARD

PORT SIDE OR RIGHT DESCENDING BANK

■ GREEN OR □ WHITE LIGHTS

FLASHING
ISO

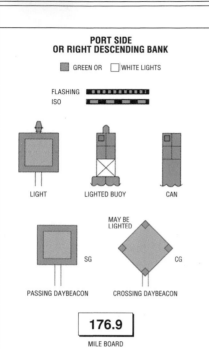

LIGHT   LIGHTED BUOY   CAN

MAY BE LIGHTED

SG   CG

PASSING DAYBEACON   CROSSING DAYBEACON

176.9
MILE BOARD

PREFERRED CHANNEL

MARK JUNCTIONS AND OBSTRUCTIONS
COMPOSITE GROUP FLASHING (2 + 1)

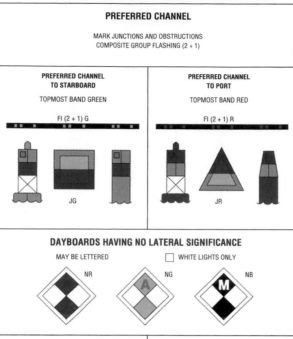

PREFERRED CHANNEL TO STARBOARD	PREFERRED CHANNEL TO PORT
TOPMOST BAND GREEN	TOPMOST BAND RED
Fl (2 + 1) G	Fl (2 + 1) R
JG	JR

DAYBOARDS HAVING NO LATERAL SIGNIFICANCE

MAY BE LETTERED   □ WHITE LIGHTS ONLY

 NR   A NG   M NB

STARBOARD SIDE OR LEFT DESCENDING BANK

■ RED OR □ WHITE LIGHTS

FLASHING (2)
ISO

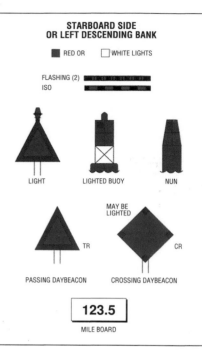

LIGHT   LIGHTED BUOY   NUN

MAY BE LIGHTED

TR   CR

PASSING DAYBEACON   CROSSING DAYBEACON

123.5
MILE BOARD

TYPICAL INFORMATION AND REGULATORY MARKS

INFORMATION AND REGULATORY MARKERS

WHEN LIGHTED, INFORMATION AND REGULATORY
MARKS MAY DISPLAY ANY LIGHT
RHYTHM EXCEPT QUICK FLASHING
AND FLASHING (2)

NW □ WHITE LIGHT ONLY

 DANGER   ⊕ EXCLUSION AREA   ◯ RESTRICTED OPERATIONS   ◇ DANGER

SPECIAL MARKS--MAY BE LETTERED

SHAPE: OPTIONAL--BUT SELECTED TO BE APPROPRIATE
FOR THE POSITION OF THE MARK IN RELATION TO THE
NAVIGABLE WATERWAY AND THE DIRECITON
OF BUOYAGE.

■ YELLOW LIGHT ONLY

FIXED
FLASHING

 A   C   NY A   B

UNLIGHTED   LIGHTED

UNIFORM STATE WATERWAY MARKING SYSTEM

STATE WATERS AND DESIGNATED STATE WATERS FOR PRIVATE AIDS TO NAVIGATION

REGULATORY MARKERS

 BOAT EXCLUSION AREA
SWIM / AREA

 DANGER
ROCK

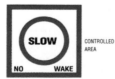 CONTROLLED AREA
SLOW / NO WAKE

EXPLANATION MAY BE PLACED OUTSIDE THE CROSSED DIAMOND SHAPE, SUCH AS DAM, RAPIDS, SWIM AREA, ETC.

THE NATURE OF DANGER MAY BE INDICATED INSIDE THE DIAMOND SHAPE, SUCH AS ROCK, WRECK, SHOAL, DAM, ETC.

TYPE OF CONTROL IS INDICATED IN THE CIRCLE, SUCH AS SLOW, NO WAKE, ANCHORING, ETC.

 INFORMATION
MULLET LAKE → / ← BLACK RIVER

FOR DISPLAYING INFORMATION SUCH AS DIRECTIONS, DISTANCES, LOCATIONS, ETC.

  5 MPH
BUOY USED TO DISPLAY REGULATORY MARKERS
MAY SHOW WHITE LIGHT
MAY BE LETTERED

LATERAL SYSTEM

MAY SHOW GREEN REFLECTOR OR LIGHT   MAY SHOW RED REFLECTOR OR LIGHT

USUALLY FOUND IN PAIRS
PASS BETWEEN THESE BUOYS

3
PORT SIDE
SOLID BLACK BUOY

—— LOOKING UPSTREAM ——

4
STARBOARD SIDE
SOLID RED BUOY

CARDINAL SYSTEM
MAY SHOW WHITE REFLECTOR OR LIGHT

RED-STRIPED WHITE BUOY

MAY BE LETTERED
DO NOT PASS BETWEEN
BUOY AND NEAREST SHORE

7
BLACK-TOPPED WHITE BUOY

PASS TO NORTH
OR EAST OF BUOY

MAY BE NUMBERED

RED-TOPPED WHITE BUOY

PASS TO SOUTH
OR WEST OF BUOY

MOORING BUOY

WHITE WITH BLUE BAND

MAY SHOW WHITE REFLECTOR OR LIGHT

Plate 4

7

Piloting—Plotting a Course

1 Navigation is the science of directing the movements of a boat from one place to another in a safe and efficient manner. Basic navigational skills are desirable for operators of boats of all sizes; power and sail. You will become aware of the need for these skills the first time you encounter darkness, fog, haze, rain, sleet, or unfamiliar waters.

2 In this course we will deal only with that part of navigation known as piloting. Piloting is operating a boat using landmarks, navigational aids, and soundings (the depth of the water) as primary tools. Most advanced forms of navigation, including electronic and celestial methods, are based on the principles of piloting.

3 Operating a boat in shallow, rock-strewn, near-shore waters requires constant attention to a boat's position and course. Knowledge of piloting will be of great value in the safe operation of your vessel. It will provide you with two valuable safety skills:
   1) the ability to determine your position at any time
   2) the ability to select the safest and most efficient route from one place to another

4 In this course we will divide the basic principles of piloting into four chapters: Plotting a Course, in this chapter; The Mariner's Compass, in Chapter 9; Distance, Speed, and Time, in Chapter 11; and Determining Position, in Chapter 13. Learn this material and use it on the water. Practice is the key to successful piloting.

Plotting a Course

5 In this chapter we describe how to plot and label a course on a chart. This is an important step in determining your position and selecting your route from one place to another.

Tools for Plotting

6 *Plotting* is drawing a boat's course on a chart. The tools to do this vary with the size of the boat and the amount of charting space available. We will use the following tools in this course:
   • a chart-you will find a practice chart inside the back cover of this manual
   • dividers for measuring distances
   • sharp pencil (preferably a #2) for drawing course lines
   • an eraser to correct mistakes or remove previous work
   • an angle-measuring tool-we will use the USPS course plotter

7 **The USPS Course Plotter** is simple, easy to use, and accurate. You may use it as a straightedge to draw course lines, and as a protractor. (A *protractor* is a tool for measuring and constructing angles.)

8 Figure 56 shows the USPS course plotter. Note the protractor scales and the parallel lines that form a rectangular grid. Four templates in the center of the plotter aid in neatly labeling positions on a chart. In this course we will use the half-circle to label a DR (deduced reckoning) position, and the circle to label a fix. You will use these when we study Determining Position in Chapter 13.

True Direction

9 Direction on a chart is measured from 000° to 360° in a clockwise direction from true north. (*True north* is the direction of the geographic North Pole.)

10 Observe the compass rose on your practice chart inside the back cover. The outer circle shows 0° (zero degrees) as true north. East is 90°, south is 180°, and west is 270°, all measured from 0°, which is true north. Note that 0° and 360° are the same. (The inner circle refers to magnetic north which we will discuss later.)

11 In Chapter 5, Charts, you learned about the latitude and longitude grid system found on charts. Meridians of longitude run true north-south through the geographic north and south poles. Parallels of latitude run true east-west, parallel to the equator. On your practice chart, note that the longitude lines are vertical and parallel to a line through the 0° and 180° graduation marks on the compass rose. The latitude lines are horizontal and parallel to a line through the 90° and 270° graduation marks.

12 North may not be at the top of some small-craft charts due to a chart's orientation. However, the compass rose and meridians of longitude will indicate true north and provide north-south direction on all charts.

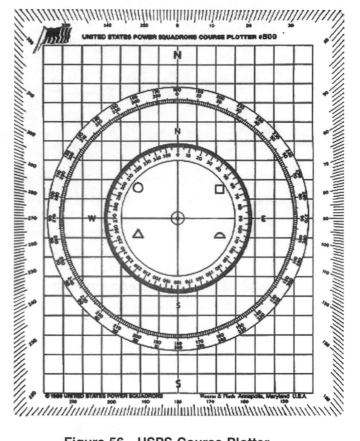

Figure 56 USPS Course Plotter

Determining a Course

13 Always label courses drawn on charts as true courses. That way the angle of a course line with any longitudinal meridian will be the same angle with true north; the direction of the earth's geographic North Pole.

14 We frequently plot courses from one known location to another. For practice, using one edge of your course plotter, draw a line on your Bowditch Bay practice chart (found inside the back cover of this manual) from G C "1" off Chapman Point to RG "D" GONG on the upper right of the chart. (When drawing a course line to or from a navigational aid, always draw the line to or through the circles or dots at the bottom of the symbols.)

15 **Measuring Course Direction.** You can determine the true course angle of your line from G C "1" to RG "D" by comparing it to the longitudinal meridians and the true North Geographic Pole:

- Place the center target of the plotter on the course line at any point
- Keeping the center on the course line, align any vertical or horizontal line on your USPS plotter with any longitudinal meridian or parallel of latitude on the chart
- Read the true course in any of three places where the course line crosses
    1) the outer edge of the plotter
    2) the inner scale of the large circle or
    3) the single scale on the small circle

16 Always state a course direction to the nearest whole degree. In this example, the true course is 067°. If your plotter reads a degree more or less, do not be concerned. Chart paper will shrink or stretch depending upon the moisture content of the air.

17 **Reciprocal Courses**. Note that if proceeding in the opposite direction (from RG "D" to G C "1"), your true course is 247°. This is called a reciprocal course, and is an opposite direction of 180° from the original direction. The outer scale of the large circle on your plotter shows reciprocal courses.

18 Always refer to a chart's compass rose to check the general direction of your course line. Unless you know the approximate direction of your course line, it is easy to make an error in reading the angle on your plotter.

19 **Labeling a Course Line for Direction.** A course plotted on a chart is of little value unless you label the direction on the course line. This is necessary because we often plan our cruises before setting sail. Once underway, you need only to refer to the chart for the true course directions previously plotted.

20 It is important to follow closely a standard method of labeling course lines. Do so, and anyone with basic skills can pick up your chart and understand and continue the work you've begun.

21 The basic rule is: Label a course line for direction *on and above the line,* as near as practicable to the start of the course. The area above the line is that portion that is nearest the top of the chart.

22 A true course label always starts with the letter "C". When labeling a course line for direction, always use three digits to the nearest whole degree, for example 005°, 015°, or 150°. Note that you use preceding zeros if necessary. The degree symbol is not used, only the three digits for the course angle. The label for a course of 5° is C 005.

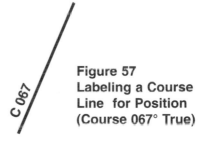

**Figure 57
Labeling a Course
Line for Position
(Course 067° True)**

Finding Your Way Digitally

23 Many boaters use GPS (Global Positioning System) or LORAN to aid with their navigation tasks.

24 When using a GPS receiver, you still will need to plot a course line on the chart, but you provide the GPS with coordinates rather than course angle. Read the coordinates from your chart for the place representing the end point for your course line. This and other locations of interest are entered into the GPS and called waypoints. Each waypoint is represented by its coordinates (latitude and longitude) and a name.

25 While physically located at the starting point for your course line, you select the waypoint (end point) for navigation and the GPS computes the course direction and distance to that point for you. It is wise to compare the GPS-reported course angle (bearing to the waypoint) with the one you measured on your chart to ensure you have not made a mistake in entering the waypoint.

26 Remember: one of the reasons you plot the course on a chart is to ensure the selected path is safe to navigate. GPS does not know what lies upon a selected course, so it is your responsibility to check.

Homework

Name: _____ Date: _____ Group: _____

1. A knowledge of piloting will provide you with two valuable safety skills: 1) the ability to select the safest and most efficient route from one place to another, and 2) the ability to:
   a. forecast the weather.
   b. place the target of your plotter on a course line.
   c. steer your boat in a straight line.
   d. determine your position at any time.

2. Direction on a chart is measured from 000° to 360° in a clockwise direction from:
   a. your compass heading.
   b. true geographic north.
   c. true geographic south.
   d. the lubber's line.

3. The compass rose and _____ will indicate true north and provide north-south direction on charts.
   a. meridians of longitude
   b. chart title block
   c. parallels of latitude
   d. nautical mileage scale

4. Always label courses drawn on charts as _____ courses.
   a. compass
   b. reciprocal
   c. true
   d. estimated

5. When drawing a course line to or from a navigational aid, always draw the line:
   a. in permanent ink so that it will not smudge.
   b. parallel to the longitudinal meridians.
   c. to or through the circles or dots at the bottom of the symbols.
   d. at a right angle to the parallels of latitude.

6. Label a course line for direction _____ and as near as practicable to the start of the course.
   a. in the margin
   b. on and below the line
   c. under the nearest latitude line
   d. on and above the line

7. When labeling a course line for direction, always use three digits to the nearest:
   a. whole minute.
   b. tenth of a minute.
   c. whole degree.
   d. whole second.

8. On the practice chart, plot a course from R "6" Fl R 4s buoy (chart center right) to RW "OR" safe water buoy at the entrance to Oyster River. The true course is _____. Label your course line.
   a. 073°
   b. 118°
   c. 253°
   d. 328°

9. On the practice chart, plot a course from
   RW "OR" to RN "2" at the entrance to
   Perkins Cove. The true course is _____.
   Label your course line.
   a. 025°
   b. 096°
   c. 276°
   d. 305°

8

Boat Handling

1 Good skippers know their duties and responsibilities. As a boat operator, you are responsible for your actions and those of your passengers from the time you leave until you return. Avoid taking unnecessary risks that could lead to personal injury or property damage. Safety is the highest concern.

2 Learning to operate a boat properly, like learning to drive an automobile, is a complex experience. It involves developing skills by both study and practice. If you learn the basic principles of handling a boat before going out on the water, you will save considerable time, effort, pain, and expense. However, there is no substitute for hands-on experience in your own boat.

Operator's Responsibilities

3 As the skipper, you are responsible for the safety of everyone aboard. Operate the boat in a safe and respectful manner, including controlling engine noise and boat speed in congested or restricted waters. Remember, as the skipper, you are legally responsible for all of your boating activities, including reckless or negligent operation of the boat.

4 Upon completion of this chapter, you should know how to:
- recognize the requirements for a safe fuel system in your boat
- fuel your boat safely
- check the condition of your boat and equipment prior to departure
- load people and gear in your boat so that it will ride at its safest position in the water
- get under way and operate your boat safely and efficiently
- approach a dock or mooring and tie up securely
- anchor your boat so that it is "made fast"
- retrieve your anchor efficiently

Homeland Security Measures

5 Boaters must be aware of rules and guidelines regarding homeland security measures. The following are steps that boaters should take to protect our country and are a direct result of the terrorist attacks of 11 September 2001. Keep your distance from all military vessels, cruise lines, or commercial shipping:
- all vessels must proceed at a no-wake speed when within a Protection Zone (which extends 500 yards around U.S. naval vessels)
- non-military vessels are not allowed to enter within 100 yards of a U.S. naval vessel, whether underway or moored, unless authorized by an official patrol; the patrol may be either Coast Guard or Navy
- violating the Naval Vessel Protection Zone is a felony offense, punishable by up to six years imprisonment and/or up to $250,000 in fines

6   Observe and avoid all security zones. Avoid commercial port operation areas. Avoid restricted areas near:
  • dams
  • power plants
  • naval ship yards
  • dry docks

7   Do not stop or anchor beneath bridges or in channels. Keep your boat locked when not using it, including while at temporary docks, such as yacht clubs, restaurants, marinas, shopping, etc. When storing your boat disable the engine. If on a trailer, immobilize it so it cannot be moved.

8   Keep a sharp eye out for anything that looks peculiar or out of the ordinary, and report it to the Coast Guard, port or marine security. When boating within a foreign country make certain that you check-in with the foreign country's Customs Service upon entering the country and with the USA Customs Service and/or Immigration and Naturalization Service upon returning. Know the rules before you go abroad so there are no unpleasant surprises upon your return home.

9   **Restricted Areas** are shown on navigational charts with a broken line around the perimeter of the area or zone. Examples where these areas may be found on charts are military bases, naval docking facilities, shipyards servicing military vessels, power plants, bridges, and other areas that have been so designated.

10 **Security Zones.** At the request of the Captain of the Port, or District Commander, an area may also be designated a *Security Zone;* these may be highlighted in magenta to better standout and warn the public to stay clear. Unauthorized vessels, without specific permission to enter, must stay out of these marked areas. Armed military, harbor police, or civilian authorities will likely confront violators.

Boat Preventive Maintenance

11 A safe boater actively maintains his or her boat, and is constantly checking and inspecting it for potential problems. This includes checking:
  • through-hull fittings
  • the engine and its related equipment
  • coolant, lubricant, and fuel levels
  • fuel and electrical systems

12 Consider the problems you may encounter when you have to fix a problem while you're at the dock. Now, compare that to what may happen when you try to fix the same problem out on the water, in heavy winds or seas, while drifting into dangerous waters, with friends and loved ones aboard who can't help but are scared stiff. As the old saying goes, "An ounce of prevention is worth a pound of cure."

Fueling

13 Gasoline vapors are heavier than air and will settle into the bilge of a boat. They will not go away without forced ventilation. These fumes are explosive when mixed with air. The fumes from a half-cup of gasoline, if ignited, can create enough explosive force to totally destroy even a large boat. Take precautions each time you use your boat to prevent gasoline, either liquid or vapor, from getting into your bilge.

14 *Never* start an engine on a boat before sniffing for fuel vapors in the engine and fuel compartments! A nose is a reliable detector of gasoline fumes.

15 If your boat is equipped with a bilge blower, run it until the bilge is clear of fumes. This could take as long as four to five minutes.

Your Boat's Fuel System

16 Make sure you have a properly installed fuel system. This will include:
- heavy duty marine gasoline tank
- approved fuel line tubing
- leakproof fittings and tight connections
- flexible metallic fuel hose, where needed, to eliminate vibration-caused failure

17 Certain aluminum tanks corrode easily when enclosed in foam where moisture can collect. These tanks can develop dangerous fuel leaks in locations not usually visible. Avoid fires by checking your boat's fuel system regularly for cleanliness, leaks, corrosion, and damage. The existence of fumes is a sign of a serious problem.

18 Fuel tanks should not have drains in their sides, bottoms, or ends. Fuel gauge lines and filler, vent, and pickup pipes must enter and exit at the top of the tank. Some larger vessels have inspection and clean-out ports in the tops of their tanks. A fuel shut-off valve should be within reach and located as far from the engine compartment as possible.

19 Fuel tanks and filler pipes should be grounded to the boat's electrical system to remove static electricity that could cause a dangerous spark and ignite fuel vapors.

20 Alcohol added to today's gasoline has contributed to rapid deterioration of fuel hoses and gaskets. Make sure you equip your gasoline-powered vessel with alcohol-resistant fuel-system parts.

21 Clearly mark your deck filler caps for *gasoline* or *diesel, water,* and *waste.* Inattentive dock attendants have put diesel fuel into gasoline tanks, and gasoline into water tanks, waste holding tanks, and fishing rod holders.

22 Portable fuel tanks used in small outboard boats must meet federal standards. They

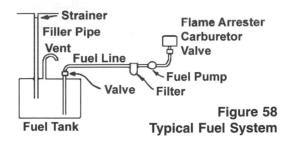

**Figure 58
Typical Fuel System**

should always be red in color and bear a certification label from an independent testing agency such as Underwriter's Laboratories, Inc. Secure your portable tanks in well-ventilated places in such a way that they are safe from damage and not exposed to sunlight. Do not store portable fuel tanks in a cabin or enclosed engine compartment.

Safe Fueling Practices

23 Careful adherence to proper fueling practices will prevent gasoline vapors from finding their way to the bilge. Using the fueling checklists, you will greatly reduce the risk of fire and explosion

24 After fueling and ventilating, start your engines and, when you are sure there is no hazard, leave the dock; lingering is discourteous.

25 **Refueling Portable Fuel Tanks:** do not refill portable fuel tanks in the back of a pickup truck, having a non-metallic bed-liner. Several explosions have been reported during refilling of portable tanks due to static electricity that had built-up during fueling. Be safe and remove portable fuel tanks and place them on the ground for refilling.

Preparing to Cast Off

26 Don't wait for emergencies to happen; make sure your boat is ready before you get underway. Planning and checking can save many hours of anxiety and distress on the water.

Table 5: Before-Fueling Checklist

☐ Fuel in daylight, if possible

☐ Tie your boat securely to the fuel dock

☐ Put out all flames (including galley stoves)

☐ *Prohibit smoking*

☐ Shut off engines and any electrical equipment that might create a spark (including blowers and radios)

☐ Close all portholes, doors, and hatches

☐ Have a working fire extinguisher close at hand

☐ Have passengers not needed for the fuel operation step off the boat

Table 6: While-Fueling Checklist

☐ Keep the pump nozzle in constant metal-to-metal contact with the filler pipe to prevent static electricity that could ignite fuel vapors.

☐ Estimate the amount of fuel needed and fill fuel tanks only 95% full to allow for expansion of the fuel and prevent spillage from overfilling. With experience you will be able to tell when the tank is near full by the sound of the entering fuel.

Table 7: After-Fueling Checklist— Before Starting Engines

☐ Close fuel filler pipe openings

☐ Wipe up any spillage (Take wipe rags ashore)

☐ Open all closed compartments

☐ Turn on bilge blower (if so equipped)

☐ Check for leaky tanks, filters, fuel lines

☐ *Sniff* in tank and engine compartments for vapors

Table 8: Fueling Portable Tanks

☐ Use approved safety cans and tanks only

☐ Fill all tanks off the boat. Tie them down when you return them to the boat

Figure 59
Fueling a Portable Tank

Check the Weather Forecast

27 Is it safe to go? Get an up-to-date forecast for the area where you plan to cruise. National Weather Service forecasts are available on your VHF radio or any radio that provides the weather frequencies. Check these forecasts regularly. They are updated several times a day, and more often when unusual weather develops. Use local radio and television forecasts, but be sure they are for your boating area.

File a Float Plan

28 A *float plan* is a plan of your cruise. It includes a description of your boat, who is on board, the safety equipment you are carrying, and, most importantly, where you expect to be and when. Leave a float plan with your marina, yacht club, or friend; not with the Coast Guard. If you launch at a ramp, leave a copy under your auto windshield wiper. (You can find a float plan in Appendix I, and a form to complete and print, using your computer, at the USPS website, www.USPS.org.)

29 If you do not return as planned, the person holding the float plan should notify the Coast Guard or some other marine law enforcement agency. If your plans change, notify that person so that false searches will not occur. Also notify them when you return. See a sample Float Plan in Appendix H of this manual.

Check Your Equipment

30 Make a last minute check to see that you have all required equipment and needed supplies aboard. Use the checklist in the next column as a reminder.

Passenger Communication

31 The skipper is obligated to educate everyone on board about matters of safety. This includes information on the location and proper use of life jackets (PFDs), fire extinguishers, visual distress equipment, and the first-aid kit. You are required to explain:

- Emergency procedures
- Rules against discharging waste overboard
- Basic operation of the marine radio (if one is installed)
- Other items, such as the operating, weather, and/or water conditions you may encounter

Load Your Boat Properly

32 Always step into a boat-never jump! Hold onto something, if possible. Step into the center of small boats, never on the *gunwale* (the upper edge of the hull). Try to avoid climbing in over the bow. Be sure of your footing–be especially careful of wet surfaces. Always load gear from the edge of the pier–never try to carry it aboard.

33 *Trim your boat* so that it rides evenly in the water (Figure 60). Tie down all loose gear to avoid injury and damage.

Table 9: Equipment Checklist

☐ **Personal papers (operator's certificate or license if required)**
☐ **Ship's papers (registration or documentation certificate)**
☐ **Life preserver for each person**
☐ **Throwable flotation aid**
☐ **Fire extinguishers**
☐ **Visual distress signals**
☐ **Horn and/or bell**
☐ **Anchor and anchor line**
☐ **Compass**
☐ **Charts and navigation tools**
☐ **Boat hook**
☐ **Paddles or oars**
☐ **Tool kit and spare parts**
☐ **Dock lines**
☐ **Flashlight and spare batteries**

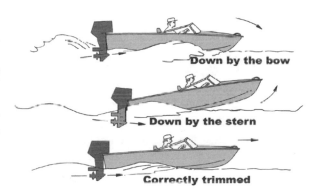

Figure 60   Trimming Your Boat

34 Overloading is a major cause of accidents in small boats. You will find a Coast Guard Maximum Capacities Label on all single-hull recreational boats under 20 feet in length manufactured after 1972 (personal watercraft are exempt, although manufacturers often make recommendations as to capacity). Never overload your boat or use a motor larger than recommended.

Life Preservers

35 Assign a life preserver, sometimes called a personal flotation device (PFD), to each person on board. Put them on and adjust them to fit.

36 The best insurance is to wear a life preserver at all times. Always wear one when underway at night. In some states, children must wear life preservers while underway unless the child is below deck or in an enclosed cabin. Most boating fatalities involve people not wearing life preservers; in most cases they were available.

Start and Warm the Engines

37 Never start your engines until you are sure the engine and fuel compartments are free of fumes. Use your nose to sniff for fuel vapors! After checking, start your engine and let it run a few minutes to ensure it is ready before leaving the pier.

Getting Under Way

38 Before casting off docklines, make a careful inspection of your immediate surroundings. Are there other boats in the vicinity? What is the direction of the wind and current? Plan what you will do if things go wrong. Warn your passengers to keep their arms and legs inside the boat at all times.

39 People should sit in the seats provided, not on the foredeck, gunwales, seat backs, or transom.

40 *Fenders* are protective devices used between the boat and other objects.

41 In nautical terms, whistle and horn are the same. It is important to sound one prolonged blast when entering a waterway, especially if there is a chance other vessels cannot see you. We will learn about whistle signals in Chapter 12, Navigation Rules.

Table 10: Boat Systems Checklist

- ☐ Bilge free of fumes and water
- ☐ Fuel supply at proper level
- ☐ Fuel system free of leaks
- ☐ Engine oil and transmission fluid checked
- ☐ Battery charge and fluid level checked
- ☐ Gauges and indicator lights operating
- ☐ Engine cooling system full
- ☐ Electronic gear working properly
- ☐ Drive belts seated and tight
- ☐ Navigation lights operative
- ☐ Steering and shift mechanisms fully operative

Table 11: Departure Checklist

- ☐ Disconnect all utility lines (power, water, etc.)
- ☐ Take in all docklines and fenders (except for those you will use in leaving the dock)
- ☐ Sound proper horn signals
- ☐ Keep a lookout at all times for other boats, persons, and objects in the water
- ☐ Keep watch for dangerous low overhead wires
- ☐ Proceed slowly whenever leaving or returning to a dock (use just enough power to maintain rudder control)
- ☐ After leaving the dock, take in all remaining docklines and fenders

Techniques for Leaving a Pier

42 Wind and current will influence the way a boat leaves a dock. Plan your actions based on which force, wind or current, has the most effect on your boat at this time.

43 **With Wind or Current From Ahead or Off the Pier,** push the bow away from the pier and move ahead slowly into a broad turn.

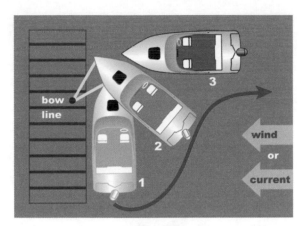

Figure 61
Leaving a Pier With
Wind or Current Toward the Pier

44 **With Wind or Current From Astern,** push the stern away, and then back the boat away enough to clear the pier.

45 **With Wind or Current Toward the Pier,** use an *after bow spring line* (a dockline leading aft from a boat's bow to the pier). With spring line fastened, and fenders protecting the boat, move slowly forward against the spring line and steer toward the pier. This will move the stern out. After releasing the spring line, you can back away.

Train an Alternate Skipper

46 *At least one* other person aboard should be competent to stop the engine, drop the sails, and use the radio in case of an emergency. Ideally, the alternate skipper will also be able to anchor the boat or take the helm and return it to the mooring.

47 Obtain a copy of the USPS learning guide, *Skipper Saver.* Use it to teach a member of the crew how to bring a boat safely back to shore if the skipper is disabled. It is a handy on-board reference.

While Underway

48 Always pay constant attention to the operation of your boat while underway. It takes skill to handle a boat well when turning, backing, stopping, and meeting tall waves and large vessels. Always use common sense and show courtesy to others.

Your Boat's Wake

49 A wake is a trail of large waves created by something moving through the water, such as those left by a moving boat. You are responsible for damage to persons or property caused by the wake of your boat. Be careful when approaching other boats or congested areas. Observe *No Wake* signs and reduce wake by slowing down a considerable distance before passing another boat.

Handling in Rough Water

50 When moving forward into large waves make sure your most qualified boat operator is steering the boat. Meet the waves at the best speed and angle for your boat for those conditions. You will have to experiment to find the correct crossing angle for your boat. The angle will vary with sea conditions, but head-on is rarely safe or comfortable.

51 When running before large waves in a planing boat, keep the stern square to the waves and run on the back of a single wave. Use engine power to keep a position about one-third of the way back from the wave's crest. Be ready to adjust speed quickly-faster or slower to maintain steerage and control.

52 In a displacement boat, you may not be able to keep up with a single wave. Keep the boat centered with its stern square to the waves coming up behind you, allowing successive waves to pass under your keel. A sea anchor on a long line trailed off the stern can help keep a boat from being pushed to the

side by a following wave. A sea anchor is a drag-producing device, usually cone-shaped.

Turning

53 Always watch the stern of your boat when turning. Boats steer from the stern; the opposite of an automobile. The front of a car turns and the back wheels follow. The stern of a boat moves out to the side so that the bow points in a new direction. Keep an eye on the stern of your boat when turning so that you don't hit anything.

54 You can lose control of your boat in high speed turns. People can be thrown overboard, and a boat can even *capsize* (overturn). Large waves increase the chance of these accidents happening. Always turn at low speed.

Backing

55 Always back slowly. Learn how your boat reacts to backing. Most single-screw boats will back to port.

Stopping

56 Boats have no brakes; you must put a boat in reverse to stop. Always come to a stop gradually. In this way you can avoid running into a pier or other boat. Practice with your boat to determine its stopping distance at various speeds.

Passing Large Vessels

57 Large ships and long barge tows take great distances to stop. For many of them, the only way to stop the propeller is to stop the engine! Even if the Navigation Rules say you are the stand-on vessel, give way to these vessels and stay as far away from them as possible.

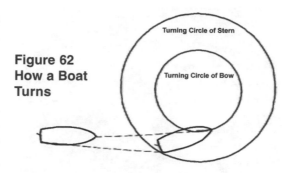

**Figure 62
How a Boat Turns**

58 Large vessels often create a dangerous rolling wake that is not apparent to the operator of a small boat. In addition, they can create huge whirlpools in the water astern that may remain for thousands of feet behind them. There is an unwritten rule for recreational vessels: If the other boat is larger, stay out of its way! Even large Coast Guard cutters follow the adage, Tonnage rules!

59 Five or more short blasts on a ship's whistle is a danger signal. If you hear this, immediately check to see if it is for you. If it is, get out of the way fast. You may use VHF channel 13 to talk with large ships.

Boating Courtesy and Ethics

60 Lack of courtesy and common sense on your part can prevent other boaters and shoreline property owners from enjoying the open water and beaches. This will result in more restrictive laws and regulations. The Golden Rule of doing unto others as you would have them do unto you is an excellent guide.

61 **Respect the Rights of Shoreline Property Owners.** Noise carries a great distance on the water, particularly at night. If you anchor off a waterfront home, keep voices down, music low, and leave with a minimum of noise. Always consider wind and tides. Do not anchor where your boat might drift too close to shore or another boat.

62 **High Speed Boating in Restricted or Congested Areas** is dangerous and against the law. Operate your boat at a reasonable speed when close to shore or near moored or drifting boats, floats, docks, launch ramps, swimmers, or downed water skiers. Your wake must never endanger any person or property.

63 **Rendering Assistance to Others in Distress** is required by law, providing it does not endanger your own boat or crew. The rules are intended to protect you from liability if you act reasonably and carefully.

64 **Give Consideration to Sailing Vessels.** Sailors have much less maneuverability than power boaters, especially when there is little wind. Give way to sail races and powerboat navigation contests. Go around them, not through them.

65 **Show Courtesy to Fishing Boats** by controlling your wake when near them. Give wide berth to fishermen trolling, pulling pots, tending fish traps, or shell fishing.

Docking

66 Docking or undocking a boat can be either a source of pride or an embarrassment. The only way you will become proficient in docking is to practice with your boat under various wind and current conditions.

Plan in Advance

67 Plan your approach to a dock or pier. You will have more control of your boat if you approach against the wind or current. Think ahead of things that might happen; have an idea of what you might do to recover. Tell your crew what you want them to do.

68 Install fenders on the correct side of the boat. Train someone to handle the docklines; they should be coiled and ready. Always hand

---

The following is an excerpt from Title 46 of the United States Code, Chapter 23 Operations of Vessels Generally (enacted August 26, 1983):

Par. 2303 Duties Related to Marine Casualty Assistance and Information

(a) The master or individual in charge of a vessel involved in a marine casualty shall:

1) render necessary assistance to each individual affected to save that affected individual from danger caused by the marine casualty, so far as the master or individual in charge can do so without serious danger to the master's or individual's vessel or to individuals on board: and

2) give the master's or individual's name and address and identification of the vessel to the master or individual in charge of any other vessel involved in the casualty, to any individual injured, and to the owner of any property damaged.

(b) An individual violating this section or a regulation prescribed under this section shall be fined not more than $1000 or imprisoned for not more than 2 years. The vessel also is liable in rem to the United States Government for the fine.

(c) An individual complying with subsection (a) of this section or gratuitously and in good faith rendering assistance at the scene of a marine casualty without objection by an individual assisted, is not liable for damages as a result of rendering assistance or for an act or omission in providing or arranging salvage, towage, medical treatment, or other assistance when the individual acts as an ordinary, reasonable, and prudent individual would have acted under the circumstances.

Par. 2304 Duty to Provide Assistance at Sea

(a) A master or individual in charge of a vessel shall render assistance to any individual found at sea in danger of being lost, so far as the master or individual in charge can do so without serious danger to the master's or individual's vessel or individuals on board.

(b) A master or individual violating this section shall be fined not more than $1000, imprisoned for not more than two years, or both.

lines to dock attendants. If you must throw the lines, toss them underhanded to one side of the attendants, never at them.

69 Alert your passengers to keep bodies, arms, and legs inside the boat. A boat hook is helpful for placing lines on pilings or cleats. However, neither a boat hook nor a person will be able to stop the movement of a heavy boat. Many arms and legs are broken by people using them to try to fend off a moving boat.

70 Make your approach cautiously and slowly, with just enough speed to maintain rudder control. You do not want to plow into the pier, and you want to avoid being pounded against the pilings by your own wake. Sailboats should approach a dock under power, when so equipped.

Docking Techniques

71 Wind and current are important considerations when docking. Plan your approach on the basis of which will have the most effect on your boat.

72 **With Wind or Current Ahead or Astern,** docking is not usually a problem. The bow line should be the first line to the pier or piling. Loop it over a piling, or fasten it to the pier, and move the boat slowly ahead. Use right rudder when placing port side to the pier; left rudder if docking to starboard. The stern will usually move into the dock. With wind or current from astern, you may want to make the stern line the first line to the pier.

73 **With Wind or Current Off the Pier,** approach at an angle of about 15–20 degrees and fasten a bow line to the pier. Turn outboard or stern-drive boats towards the pier and put the engine(s) in reverse. This should bring the stern to the pier where a stern line can be fastened.

74 With inboard boats, move the boat ahead against an after-bow-spring line and turn the bow away from the pier. This should force the stern to the pier. An *after-bow-spring line* runs from the bow aft to a cleat on the pier.

75 **With Wind or Current Towards the Pier,** ease your boat alongside the pier and let the wind push you in to it.

Tying Up

76 To tie your boat alongside a pier properly, you will need a minimum of four dock lines: a bow line, stern line, and two spring lines. Spring lines keep a boat from moving ahead or astern. Some sources recommend $1/8$ inch

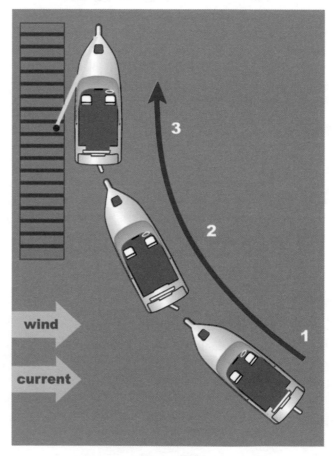

Figure 63
Docking an Inboard Boat
With Wind or Current Off the Pier

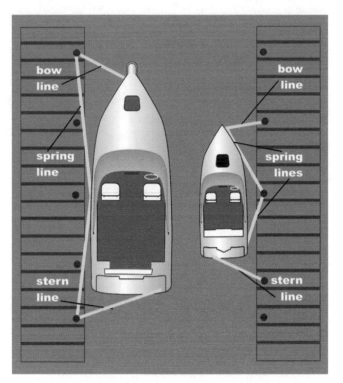

Figure 64
Tying Up Alongside a Pier

of line diameter for each nine feet of boat length. Bow and stern lines should be ²/₃ the length of the boat; spring lines, the length of the boat. If in doubt, seek advice from a professional marine dealer for your specific dock line needs. Your boat's weight, size, and the conditions where you dock can have a bearing on which size rope you should use.

77 Keep the engine running until the boat is tied securely to the pier. Fasten the bow line, stern line, and spring lines as shown in Figure 64. If you plan to leave your boat for any length of time, use chafing gear where lines run through chocks. A chock is a fitting to guide a line. *Chafing gear* is sacrificial wrapping placed around lines, rigging, or spars to prevent wear. It is often made of cloth, cord, tape, leather, rubber, or plastic.

78 In Chapter 4 of this course, you learned the appropriate knots for tying up your boat. When adjusting the length of docklines in

tidal areas, be sure to consider tidal range, the difference in height of water between any successive low tide and high tide.

Leaving the Boat

79 It is unsafe to jump from a boat onto a pier. Make sure of your footing—observe wet surfaces that may be slippery. Pass your gear onto the pier, then step ashore. Do not try to carry it out of the boat.

Tying to a Mooring Buoy

80 Mooring buoys are the only buoys to which recreational boaters may legally tie their boats. It is illegal to tie to a navigational aid.

Permanent Moorings

81 A permanent mooring usually has five parts:
   1) a heavy anchor
   2) a chain rode
   3) a surface buoy attached to the rode
   4) a mooring pendant attached to the rode
   5) a small pickup float or mast buoy attached to the pendant

82 A *pendant* (pronounced *pen'ant*) is a short line that lengthens a mooring rode. It is usually the largest diameter nylon rope that will fit into a boat's chock and around its bow cleat. Pendants are very helpful in picking up a mooring rode, especially when they are equipped with a mast buoy. A *mast buoy* is a small buoy with a 4-foot to 8-foot mast that may be picked up by just leaning over the side of the boat.

83 For maximum control, approach a mooring buoy slowly, heading into the wind or current. When picking up or leaving a mooring buoy, constantly watch the position of the mooring rode. It is very easy to catch it or the pendant in your propeller or rudder.

Anchoring

84 Master the art of anchoring if you want to cruise with peace of mind. Poor equipment and bad anchoring practices can lead to great inconvenience.

85 If your boat drags its anchor, you may find yourself drifting into other boats or onto rocks or beaches. If you drift into and damage other vessels, or foul their anchors, you are responsible for any damage incurred.

Choose the Correct Anchor

86 The correct anchor for your boat depends on the
- size and type of your boat
- kinds of seabed where you intend to anchor
- amount of wind and current you expect to encounter.

87 There are many kinds of anchors. No one anchor is best—each has its strengths and weaknesses.

88 As a starting point, ask marine supply stores and fellow boaters in your area what they recommend. While local knowledge is always valuable, only personal experience in anchoring your boat will tell you if you have made the correct choice.

89 What you are purchasing in an anchor is *holding power*. Factors affecting holding power include design, weight, and material of construction. Anchors almost always hold by digging in to the bottom, seldom by weight alone. Design strongly influences an anchor's ability to hook itself into the bottom. Always purchase a quality anchor. Avoid bargain copies of name-brand anchors.

Figure 65
Typical Permanent Mooring

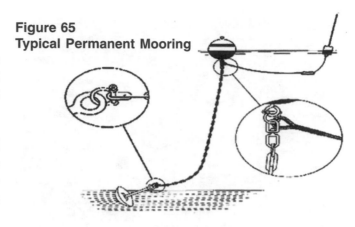

Types of Anchors

90 Today's anchors are mostly lightweight types. Known by the names of their manufacturers, most have outstanding holding power for their weight.

91 The typical anchor is designed so that a horizontal pull will cause it to dig itself firmly into the bottom. An upward pull should dislodge it easily. There are two types of anchors found on today's recreational boats:

92 **Lightweight High-Penetration Anchors.** The Danforth® anchor (Figure 66) is a twin fluke anchor developed during World War II to pull landing craft off the beachheads of the Pacific. Light in weight, its long, narrow, twin flukes engage the bottom quickly. The anchor tends to bury itself in sand and mud when under heavy horizontal strain. However, it has limited penetration in grass, rocks, or clay. There are many copies of this design with a variety of brand names. (Fortress® and West® anchors are examples.)

Figure 66
Danforth®
Anchor

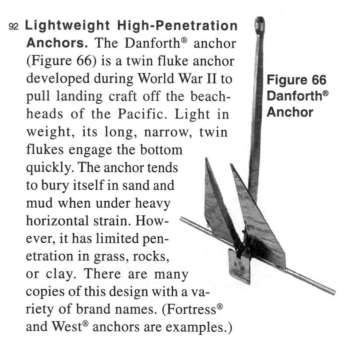

93 **Heavy Partial-Penetration Anchors.** The CQR® ("secure") anchor (Figure 67) is a *plow* anchor with a single fluke, shaped like a plowshare that digs itself deeper under heavy horizontal strain. Although it has limited holding power in deep mud, the CQR anchor will penetrate weeds, sand, and grass, and hook itself into rocks. It is claimed to remain buried over moderate changes in direction of pull due to current or wind changes. However, a CQR anchor is difficult to stow unless hung on an anchor roller off the bow.

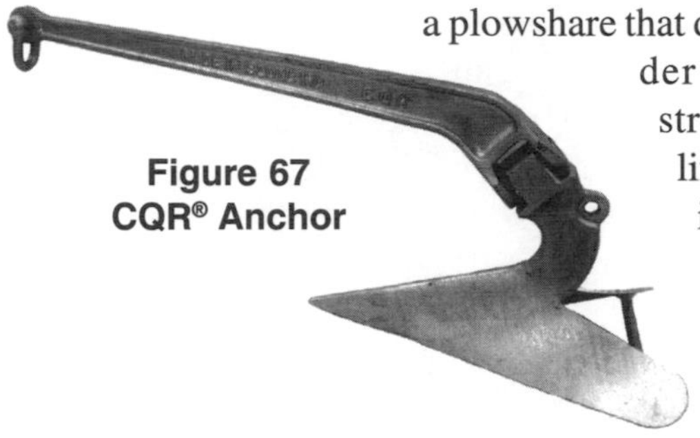

**Figure 67
CQR® Anchor**

94 The Bruce® anchor (Figure 68) is another plow anchor developed for use with offshore oil well rigs and scaled down for small craft use. It is designed to right itself no matter how it lands on the bottom and is claimed to resist breaking out through 360° changes in the direction of pull. The Bruce works well in mud, sand, clay, gravel, weeds, and rocks. It is also difficult to stow unless you hang it from an anchor roller. (The Delta® anchor is similar to the CQR and the Bruce.)

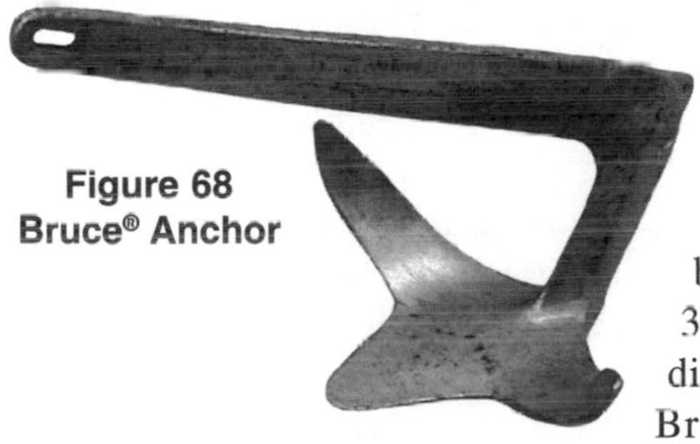

**Figure 68
Bruce® Anchor**

95 **Specialty Anchors.** A *grapnel* anchor (Figure 69) has four or five arms to snag projections on the sea bed. Often used on inland rivers and lakes, it has even been hung in trees to anchor boats. It has poor holding power in mud, sand, and gravel, but is good in rocks. The grapnel can also be used to drag for lost objects.

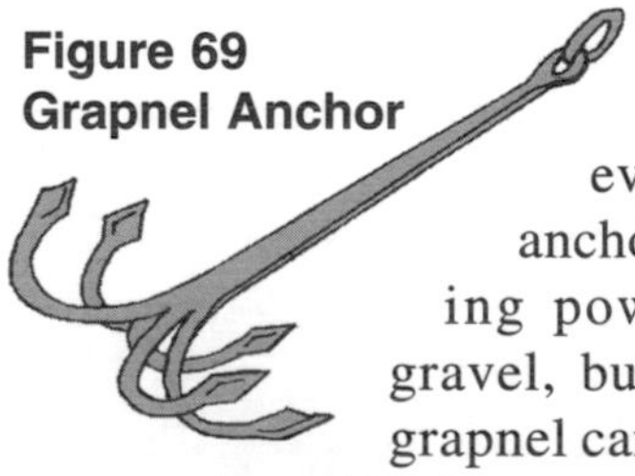

**Figure 69
Grapnel Anchor**

96 Attach a trip line if you use a grapnel for an anchor. (A *trip line* is a buoyed line attached to the crown of an anchor. Pulling the trip line will free a fouled anchor.)

97 Large *mushroom* anchors (Figure 70) are ideal for permanent moorings. They have a history of being used to anchor dredges and lightships in soft sea beds. The mushroom shape tends to sink deeply into the bottom and, when so embedded, has tremendous holding power.

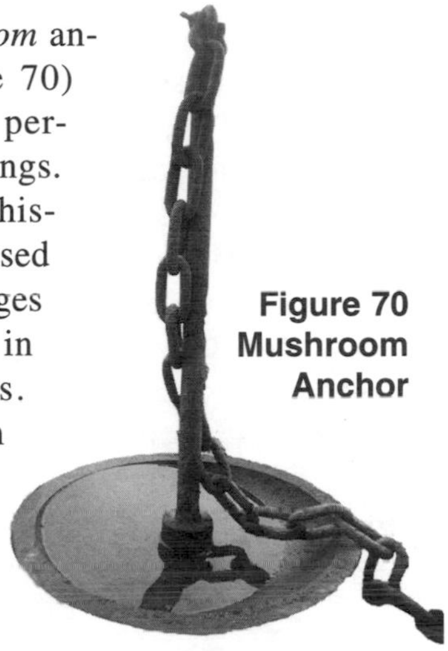

**Figure 70
Mushroom
Anchor**

98 All the anchors described here are made in an assortment of sizes for various boats. It's a good idea to carry two anchors, of different designs, to handle nearly any condition you might encounter. If you lose an anchor, the second anchor also serves as a backup. Attach both anchors to anchor lines and carry them at the bow so they will be ready for instant use.

Rode

99 The nautical term for anchor line is *rode,* which may be rope or chain. Nylon rope is strong, with good resistance to chafing and rubbing. It can stretch without damage to its fibers and will not rot when stowed wet. It is easy on the hands and will not float.

100 Chain is excellent on larger vessels. Although heavy, it has great strength, stows compactly, and can be stowed wet if rust-proofed.

101 You will find the relative strengths of various kinds and sizes of materials used for anchor rodes in *Chapman,* marine catalogs,

and other reference books. You may also seek advice from the manufacturer of your boat as to the diameter of rode recommended.

Anchor Systems

102 Anchor chain should be installed between a rope and an anchor (Figure 71). The weight of the chain reduces the pulling angle and keeps the direction of the pull of the rode as near to horizontal as possible. Chain also reduces damage to the rode from bottom conditions. Obtain expert advice on the size and length of chain for your particular boat and then experiment. Chapman and other sources suggest a length of good quality $^3/_{16}$ to $^1/_2$-inch chain, from 6 to 30 feet in length, depending on the size of the boat.

103 **Fastening Rode to the Anchor or Chain.** The recommended method of connecting rope rode to an anchor or chain is to splice an eye around a thimble in the end of the rode. (An *eye* is a fixed loop in the end of a line. A *thimble* is a grooved metal loop around which a rope eye may be spliced, thus making it more resistant to chafing.) Non-metal thimbles are not recommended.

104 A shackle is then used to fasten the thimble to the chain or anchor. (A *shackle* is a U-shaped metal piece of hardware with a re-movable pin, used to connect a line, sail, or fitting.) We recommend that you wire the shackle pin to the shackle so that it will not vibrate loose. It is also a good idea to se-cure the rode to the legs of the thimble with small twine or wire.

Anchoring Techniques

105 In order to gain a nearly horizontal pull on an anchor, the rode must be relatively long compared to the vertical distance to the bot-tom of the seabed. This ratio (comparison) is called *scope*.

106 **Note:** *vertical distance to the bottom* in-cludes:
   1) the height of the bow of the boat from the surface of the water
   2) the depth of the water, and
   3) any anticipated difference in water depth due to rise and fall of the tide

107 The amount of scope required depends on your anchor's ability to hold a particular type of bottom, considering wind and sea conditions. Scope will vary from a minimum of about 5:1 for calm conditions to 10:1 in severe conditions (7:1 is considered normal).

108 For example: you wish to anchor in 10 feet of water using a scope of 7:1; the bow of your boat is 5 feet above the surface of the water; you expect the tide to rise 3 feet while you are anchored. You will need 126 feet of rode: $(10 + 5 + 3) \times 7 = 126$. If severe weather develops, you would increase your scope to 10:1, using 180 feet of rode.

109 The longer the rode, the more horizontal the pull: the better the anchor will dig in. In a storm, a longer rode will not allow a sharp enough angle for the anchor to pull out. The elasticity of the longer rode will help cush-ion the boat against wave surges.

110 *Be sure the end of the rode is fastened to your boat!* Anchors have been lost due to boaters' oversight of this simple precaution.

111 **Anchor Line Markers** are available to in-sert between the strands of a rode to mark the length to that point. Some manufactur-ers offer anchor line that is color-coded at various lengths.

112 **Setting an Anchor.** Approach the place you intend to anchor *against* the wind or cur-rent, whichever is stronger. When you reach the desired position, bring the boat to a standstill. Lower (never throw) the anchor over the bow. Allow the boat to drift with the wind or current. Apply power in slow

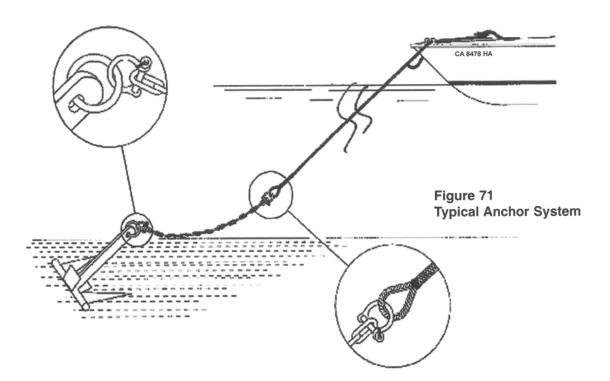

**Figure 71
Typical Anchor System**

reverse if necessary. Let the rode out slowly to keep it from fouling the anchor. Make sure the line does not wrap around your legs as you pay it out.

113 Use more rode than you need for your planned scope. This will increase the horizontal pull necessary to dig in the anchor. When sufficient line is out, *snub* it by taking a turn around your bow cleat. Then

place an easy strain on the line with the engine. When satisfied that the anchor is *set* (dug in), take in any extra rode, run it through a chock, and tie it to the bow cleat with a cleat hitch. (The cleat hitch is described in the Chapter 4, Knots and Lines, of this manual.)

114 Sailing vessels without power must pay particular attention to insure that their anchor is set into the bottom.

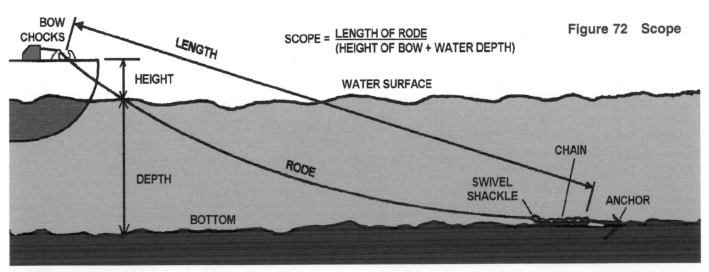

SCOPE = LENGTH OF RODE / (HEIGHT OF BOW + WATER DEPTH)

Figure 72   Scope

115 Always observe the relationship of the boat to objects on shore and check periodically to see that the anchor is not dragging. Never anchor a vessel only from the side or stern; strong current, heavy seas, or large wakes can swamp or sink you.

Retrieving an Anchor

116 When ready to hoist anchor, approach the anchor position slowly, taking in the line to avoid fouling it around your boat's propeller or rudder. When directly over the anchor, it should break out easily. If deeply embedded, it may be necessary to snub the rode around the bow cleat and run the boat forward, breaking it out with the force of the boat. If that is not successful, move the boat slowly in a circle. Always take extreme care that the rode is kept away from propellers and rudders.

Boat Theft Protection

117 Theft of boats and equipment is a major problem. Boats are left unattended for days at a time and it is not unusual for thieves to slip into a harbor at night and tow off a boat or steal equipment.

118 No nationwide system for tracing and identifying boats exists, such as there is for motor vehicles. You cannot stop a determined thief, but you can slow him down and perhaps discourage him enough that he will look for easier prey.

119 Keep valuable items, particularly portable ones, out of sight. You may want to take valuable items with you when you leave the boat. Locks are available to help secure outboard motors, trailers, etc. Add a padded chain and lock to the mooring lines securing your boat to a pier or trailer. Consider installing a hidden ignition switch or fuel cutoff valve.

120 If you purchase a security alarm, chose one that is designed for a boat. Automobile alarms often work on principles that are not compatible with a boat. Perhaps the best protection is to enlist your boating neighbors in a mutual boat-watch project, where everyone helps to keep an eye on the boats in your marina or mooring field.

Personal Watercraft Considerations

121 Remember, a PWC is a boat! As such it is subject to many of the same requirements for equipment and operation as any other powered vessel under sixteen feet in length. Use courtesy and good judgment just as you would with any other boat. Respect the rights of shoreline property owners, other boaters, and persons enjoying the water. Keep noise down. Operate your PWC at a minimum speed when in close proximity to shore, other boats, persons in the water, and wildlife.

122 Always operate your PWC in such a way that accidents will not occur. Remember that a PWC will turn only when the jet pump is operating and pushing a stream of water out of the stern of the craft and creating thrust. If you release the throttle to avoid a collision while operating at high speed, your PWC will not turn. It will probably continue in the direction you were moving, often into the object you were trying to avoid.

123 Chapter 16 of this manual, Personal Watercraft Operation, covers how PWCs work and other considerations for safe PWC operation. Consider taking a course in PWC operation. The USPS home study video course entitled *Jet Smart* includes an action-packed video tape demonstrating proper PWC techniques. USPS also publishes the learning guide, *Water Sports*.

Homework

Name: _____ **Date:** _____ **Group:** _____

1. A safety-conscious skipper never starts the engine on a boat before:
   a. all passengers are comfortably seated on the foredeck, gunwale, or transom.
   b. checking to see that there is enough alcohol and additives in the fuel.
   c. checking the previous day's newspaper for a weather forecast.
   d. sniffing for fuel vapors in the engine and fuel compartments.

2. Before fueling a boat with a built-in fuel tank, you should:
   a. close all portholes, doors, and hatches.
   b. turn on the bilge blower, if so equipped.
   c. open all portholes, doors, and hatches.
   d. turn off all electronic equipment except your VHF radio.

3. An important safety instruction to follow when refilling portable fuel cans and tanks is to:
   a. always use approved yellow marine safety tanks.
   b. always fill them inside the boat where fuel will not spill.
   c. use only approved safety tanks and fill them outside the boat.
   d. step carefully onto the gunwale when carrying full tanks aboard.

4. A float plan includes a description of your boat, who is on board, your safety equipment, and, most importantly:
   a. the name of your radio operator.
   b. where you expect to be and when.
   c. the name of your alternate skipper.
   d. what mechanical equipment on your boat is not in the best condition.

5. An alternate skipper should have enough knowledge to:
   a. stop the engines, drop the sails, and use the radio in an emergency.
   b. make mechanical repairs if necessary.
   c. empty the boat's holding tank at a pump-out station.
   d. fly burgees and ensigns in their proper places.

6. When approaching other boats or congested areas, check your wake because:
   a. it can disturb the smooth operation of personal watercraft.
   b. your wake must never be more than three inches high.
   c. you are responsible for damage to persons or property caused by the wake of your boat.
   d. you may see beautiful colors created by the oxidation of phosphorus in the water.

7. When docking and undocking your boat, it is desirable to:
    a. always operate your boat at cruising speed.
    b. approach against the wind or current for more control of your boat.
    c. give instructions in a loud authoritative tone so that the crew will know who is in charge.
    d. teach the crew how to keep the boat away from the pier using their arms and legs.

8. The correct anchor for your boat will depend not only on the size and type of your boat but on the:
    a. cost-always purchase the cheapest anchor available.
    b. size and length of your anchor rode.
    c. types of seabed and amount of wind and current you expect to encounter.
    d. location-bow or stern-from which you anchor.

9. The ratio of the length of a rode to the vertical distance to the bottom of the seabed is called a:
    a. chock.
    b. spring.
    c. scope.
    d. wake.

10. Under normal conditions, the recommended scope of an anchor line should be approximately:
    a. 25:1
    b. 15:1
    c. 7:1
    d. 2:1

11. Never anchor a boat only from the side or stern because:
    a. strong current, heavy seas, or large wakes can swamp or sink you.
    b. the bow should always be pointing away from the wind.
    c. it is difficult to adjust the rode for proper scope.
    d. it is difficult to bring persons over the bow in an emergency.

9

Piloting—The Mariner's Compass

1 The compass is a direction-finding instrument. It is used to determine the direction a vessel is heading and to take bearings to establish position. It is an important navigational tool, and every boat should be equipped with one.

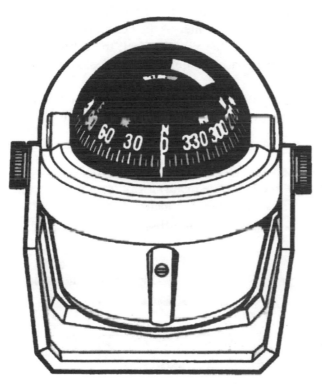

Figure 73   A Typical Mariner's Compass

How a Compass Works

2 An irregular and constantly changing magnetic field surrounds the earth. The poles of this magnetic field are not in the same location as the earth's true geographic poles where the longitudinal meridians converge.

The magnetic North Pole is more than 600 miles away from the true North Pole.

Compass Design

3 An iron bar or needle that is free to rotate in a magnetic field will align itself in the direction of the lines of force that make up the field. If the needle is also a magnet, alignment is quicker. A magnetic compass operates in the same manner. Its magnets will align the compass card with the magnetic North Pole.

Compass Construction

4 A compass consists of parallel bar magnets attached to the bottom of a nonmagnetic circular compass card. A jeweled bearing on a pivot pin supports the card. Friction at the pivot is reduced by floating the card in an oil contained in the compass bowl. The oil serves an additional purpose of making the card more stable.

5 The bar magnets align themselves and the compass card with the earth's magnetic field, in the direction of the magnetic North Pole. The edge of the compass card is marked in degrees, reading clockwise 360° in a full circle.

6 Marked on the inside of the compass bowl is an index mark, called a lubber's line. If the compass is properly mounted, the numbers on the compass card-when read at the lubber's line-will indicate the direction the

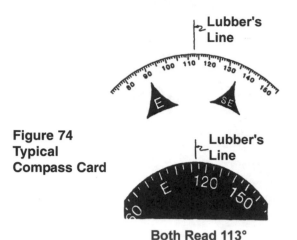

**Figure 74
Typical
Compass Card**

Both Read 113°

boat is heading in reference to magnetic north. On better compasses, you will find the lubber's line on the far side of the compass bowl from the helmsman. Note that in Figure 74, the compass cards read 113°.

Selecting a Compass

7   Select a compass carefully and pay special attention to its installation and care. Your compass is your most important piloting tool.

Size

8   A large compass will be much more stable, of better quality, and easier to read than a small one. However, the space available to mount it may limit size. In mounting a compass, consider where it can best be viewed by the helmsman.

Quality

9   Compasses vary widely in quality. However, price is not the best indicator of quality. Minimum pivot friction is an important consideration. Excessive pivot friction causes a compass card to move very slowly and is apt to cause inaccuracy.

10 Test for pivot friction by moving a magnet near the compass to draw the compass card to one side.

11 Observe the movement of the card when you remove the magnet. Does it return smoothly and easily to its original position? Reverse the magnet and test the compass in the same way in the opposite direction. If the compass does not pass this test, it has excessive pivot friction and you should reject it. Test even new compasses in this manner. The type of fluid in the bowl can affect the movement of the compass card.

Installing a Compass

12 Mount your compass where you can easily read it; preferably directly in front of the steering station. A line through the lubber's line and the center of the compass must be parallel to the vessel's keel, the centerline of the boat. Illuminate the compass bowl at night with a dim red or filtered light. Chapman's Piloting, Seamanship, and Small Boat Handling is one source of instruction on methods of installing a compass.

13 Ideally you should mount a compass at least three feet (one meter) away from any electrical or magnetic influence. In practice, however, this may be difficult. Twist each pair

**Figure 75
Compass Installation**

Mounting Line

Keel Line

Lubber's Line

Compass   Compass

of electrical wires near the compass along the full length of the wires to cancel magnetic effects of current. Engines, windshield wipers, and panel instruments (especially an ammeter) when running, can affect accuracy, as can a steering wheel with a steel core.

14 Try to keep the compass in the center of a three-foot spherical space that is free of magnetic material. Be careful where you put items such as radios, remote speakers, clocks, fans, tools, pocket knives, steel food cans; anything metal. These can have adverse influences on your compass.

15 Before fastening down the compass, move it slowly to the desired location and watch the effect on the compass card. If the helmsman is not directly in front of the compass, he must be aware that compass readings can be distorted by the glass of the compass bowl, possibly resulting in inaccurate readings.

16 Once you have installed a compass, you must be sure that its readings are correct. You may have a compass checked and adjusted by a professional compass adjuster. Or, learn to do this yourself in advanced courses such as the USPS Piloting course or the USPS Learning Guide, Compass Adjusting.

Compass Care

17 Keep your compass in top condition. Direct sunlight may discolor the card and fluid, making the compass hard to read. To avoid this, use a cover that will not allow sunlight to penetrate. Remove compasses from boats during storage or trailering. Storing a compass on its side removes pressure on the pivot and reduces pivot wear. In cold weather, bubbles may form in the compass bowl due to contraction of the fluid. If they do not disappear when warm weather arrives, take the compass to a repair shop.

The Compass Course

18 A compass will point to true north only along an imaginary line that runs irregularly from the west coast of Florida north through the Great Lakes to Hudson Bay. This line is called the agonic line. Everywhere else, east and west of this agonic line, the earth's magnetic field varies as much as 25 degrees from true north.

Variation

19 Variation is the angle between the true north geographic pole and the magnetic North Pole. When the earth's magnetic field causes the compass to point west of true north, the variation is a westerly variation. Conversely, when the magnetic field causes the compass to point east of true north, the variation is an easterly variation.

20 Variation changes with geographic position. (It is 0° along the agonic line.) The variation for a given location can be found on the chart. It is in the center of the compass rose closest to the location. The annual change is also shown. When used for piloting, variation is always expressed in whole degrees. (Note that the variation on our practice chart is westerly due to its geographic location.)

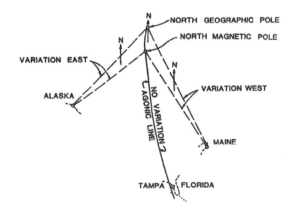

Figure 76   Variation

Deviation

21 Magnetic fields created by electrical and magnetic materials aboard a boat can cause a compass to show improper readings. This effect is called deviation.

22 Careful placement of instruments and metallic materials, combined with accurate adjustment of the compass, can reduce deviation to almost zero. As a practical matter, the deviation for a well-placed compass in a fiberglass, aluminum, or wooden boat can be insignificant if the compass is corrected for onboard influences.

23 In this course, we will consider a vessel's deviation to be 0°. This subject is discussed more fully in advanced courses such as the USPS Piloting course.

Calculating a Steering Course

24 When we drew the course line from G C "1" to RG "D" GONG on our Bowditch Bay practice chart, we found the true course to be 067°. We referenced it to true north, because true is the language of the chart.

25 However, the helmsman steers by a compass. Magnetic is the language of the compass.

26 In order to steer the desired course, we must make a correction to convert the true course of the chart to the magnetic course of the compass. That correction is variation, the angle between true north and magnetic north, as explained above. (We must also correct for deviation, but here we are assuming no deviation.)

27 There is a simple rule: When going from true to compass, add westerly variation and subtract easterly variation.

28 Example: In our practice exercise, true course was 067°. We note from the closest compass rose that the variation for that area is 15° W. Our steering course would then be 082°.

True Course	T	067°
Variation	V	15° W (+)
Magnetic Course	M	082°
Deviation	D	0° (Assumed)
Compass Course	C	082°

29 As a second example, assume that the true course (T) is 035° and the variation (V) is 8° E. Then the compass course (C) is 027°.

True Course	T	035°
Variation	V	8° E (−)
Magnetic Course	M	027°
Deviation	D	0° (Assumed)
Compass Course	C	027°

Outside Influences

30 Wind and current can affect the course of a vessel. Make allowances based on personal experience for the way these forces affect the progress of your boat. Advanced navigation courses such as the USPS Advanced Piloting course will teach you how to estimate these outside influences.

Homework

Name: _____ **Date:** _____ **Group:** _____

1. A compass is an important navigational tool on board a vessel because it:
   a. is a speed-determining instrument.
   b. can be used to establish position and determine the direction a boat is heading.
   c. is required by federal, state, and local laws.
   d. will show the direction of true north at a glance.

2. If a compass is properly mounted, the numbers on the compass card-when read at the lubber's line-will indicate the direction the boat is heading in reference to:
   a. magnetic north.
   b. the north star.
   c. true north.
   d. the boat's centerline.

3. Size and quality are two key factors in choosing a compass. The size will often be limited to the:
   a. shape of the compass bowl.
   b. space available to mount it.
   c. position of the lubber's line.
   d. amount of pivot friction.

4. Mount a compass so that:
   a. the compass card can be seen from anywhere in the boat.
   b. it is as close to your VHF radio as possible.
   c. it will not be in the way or anywhere you can find a place.
   d. a line through the lubber's line and the center of the compass is parallel to the keel.

5. Keep your compass in top condition by keeping it out of direct sunlight and by:
   a. storing it on its side to remove pressure on the pivot.
   b. not using it in stormy weather.
   c. not adding too much oil to the compass bowl.
   d. avoiding exposing it to moisture.

6. The angular difference between the true geographic pole and the magnetic North Pole is called:
   a. variation.
   b. magnetization.
   c. deviation.
   d. a line of force.

7. Variation:
   a. is established by the Coast Guard.
   b. can usually be ignored.
   c. changes with geographic position.
   d. does not show on a chart.

8. To convert true course to magnetic course:
   a. add easterly variation.
   b. subtract westerly variation.
   c. add westerly variation.
   d. consult Local Notices to Mariners.

9. Referring to the course you plotted on the practice chart from R "6" to RW "OR", what would be your compass course? (Variation is 15° West, Deviation is 0°)
   a. 087°
   b. 193°
   c. 268°
   d. 323°

10. What would be the magnetic course from
    RW "OR" to R N "2" if the variation
    was 5° East? (Deviation is 0°)
    a. 060°
    b. 091°
    c. 180°
    d. 271°

10

Government Regulations

1 You, as a skipper, are responsible for the safety of your boat and the people aboard. The federal government has created regulations to help reduce the number of boating accidents. Therefore, it is essential that you know and follow these regulations. You must also know your state and local boating laws.

2 The expression "ignorance of the law is no excuse" also applies to boating.

3 Upon completion of this chapter, you should:
- know the boat registration requirements
- know the equipment required on board
- realize the required equipment is not enough to guarantee safe and pleasurable boating
- be familiar with important U.S. Coast Guard safety standards
- be informed of federal rules and regulations enforced by the Coast Guard, state, and local agencies

Required Equipment

4 It is important that you have the required equipment on board your boat and know how to use it. The following chapter will help you determine the equipment required for your type and size of boat.

Boat Registration

5 Motorboats must be registered in the state where they are primarily used, or documented with the Coast Guard. (Documentation is an optional form of national registration for yachts of five or more net tons.)

6 When you register your boat, you will receive a certificate; it must be on board whenever the vessel is in use. Keep it in a waterproof container to protect it from the elements.

7 Attach your assigned numbers permanently to each side of the forward half of your boat; they should read from left to right. Use block letters at least three inches high. The color of the letters must contrast well with the color of your boat. Examples would be black on white, or white on black.

8 Boat numbers include two letters that identify your state, followed by a combination of numbers and letters that identify your boat. Use spaces or hyphens to separate blocks of numerals from letters. Attach state registration stickers within six inches of the boat number. Do not display any other numbers nearby.

RI 1635 H

**Figure 77
Typical Boat Registration Number**

9 The law allows each state to create its own numbering system. Find out the requirements in your state. Notify the state agency that issued your registration within 15 days, if your:
- boat is transferred, destroyed, abandoned, lost, stolen, or recovered
- registration certificate with assigned number is lost or destroyed
- address changes

10 Surrender your certificate within 15 days if it becomes invalid for any reason.

Classes of Boats

11 Federal regulations divide motorboats into four classes according to length. Required equipment is different for each length.
- Class A—Less than 16 feet (4.9 meters)
- Class 1—16 feet to less than 26 feet (7.9 meters)
- Class 2—26 feet to less than 40 feet (12.2 meters)
- Class 3—40 feet to not more than 65 feet (19.8 meters)

12 **Length Determination (LOA).** Measure boat length along the centerline from the foremost part of the hull to its aftermost part. Bowsprits, rudders aft of the transom, swim platforms, and outboard motor brackets are not part of the length unless they are part of the hull.

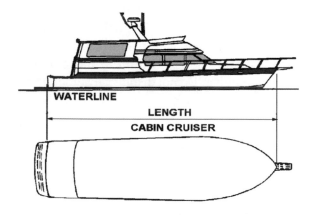

Figure 78   Measuring the Length of a Boat

Life Preservers

13 Everyone who goes boating needs a life preserver. A life preserver is sometimes referred to as a Personal Flotation Device (PFD). Purchase one that you will wear, then wear it; life preservers float—you don't!

14 Coast Guard statistics show that most boating fatalities occur from capsizing or falling overboard. Most drownings occur within a few feet of safety, and the victims owned life preservers but died without them. A wearable life preserver can save your life only if you wear it.

15 **Life Preserver Requirements.** Regulations require a wearable life preserver for each person on board a recreational boat; this includes canoes and kayaks. Life preservers must have a Coast Guard Approval Number on the label. This approval means the preserver has met minimum testing standards in calm water. It is not a guarantee of its performance in all rough water conditions.

16 Life preservers must be in good condition, the right size for the wearer, and easily reached. Have each crew member adjust his or her life preserver for proper fit. Mark them with the wearer's name and, when not worn, stow them so that you can read the names easily.

17 Boats over 16 feet must also carry a Type IV throwable device or equivalent Type V device, ready to toss to a person in the water (see below).

18 **Features of Life Preservers.** The buoyancy of a life preserver, rated in pounds, is what keeps you afloat. Your weight is not the only factor in finding out how much "extra lift" you need in the water. Body fat, lung size, clothing, and whether the water is calm or rough, all play a part in staying on top. In general, the more physically fit you are, the more "lift" you need.

19 Life preservers come in a variety of shapes, colors, and materials. Obtain one that fits you and your type of boating. Try on a preserver before you purchase it. Make sure it is for your weight and size and is easy to put on, take off, and adjust. A highly visible color will make you easier to find.

20 **Types of Life Preservers.** There are five types of USCG-approved life preservers:
- Type I—Offshore Life Jackets
- Type II—Near-Shore Buoyant Vests
- Type III—Flotation Aids
- Type IV—Throwable Devices
- Type V—Special Use Devices

21 For Types I, II, and III, the lower the type number, the better the life preserver's performance; for instance, Type I is better than Type II.

22 **Classes of Life Preservers.** The five types of life preservers fall into three classes:
1. inherently buoyant
2. inflatable
3. hybrid inflatable

23 *Inherently Buoyant Life Preservers* have buoyant material built in-usually foam or kapok. They are the traditional rugged, low maintenance life preservers that are available in adult and child sizes. They are available for both swimmers and non-swimmers in all five types; four wearable and one throwable, as described in Table 1 on page 94.

24 Inherently buoyant preservers in Types II, III, and V are also produced in high-impact models for active sports such as waterskiing and riding personal watercraft. They have various ratings such as 50 miles per hour and 75 miles per hour. These ratings mean that the preservers were tested to determine if they could withstand impact at that rate of speed without tearing or disintegrating.

25 The tests were not made on real people. The ratings do not guarantee personal protection for someone hitting the water at these speeds, or even that the life preserver will stay on the person.

26 *Inflatable Life Preservers* are the most recent class approved by the Coast Guard. They can be manufactured in Types I, II, III, and

V. There are no throwable types. They inflate either orally, manually, or automatically.

27 All types inflate orally with an inflation tube that allows you to use your own breath to inflate the vest. The tube also deflates the vest. Manual vests inflate by pulling a cord that triggers a device that inflates the vest within seconds. The automatic version inflates within five seconds of full impact with the water, but may also be inflated manually. The advantage of inflatables is that they are comfortable and more likely to be worn continuously to prevent a person from being suddenly caught without protection.

28 Inflatable life preservers have no buoyancy unless inflated and are not for use:
- by non-swimmers or weak swimmers, unless worn inflated
- by children younger than 16 years of age or persons weighing less than 80 pounds
- in water sports where water impact is expected, such as waterskiing, riding personal watercraft, or white water paddling-inflatables are not made in high-impact models
- under restrictive clothing-automatic or accidental manual inflation can restrict breathing and injure the wearer

29 Inflatables are available only in adult sizes. *Belt packs*, which are worn around the waist and pulled up over the wearer's head when inflated, are also available. Automatic inflatables should inflate within five seconds of immersion in the water. All types can be inflated by pulling a lanyard or blowing into an inflation tube.

30 Inflatable life preservers require regular user checks and maintenance; more than inherently buoyant life preservers. Always check the status of the inflator and cylinder before each outing.

Table 12—Inherently Buoyant Life Preservers

Features	Type I Inherently Buoyant Offshore Life Jacket	Type II Inherently Buoyant Near-Shore Buoyant Vest	Type III Inherently Buoyant Flotation Aid
Best For	All waters; especially off-shore, remote waters where rescue may be delayed	Protected waters, near shore, where there is a chance for fast rescue	Calm, protected, inland, near-shore waters where there is a chance for fast rescue
Minimum Buoyancy	22 lbs. Adult 11 lbs. Child	15.5 lbs. Adult 11 lbs. Child 7 lbs. Infant	15.5 lbs. Adult 11 lbs. Child 7 lbs. Infant
Rough Water Support	Excellent	Poor	Poor
Flotation Posture	Will turn most unconscious victims face-up	Will turn some unconscious victims face-up	Will not turn victims face-up
Body Heat Retention	Fair	Poor	Fair
Visibility	Excellent: only available in orange color	Excellent when color is orange or yellow	Excellent when color is orange or yellow
Comfort	Bulky; restricts movement	Lightweight; more comfortable than Type I	Comfortable

Features	Type IV Inherently Buoyant Throwable Device	Type V Inherently Buoyant Special Use Device
Best For	Throwing to a person in the water to grasp and hold until rescue	Only for special uses or conditions. Label states limits of use which may include approval only when worn. Includes boardsailing vests, deck suits, pullover vests, work vests.
Minimum Buoyancy	16.5 lbs. ring buoy 18.0 lbs. cushion	15.5 lbs.
Rough Water Support	Poor	Good if so indicated on label
Flotation Posture	Not acceptable as a wearable life preserver	Will turn most unconscious victims face up; but always check label for this information
Body Heat Retention	None	Excellent (coveralls) to fair (vests)
Visibility	Excellent if orange in color	Good if orange or yellow in color
Comfort	Not a wearable preserver	Most comfortable, convenient, and useful

Table 13—Inflatable Life Preservers

Features	Type I Inflatable Offshore Life Jacket	Type II Inflatable Near-Shore Buoyant Vest	Type III Inflatable Flotation Aid	Type V Inflatable Special Use Device
Best For	All waters; especially offshore, open, rough, remote waters where rescue may be delayed	Protected waters, near shore, with chance for fast rescue	Calm, protected, inland, near-shore waters with chance for fast rescue	Only for special uses or conditions; see preserver label for limits of use, which may include that they are approved only when worn
Minimum Buoyancy	34 lbs. Adult; only adult types available	34 lbs. Adult; only adult types available	22.5 lbs. Adult; only adult types available	22.5 lbs. Adult; only adult types available
Rough Water Support	Excellent	Poor	Poor	Good if used according to label conditions
Flotation Posture	Will turn most unconscious victims face-up	Will turn some unconscious victims face up	Will not turn victims face-up	Will turn most unconscious victims face up when inflated
Body Heat Retention	Poor	Poor	Fair	Poor
Visibility	In all four types; excellent visibility when inflated; orange and yellow are only colors available			
Comfort	In all four types; best combination of convenience and comfort (especially in hot weather) among all life preservers			

31 The inflator will have a red and green indicator that shows if it is ready for use. If the indicator shows red, do not use the preserver until you recharge it. If it shows green, it is ready for use.

32 Check the cylinder to make sure it is installed properly and not punctured. Inspect all parts for corrosion. Blow up the vest with the inflation tube regularly to check for rips, tears, and punctures. Do this in accordance with the owner's manual. See Table 2, Inflatable Life Preservers.

33 *Hybrid Inflatable Life Preservers* are available in Types I, II, III, or V. These preservers combine inherently buoyant flotation material with an inflatable bladder for extra lift, thus they are different from *Inflatable Life Preservers* that don't contain any inherently buoyant flotation material. Hybrid Inflatables are available in both adult and child sizes.

34 Minimum inherent buoyancies for adult preservers are: 15.5 lbs. for Type I, 10.0 lbs. for Types II and III, and 7.5 lbs. for Type V. Body heat retention properties will vary with the style and design of the jacket or suit. The label will indicate if hypothermia protection is particularly good.

35 These preservers are stylish, convenient and useful for specific activities, and offer the

Table 14—Hybrid Inflatable Life Preservers

Features	Type V Hybrid Inflatable Jacket
Best For	Best for Restricted use per label which may include that it be worn to meet requirement
Minimum Buoyancy	7.5 lbs. uninflated 22.5 to 34 lb. inflated
Rough Water Support	Good when inflated
Flotation Posture	Will turn most unconscious victims face-up when inflated
Body Heat Retention	Fair to good; see label
Visibility	Good if bladder is orange
Comfort	Comfortable

best comfort for non-swimmers. Type Vs are less safe than other types if not used according to conditions specified on the labels; some meet the requirement only when worn.

36 **Children's Life Preservers**. Teach your children to wear a life preserver whenever they are on a boat or around the water. Some states require this; check your local regulations. A USCG rule went into effect 23 December 2002 requiring all children less than 13 years of age to wear USCG-approved life jackets while aboard recreational vessels underway, except when children are below decks or in an enclosed cabin.

37 Children's life preservers come in child weight ranges: less than 30 pounds, 30–50 pounds, and 50–90 pounds.

38 Some manufacturers specify a chest size. Measure your child's chest under the arms before shopping for a life preserver.

39 Children often panic and move their arms and legs violently when they fall into the water. Their life preservers must fit properly. Pick the child up by the shoulders of the jacket. If the preserver gives more than three inches or slips over the chin or ears, it is too large. Fit it with a crotch strap to help keep it in place. Purchase one in a highly visible color. A white preserver is a poor choice-it looks like a whitecap in the water.

40 Test the preserver in shallow water. Children may not float face up in the water as easily as adults due to a different distribution of body weight.

41 An adult should always be with a child on or near the water. Never use a life preserver as a babysitter. Never use inflatable toys or rafts as a substitute for a life preserver. Don't leave a child alone while aboard a moving boat, regardless of the boat's size!

42 **Wear Your Life Preserver** whenever you are on the water: you may not have time to put it on when you need it, especially when injured. Life preservers are hard to put on in the water. Try it sometime, and you will find out firsthand the difficulty of trying to fasten them while treading water!

43 Even strong swimmers can tire and succumb to exhaustion or hypothermia. The extra buoyancy of a life preserver keeps you afloat. Some life preservers will help retain body heat, thus extending survival time.

44 If you have not been wearing your life preserver because of the way it makes you look or feel, there is good news. Today's life preservers fit better, look better, and allow easy movement. Brightly colored life preservers can increase your chances of rescue.

45 Before you shove off, make sure all on board are wearing life preservers. To work best they must be worn with all straps, zippers,

and ties fastened. Tuck in any loose straps to prevent getting hung up.

46 When you *don't* wear your life preserver, the odds are against you. You are taking a chance with your life.

47 **Care of Life Preservers.** Life preservers must be in good condition. Store and care for them properly. Dry them before storing. Do not crush them under heavy weights or use them for boat fenders or seat cushions. Oil and grease may deteriorate life jackets and reduce their buoyancy.

48 Make regular checks for tears, holes, broken straps, and hardware. Squeeze the jacket; does it feel the same as when you bought it? Yank on the straps to be sure they are securely fastened. Replace any preservers that are not in first-class condition.

The 20% Who Wore PFDs and Still Drowned

49 Why, in boating mishaps, did the 20% who *were* wearing life jackets still drown? A significant number of these victims were paddlers, such as canoeists and kayakers. Paddlers have a few things working against them if they have a mishap. They tend to boat in remote areas, far from rescue resources or help from passersby. They frequently paddle alone or with only one other person. Their vessels tend to be relatively unstable and prone to frequent capsizing.

50 Paddlers are particularly at risk for a dangerous situation called *entrapment*. This occurs in flowing water when a boater becomes snagged on rocks or debris at a hazardous point (referred to as a *strainer*), then goes under due to the severe hydraulics of the water pressure. If the boater is either unable to escape the craft or unable to escape the hydraulic pressures, regardless of what

kind of PFD the boater is wearing, the resulting cause of death will be drowning.

Fire Extinguishers

51 There are three common types of fire extinguishers (A, B, and C) to match the class of fire they extinguish:
  • Class A fire-wood, paper, rubber, plastic, textiles
  • Class B fire-flammable liquids (gasoline, oil, and grease)
  • Class C fire-electrical equipment

Figure 79   Typical Fire Extinguisher Label

52 The most available and least expensive fire extinguisher for a recreational boat is a dry chemical type that is made to put out all three classes of fires, A, B, and C. Just plain water, which is almost always available, will extinguish a Class A fire. Dry chemical extinguishers leave a messy residue that will cause corrosion unless cleaned up immediately.

53 Other effective extinguishing agents, such as carbon dioxide, foam, and Halon, are not often found on small recreational boats for various reasons.

**Figure 80
Dry Chemical Fire
Extinguisher**

54 Manufacturers have voluntarily halted production of Halon. It allegedly causes damage to the ozone layer that protects the earth from ultraviolet radiation. If you own a Halon extinguisher, you may keep it and use it for the life of the product. Halon replacements are now available on the market.

55 **Sizes of Fire Extinguishers.** There are two sizes of extinguishers, I and II. The size describes the amount of extinguishing chemical an extinguisher holds. The Coast Guard requires that a Size I dry chemical extinguisher contain a minimum of 2 lbs. of dry chemical. Size II requires at least 10 lbs.

56 **Fire Extinguisher Requirements.** Fire extinguishers are required on boats with:
  • inboard engines, and outboard boats with closed compartments for storing permanent or portable tanks
  • permanently installed fuel tanks
  • closed compartments or living spaces

57 Since a flammable liquid fire (gasoline, oil, or grease) is the most serious type of fire on a boat, Class B extinguishers are the best for recreational boats. Many Class B extinguishers also put out Class A and Class C fires.

58 Purchase only extinguishers certified as Coast Guard approved by an independent testing agency such as Underwriter's Laboratories, Inc.

59 The minimum requirements for portable extinguishers depend on the length of the boat.

60 You may substitute one B–II extinguisher for two B–I extinguishers. A boat with a fixed extinguishing system in the engine room may carry one less B–I extinguisher.

61 Mount portable extinguishers in USCG-approved mounting brackets with quick-release catches.

62 **Choose the Correct Extinguisher.** You can make a fire worse by using the wrong type of extinguisher on a fire. For instance, never use a stream of water on a Class B flammable liquid fire because oil and gasoline will float on the water and spread the fire.

63 The federal requirements listed above are bare minimums. We recommend you equip your boat with at least one more extinguisher than required. A B–I extinguisher will completely discharge its contents in 8 to 10 seconds!

64 The key to controlling a fire is to put it out while it is still small. Your chances are better if you have more than the minimum required extinguishers.

65 **Learn How to Use Your Extinguishers.** Pull the safety pin and direct a stream of halon from a Halon extinguisher or powder from a dry chemical extinguisher at the base of the fire. Hold the extinguisher upright and sweep from side to side or use a series of short blasts. The powder blankets the fire, cutting off oxygen that fuels the flames.

66 Be careful when putting out galley fires. Too much pressure from the extinguisher can cause liquids or grease to splatter and spread the fire. Watch for hot embers and repeat if a flashback occurs. Many local fire departments provide practice opportunities.

67 Never partially discharge extinguishers to test them; they may leak and be unusable. Always recharge or replace partially discharged extinguishers. Purchase only extinguishers

Boat Length	Number of Extinguishers	Type and Size
Less than 26 ft.	1	B–I
26–39 ft	2	B–I
40–65 ft	3	B–I

Table 15   Fire Extinguishers Required

approved by an independent testing agency such as Underwriter's Laboratories, Inc.

68 **Fire Extinguisher Locations.** Mount your extinguishers away from fire hazards so that you will be able to get to them safely. Make sure they do not project into a busy passageway. Steering stations, galleys, and passenger cockpits are logical locations. If you sleep aboard, keep one near your bunk.

69 **Maintenance.** Check the gauges on your extinguishers monthly to make sure they are at full pressure. Gauges may occasionally be unreliable. Be sure the discharge nozzle is clean; insects love to build nests inside. Slowly rock your dry chemical extinguishers from an upright to an upside down position several times. If you feel a thud, it means that the chemical is stuck together and the extinguisher will no longer function properly.

70 Immediately replace and properly dispose of old extinguishers. Check for corrosion or mechanical damage to the extinguisher case. If they are the rechargeable-type metal head—not plastic—take them to a qualified fire extinguisher service for an annual inspection.

Flame Arrestors

71 All gasoline engines, except outboard motors, must be equipped with acceptable flame arrestors. A flame arrestor is a screen-like metal fitting fastened over a carburetor air intake. It keeps flames from flashing out into the engine compartment where they could ignite gasoline fumes. Flame arrestors work by spreading and cooling the ignited fumes. They must comply with Underwriter's Laboratories or Society of Automotive Engineers standards.

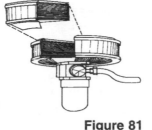

**Figure 81
Flame Arrestor**

72 Keep your flame arrestors in good condition. There should be no holes in the grids through which flames might advance. Keep them clean, not only for safety purposes, but to allow your engine to operate efficiently.

Visual Distress Signals

73 Federal law states that all boats used on coastal waters, the Great Lakes, and those waters connected directly to them, up to a point where a body of water is less than two miles wide, must be equipped with USCG-approved visual distress signals. They must be in serviceable condition and readily accessible.

74 The following vessels are not required to carry day signals but must carry night signals when operating from sunset to sunrise:
  • recreational boats less than 16 feet in length
  • open sailboats less than 26 feet in length, not equipped with motors
  • manually propelled boats

75 Electronic devices such as a VHF radio are very helpful in an emergency. However, never depend only on electronic equipment that may go out of service. Visual distress signals will help you attract attention and get help when needed.

**Figure 82
Pyrotechnic Distress Signals**

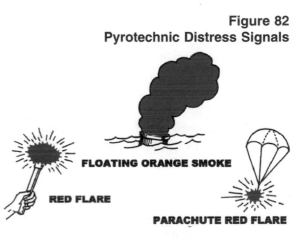

FLOATING ORANGE SMOKE

RED FLARE

PARACHUTE RED FLARE

76 **Types of Visual Distress Signals.** There are two kinds of distress signals pyrotechnic and non-pyrotechnic.

77 *Pyrotechnic signals* resemble fireworks. They include:
  • red flares, handheld or aerial meteor, and parachute flares
  • orange smoke, handheld, or floating

78 Flares are marked with an expiration date beyond which they will not meet requirements. Keep those with expired dates as backup devices. Small seven-second meteor flares are only minimally adequate, even though they satisfy USCG requirements. Bigger is better.

79 Store pyrotechnic signals in a cool, dry location in a red or orange watertight container clearly marked *Distress Signals.*

80 Use pyrotechnic signals safely. They can cause personal injury and property damage if you do not handle them properly. These signals produce a very hot flame, and the residue can cause burns or ignite flammable material. For safety's sake, tape your flares to the end of a mop handle or boat hook. This will allow you to hold the burning flare downwind and away from the boat to avoid burns from dripping slag.

81 Always consider wind direction when you use a rocket-propelled distress signal. To avoid starting a fire, never fire a pyrotechnic device straight up or in such a direction that it may land in your boat, another boat, or on land.

82 Pistol launched and hand-held parachute flares and meteors have many characteristics of a firearm and must be handled with caution. In some states they are considered a firearm and prohibited from use. You should also declare pistol launched devices when checking in with Customs in foreign countries.

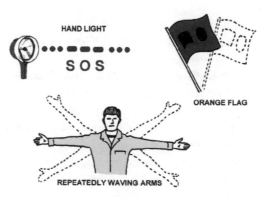

Figure 83
Non-Pyrotechnic Distress Signals

83 *Non-pyrotechnic Signals* must be in serviceable condition, readily accessible, and certified by the manufacturer as complying with USCG requirements. They include the following devices:
  • orange distress flags-black square and ball displayed against an orange background at least 3 feet square (day signal only)
  • mirror-very effective in sunlight and requires no power (day signal only)
  • dye markers-mostly for offshore use (day signal only)
  • electric distress lights (for night use only) must automatically flash the SOS international distress signal:
    [• • • – – – • • •]

84 Under Inland Navigation Rules, a high-intensity white light that flashes at regular intervals from 50 to 70 times per minute is considered a distress signal.

85 The international distress signal of slowly and repeatedly raising outstretched arms to each side is a simple attention-getter. *Do not* wave your arms over your head: it looks like a greeting.

86 **Visual Distress Signal Requirements.** The following are examples of the variety and combination of devices that meet *all* of the following requirements:

- three handheld red flares (day and night)
- one handheld red flare and two parachute flares (day and night)
- one handheld orange smoke signal and two floating orange smoke signals (day)
- one electric distress signal (night only)

87 The use of visual distress signals is prohibited except for emergency situations. The Coast Guard dispatches a vessel and/or aircraft each time a distress signal is reported. Do not fire flares until you are sure there is a chance of their being seen.

Lights

88 The Navigation Rules require vessels to display lights between sunset and sunrise and during periods of restricted visibility; i.e., fog, rain, haze, etc. Lights alert other vessels of your presence. They also convey information about your boat's approximate length, and its type. Chapter 12, The Navigation Rules, and Appendix G of this manual describe navigation lights in detail.

Sound-Producing Devices

89 The Navigation Rules require you to use sound signals during periods of limited visibility and in meeting, crossing, and overtaking situations.

**Figure 84
Typical Sound-Producing Devices**

90 The law states you must have some means of making an efficient sound signal. Canister-powered horns are ideal for a small boat.

91 A whistle and a bell are additionally required on vessels more than 39.4 feet (12 meters). Check your local laws; they frequently differ from federal regulations.

When You Rent a Boat

92 A skipper is always responsible for a boat's equipment and operation, and for the safety of its passengers. When you rent a boat, you are the skipper. You are responsible for having the required equipment on board, not the boat rental agency.

Recommended Equipment

93 For safe, comfortable boating, you need more equipment than that legally required.

94 Imagine being out in a small boat without such basic necessities as oars, paddles, anchor, rode, bailer, compass, and charts. The following is a checklist of additional equipment to consider.

Large Boats—Need to Have

- anchor and rode
- compass
- first-aid kit
- automatic bilge pump
- high-volume, manual bilge pump
- charts and plotting tools
- food and water for emergencies
- VHF radio
- spare anchor
- docking lines
- flashlight

Large Boats—Nice to Have

- extra clothing
- spare propeller
- sea anchor
- spotlight
- spare tiller
- towline
- fenders
- spare sails
- spare parts
- swim ladder
- tools

Small Boats—Need to Have

- anchor and rode   • bailer
- compass   • first-aid kit
- oars and paddles

Small Boats—Nice to Have

- spare anchor   • fenders
- spare propeller

USCG Boating Safety Standards

95 Over time, the Coast Guard has developed a number of safety standards for boats.

Hull Identification Number

96 Boats manufactured after 1972 must have a hull identification number (HIN). This consists of 12 letters and/or numbers. A country-of-manufacture designator may precede these numbers and letters. The HIN has an important safety purpose; it enables manufacturers to locate boats involved in defect notifications and recalls. It is not the same as the state registration number that you display on the bow of your boat, but it does appear on your state registration certificate.

97 You will find the HIN near the top of the outboard starboard side of the transom, or near the top outboard portion of the starboard hull near the stern. On catamarans and pontoon boats, it is on the aft crossbeam near the starboard hull attachment.

98 Newer boats have duplicate identification numbers in unexposed locations inside the boat or under items of hardware. This duplicate number aids authorities in identifying

ABC 45678C 393

Figure 85
Typical Hull Identification Number

your boat if the primary identification number is damaged or removed.

99 The first three digits "ABC" identify the manufacturer. The second five digits "45678" are the hull serial number. The next two digits "C3" are the date of certification (the letter "C" represents the month of March, and the number "3" the year 1993). It is illegal to alter or remove an HIN. If your boat does not have an HIN, your state will assign one.

Maximum Capacities Label

100 A small boat will often accommodate more people and gear than the boat can safely carry. Overloading a boat reduces freeboard and makes it easy to swamp or capsize in heavy waves.

101 A USCG safety standard requires a maximum capacity label on all single-hull boats less than 20 feet in length. It does not apply to personal watercraft, canoes, kayaks, inflatable boats, or sailboats. The maximum capacity label states the maximum:
- number of persons for which the boat is rated
- total weight of those persons
- combined weight of persons, motor, and gear for which the boat is rated
- horsepower of any motor used on the boat

102 The rating for maximum number and weight of persons is only a guide. The most important information is the maximum combined weight of persons, motor, and gear. Use it as the controlling figure. Although not required by federal law, many boat manufacturers have their own voluntary standards for boats up to 26 feet in length.

103 The safety standard for maximum capacities described above is a federal standard.

State and local governments may have different standards. Always check for local laws and regulations with law enforcement agencies in the area where you operate your boat.

104 Excessive engine power can make a boat difficult to control. Overpowering leads to excessive speed on turns with great risk of capsizing. It also puts too much stress on the hull.

105 The greater the horsepower, the greater the weight of the motor. This extra weight can lead to stability problems and reduce freeboard at the stern. The latter increases the likelihood of following seas or wake coming aboard over the transom.

106 Most marine law enforcement agencies consider operating a boat in excess of its capacity rating as negligent operation. Insurance companies often refuse to insure a boat powered with an outboard engine that exceeds the horsepower rating on the capacity label. In addition, manufacturers may refuse to honor warranty claims for boats with oversized motors.

Vessel Certification Label

107 Boat manufacturers affix a certification label to each boat, stating the boat complies with applicable USCG Safety Standards. It is illegal to alter or remove a certification label. It may be a separate label or combined with the maximum capacities label.

Flotation Standard

108 A 1978 flotation standard requires that single-hull outboard and manually propelled boats less than 20 feet long have flotation material. There must be enough to keep the boat at or just below the surface of the water if holed or swamped, even when loaded with passengers, motor, and gear.

109 Sailboats, canoes, kayaks, and inflatable boats don't have to comply with this standard. However, extra flotation adds a measure of safety for all boats. Single-hull inboard and stern-drive boats under 20 feet in length also have flotation requirements but they are not as stringent.

Ventilation Systems

110 Ventilation systems bring fresh air into each engine and fuel tank compartment, and conduct dangerous fumes out of the vessel. Ventilation requirements apply to any boat that has a permanently installed gasoline engine for electrical generation or mechanical power propulsion, and any outboard boat with a fuel tank in an enclosed compartment.

**Figure 87
Typical Ventilation System**

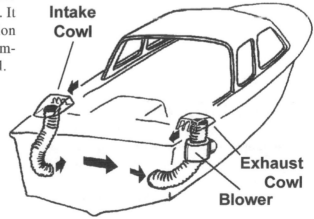

Intake Cowl

Exhaust Cowl
Blower

**U. S. COAST GUARD
MAXIMUM CAPACITIES**

6 PERSONS OR **800** lbs.
1,325 LBS. PERSONS, MOTOR, GEAR
120 H.P. MOTOR

THIS BOAT COMPLIES WITH U.S. COAST GUARD SAFETY
STANDARDS IN EFFECT ON THE DATE OF CERTIFICATION
MANUFACTURER: ABC MARINE, INC.
MODEL: 2050   METRO, NY USA
LOAD AND H.P. CAPACITY • LEVEL FLOTATION
COMPARTMENT VENTILATION • MANEUVERABILITY

**Figure 86
Maximum Capacities
and Certification Label**

111 A typical ventilation system has two ducts. One brings outside air in below the level of the carburetor. The other exhausts inside air from the lower bilge to the outside. Some ventilation systems include ducts equipped with blowers. Ducts in these systems must be in the lower one-third of the compartment and above the normal accumulation of bilge water. A powered ventilation system is required for each compartment in a boat that has a permanently installed gasoline engine with a cranking motor for remote starting.

112 If your boat bears a label containing the words, "This boat complies with U.S. Coast Guard safety standards," you can assume that your boat's ventilation system meets regulations.

Law Enforcement

113 There are many laws enforced by the U.S. Coast Guard and other law-enforcement agencies. You should be aware of all of the things they will be looking for.

Boarding

114 The Coast Guard and most law enforcement officials may board your boat any time it is underway to conduct a safety inspection. If hailed by a law enforcement vessel, follow the boarding officer's instructions. Avoid penalties by following the Navigation Rules and all regulations described in this chapter.

Negligent Operation

115 The Coast Guard imposes penalties for negligent operation that endangers life and property. Examples of negligent operation are:
- operating a boat in a swimming area
- operating a boat while under the influence of alcohol or drugs
- excessive speed in the vicinity of other boats or in dangerous waters
- hazardous waterskiing practices

- bow riding-also riding on a seat back, gunwale, or transom
- wake jumping

Responsibility for Wake

116 You are responsible for damage to persons or property caused by the wake of your boat. You are liable for both criminal and civil actions if your boat creates a wave that rocks another boat enough to injure a person or damage the boat or equipment.

117 Anticipate wake problems. Observe the water-not just behind you-but at a distance where your wake may be hitting other boats or objects. Heavy wakes striking the shore may cause serious erosion. Consider the effects of your wake on boats you meet. Slow down some distance away to reduce the effect of your stern waves.

Boating While Intoxicated

118 The use of alcohol is a serious problem on the water. According to federal law, you are intoxicated if your blood alcohol content is 0.10% or higher. Nearly every state has a blood alcohol limit of not more than 0.10%; many states have limits of 0.08% or lower. Violators are subject to civil and criminal penalties.

119 *Boater's fatigue* often results after about four hours of exposure to noise, vibrations, sun, glare, wind, and other motion on the water. It can slow reaction time almost as much as if you are legally drunk. Adding alcohol or drugs to these factors multiplies the risk of accidents.

120 Alcohol and drugs reduce your ability to survive if you fall overboard. They affect your judgment and limit your ability to think clearly. It takes longer for your eyes, ears, and other senses to react. Passengers are affected as well as the boat operator.

121 Boat smart! Don't boat if you drink or use drugs. Remember that a boat's skipper is responsible for the conduct of his passengers as well as his own.

Termination of Use

122 If the Coast Guard observes a boat being operated in a hazardous condition or manner, it may direct the operator to take immediate steps to correct the condition. This can include terminating the use of the boat and returning it to port. The following are typical reasons for ordering termination of use:

- insufficient number of USCG-approved life preservers
- insufficient number of fire extinguishers
- overloading beyond the manufacturer's recommended safe-loading capacity
- improper navigation light display
- inadequate ventilation systems
- fuel leakage
- fuel in the bilge
- improper backfire flame control
- operation of an unsafe vessel

Water Pollution

123 Federal law prohibits the throwing, discharging, or depositing of any refuse matter, including garbage, sewage, oil, trash, or other pollutants, into U.S. waters.

124 **Oil Discharges** must be reported immediately to the Coast Guard. Report any discharge into the water of hazardous substance that causes a film, sheen, discoloration of the water, or emulsion beneath the surface. There are penalties for every discharge of a "harmful quantity of oil." If your boat is 26 feet in length or over, you must post a special 5-inch × 8-inch placard near the engine compartment summarizing the law.

125 **Disposal of Toxic Substances.** Federal law prohibits the discharge of oil or other hazardous substances into navigable waters.

Oil residue can build up in your bilge; and, that residue may be pumped overboard or pollute the surrounding area, if any drain plugs are removed while your boat is on a trailer or lift. Take precautions to ensure this does not happen.

126 **Sewage Discharge.** It is illegal to discharge raw sewage from a vessel in the sea within three miles of the coastline, or in sounds, bays, navigable rivers, or the Great Lakes. Recreational boats with installed toilet facilities must have an operable USCG-certified marine sanitation device.

127 These devices are of various types. Type I and II devices treat sewage in some approved manner before discharging it into the water. Type III MSDs include recirculating and incinerating devices and holding tanks.

128 Vessels equipped with Types I or II devices must have their MSDs sealed to prevent discharge when in no discharge zones. *No discharge zones* are areas that require greater environmental protection and in which the discharge of sewage, even though treated, is considered unacceptable.

Discharge of Oil Prohibited

The Federal Water Pollution Control Act prohibits the discharge of oil or oily waste into or upon the navigable waters of the United States or the waters of the contiguous zone if such discharge causes a film or sheen upon, or a discoloration of the surface of the water, or causes a sludge or emulsion beneath the surface of the water.

Violators are subject to substantial civil and/or criminal penalties including imprisonment.

Figure 88   Oil Discharge Placard

129 Due to the growing number of no discharge zones, and increasing number of boaters, the federal government and the states are assisting with funding the installation of additional pump-out stations along U.S. waterways. Be aware of local antipollution laws wherever you boat.

130 **Dumping of Garbage** into the sea is a worldwide problem. Plastic waste is particularly harmful. It kills fish and marine wildlife and fouls vessel propellers and cooling systems. The law prohibits dumping garbage and plastic refuse into the water. Never throw anything into the water that did not come out of it.

131 Boaters who witness suspected violations of garbage-dumping laws should report these violations to the United States Coast Guard. If your boat is 26 feet in length or over, you must display a special 4-inch × 9-inch placard notifying passengers of dumping restrictions (see Figure 89).

132 **Aquatic Nuisance Species.** To help prevent the spread of the latest plague of non-native fish and Zebra mussels in our waterways, boaters should follow these simple rules:

- Trailer boaters should remove visible mud, plants, fish, or animals from boats and trailers prior to transport to another body of water
- Scrape any mussels from boat or outdrive and flush hull, bilges, and water-holding compartments with hot water (at least 120° Fahrenheit), if available
- Do not release plants or fish, including bait, into a body of water unless they came out of that same body of water
- Pump fresh water through engines before leaving the area
- Drain live and transom wells, bait buckets, and bilge

Figure 89   Garbage Dumping Placard

- Remove water from trailer boats by removing the drain plug and parking on an incline to facilitate draining
- If available, use high-pressure hot water to spray down both boat and trailer.
- Let boat, trailer, and equipment dry for at least five days
- Empty water out of kayaks, canoes, rafts, etc.

133 These same rules apply to:
- scuba diver equipment
- waterfowl hunting gear
- angler's rods and equipment
- sailboats and sailboards
- PWCs
- seaplanes

134 **Waste Management Plan.** Vessels 40 feet and longer, equipped with a galley and berthing, are required to have a written Waste Management Plan aboard. The plan must describe the procedures for collecting, processing, storing, and discharging garbage and designate the member of the crew who is responsible for carrying out the plan.

135 **Environmental Summary.** We all enjoy America's lakes, rivers, and coastal waters. To keep them healthy and productive, follow good environmental boating practices.

Top 10 Green-Boating Tips

1. Keep your bilge clean—don't pump oily water overboard
2. Use bilge sorbents, not detergents
3. Don't pump your sewage in confined waters—use a holding tank
4. Observe local and federal sewage regulations
5. Bring garbage home—don't litter
6. Use detergents sparingly—even "biodegradable" cleaners are hard on the aquatic environment
7. When fueling, don't top off tanks; clean up any spilled fuel
8. Use paints approved for marine use
9. Avoid shoreline erosion—watch your wake and propeller wash
10. If fishing, practice catch and release

136 Report pollution when you see it.

Accident Reporting

137 All boating accidents described below must be reported to the proper marine law enforcement authority by the operator or owner of the vessel. All vessels involved in an accident must file a report.

138 This accident information is required:
- date, time, exact location of the accident
- name of each person who died or disappeared
- number and name of the vessel
- name and address of the owner and operator

139 The above are federal regulations regarding accident reporting; local laws may differ. The safest approach is to report any accident involving property damage or personal injury as quickly as possible to your local State Boating Office and insurance company.

140 You may call the Coast Guard Customer Infoline (see below), or your State Boating Office for additional information regarding accident reporting.

141 **Note:** An example of a Boating Accident Report form is located in Appendix H, pages 255 and 256.

Vessel Safety Check Program

142 USPS has joined with the USCGAux in conducting free Vessel Safety Checks (VSCs) of pleasure boats. This program of checking and discussing the safety equipment on board your vessel is designed to make your boating activities safer for you, your family and friends, and fellow boaters. No report of your boat is ever made to any law enforcement agency.

143 If your boat meets VSC requirements, the award of the VSC decal is your assurance that your boat is properly equipped and meets the minimum federal equipment requirements. A properly equipped boat is a safer boat.

Orally Notify Authorities Immediately	File Written Report Within 48 Hours	File Written Report Within 10 Days
Fatal accidents in which a person dies or disappears	If a person dies or disappears or if there are injuries requiring more than first aid	Accidents involving damage in excess of the state-specified limit or complete loss of vessel.

Table 16   Required Accident Reports

Figure 90   Vessel Safety Check Decal

USCG Customer Infoline

144 Infoline operators provide callers with information on boating safety recalls and take consumer complaints about possible safety defects. They answer questions about such things as safety equipment requirements, boating safety classes, how to register a boat, and how to get a commercial license. They will also respond to requests for printed safety material.

145 The Coast Guard offers a guide entitled, "Federal Requirements and Safety Tips for Recreational Boats." In the United States, including Alaska, Hawaii, Puerto Rico, and the Virgin Islands, call 1-800-368-5647 (1-800-689-0816 for the hearing impaired). Hours are 0800 (8:00 A.M.) to 1600 (4:00 P.M.), Eastern Time, Monday through Friday, excepting federal holidays.

State and Local Regulations

146 Boating regulations discussed in this student manual are those of the federal government. State and local governments often have additional rules governing the operation of boats. You will receive instruction in this course in local and state regulations that differ from federal regulations. If your state requests that the course examination include questions relative to their regulations, your course instructor will cooperate with this request.

147 Most states provide guides that describe boating regulations in their area.

Homework

Name: _____ **Date:** _____ **Group:** _____

1. In addition to federal regulations described in this course, you must be familiar with:
   a. the Federal Boat Safety Act of 1764.
   b. state and local regulations.
   c. laws of the Underwriter's Laboratories, Inc.
   d. regulations of the AARP.

2. Your boat has a yellow hull. After registering it with the state, and receiving a boat number, you purchase:
   a. a black plastic plate with 2 inch script letters and numbers to hang over the side.
   b. 3 inch black vertical block letters and numerals for both sides of the forward hull.
   c. lighter yellow letters and numbers for both sides of the forward hull.
   d. light gray 2 1/2 inch italic letters and numbers for the starboard upper transom.

3. Regulations require that all recreational boats have:
   a. a USCG approved wearable life preserver for each person on board.
   b. an anchor and rode to securely anchor the vessel under any conditions.
   c. a compass, charts, dock lines, and fenders.
   d. a radiotelephone.

4. The feature of a life preserver that keeps a person afloat is its:
   a. visibility.
   b. ability to be thrown.
   c. warmth.
   d. buoyancy.

5. You should purchase a life preserver that fits you and your type of boating and one that:
   a. can be easily stored out of the way.
   b. is easy to put on, take off, and adjust.
   c. will be stylish in keeping with current fashions.
   d. can also be used for scuba diving.

6. A dry chemical fire extinguisher:
   a. never needs refilling or servicing-it keeps its pressure indefinitely.
   b. is not very effective for fires in the cabin, galley, or cockpit.
   c. must be directed at the base of the fire to cut off the oxygen that fuels the flames.
   d. may be replaced by water on fires involving flammable liquids.

7. Visual distress signals:
   a. are required on all boats.
   b. are not needed if you have a VHF radio.
   c. help you attract attention and get help when needed.
   d. make attractive displays on national holidays.

8. When you rent a boat, the person responsible for having all legally required equipment aboard is the:
    a. dock hand who turns the boat over to you.
    b. boat's manufacturer.
    c. person who rents the boat; you.
    d. rental agent.

9. Vessel equipment required by law:
    a. is only part of that needed for safe and comfortable operation.
    b. covers all of your needs for the safe operation of your vessel.
    c. includes charts and other navigational equipment.
    d. does not include visual distress signals and fire extinguishers.

10. A hull identification number not only identifies your boat but:
    a. is the registration number on the forward part of the hull.
    b. prescribes the maximum horsepower engine for which the boat is rated.
    c. identifies the materials of construction of that boat.
    d. enables manufacturer to locate boats involved in defect notifications and recalls.

11. The most important information on a boat's Maximum Capacities Label is the:
    a. boat's registration number.
    b. seating capacity of the boat.
    c. maximum total weight of occupants of the boat.
    d. maximum combined weight of persons, motor, and gear.

12. If you are hailed by a law enforcement vessel you should:
    a. wave to indicate that you do not need help.
    b. follow the boarding officer's instructions.
    c. move quickly out of the area so that you are out of the way.
    d. maintain course and speed, for you are the stand-on boat.

13. A condition that could result in the termination of the use of your boat is:
    a. the display of navigation lights in daylight.
    b. running with your fenders hanging from the sides of your boat.
    c. overloading beyond the manufacturer's recommended safe loading capacity.
    d. failure to carry charts of your cruising area.

14. The condition that slows reaction time after several hours on the water almost as much as if you were legally drunk is called:
    a. hypothermia.
    b. saint vitus dance.
    c. sea leg fever.
    d. boater's fatigue.

15. Federal law prohibits:
    a. depositing garbage at a marina or on shore.
    b. using a marine sanitation device that utilizes disinfecting chemicals.
    c. using incinerating marine sanitation devices.
    d. throwing, discharging, or depositing oil, garbage, sewage, or other pollutants into U.S. waters.

16. If involved in a boating accident, the safest approach is to:
   a. report to the proper authority immediately any accident involving damage in excess of $3000.
   b. file an accident report with the local Motor Vehicle Department within 30 days.
   c. file a report on VHF radio with the Federal Communications Commission as quickly as possible.
   d. report any type of accident involving property damage or personal injury as quickly as possible to your State Boating Office and insurance company.

11

Piloting—Distance, Speed, Time

1 You have learned to plot simple true courses from one navigational aid to another. In real situations you will need more information, such as an estimated position of your vessel at a specified time. To obtain this information, you need to know how to compute distance, speed, and time.

The DST Formula

2 There is one basic formula for computing distance, speed, and time when any two of the values are known:

$$60 \times D = S \times T$$

- **D** = *Distance* in nautical miles (nm); the distance from one place to another. A *nautical mile* is 1.15 statute miles, (1.84 kilometers). (In areas where charts show distance in statute miles, the formula may be used, providing that speed is in statute miles per hour.)
- **S** = *Speed* in knots (kn); a *knot* is a nautical mile per hour
- **T** = *Time* in minutes (m); the time to get from one place to another
- Multiplying distance by 60 allows us to use time in minutes

3 Thus, 60 multiplied by the distance (D) is equal to the speed (S) multiplied by the time (T). By substituting known values in the DST formula, the unknown value can be calculated by simple multiplication and division.

4 Of the three values (distance, speed, and time) two will always be known and used to calculate the value of the third. It may be convenient to remember this formula as a street address:

60 D STreet

Distance

5 Always express distance in nautical miles to the nearest one-tenth of a nautical mile (such as 2.8 nm). On charts where distance is shown in statute miles, express distance to the nearest one-tenth of a statute mile.

6 **To Compute Distance (D),** start by writing the formula. Then fill in the information you know. For example, if speed is 10 knots and time is 30 minutes

Formula:	$60 \times D = S \times T$
Known information:	$60 \times D = 10 \times 30$
Multiply two numbers:	$60 \times D = 300$
Divide by the other number:	$D = 5$ nm

7 Sample Problem: If you run your boat at a speed of 12 knots for 40 minutes, how far will you go?

Formula:	$60 \times D = S \times T$
Known information:	$60 \times D = 12 \times 40$
Multiply two numbers:	$60 \times D = 480$
Divide by the other number:	$D = 8$ nm

8 **To Measure Distance.** On coastal charts, distance is measured in *nautical miles* (6076 feet). In inland waters, distance is measured in *statute miles* (5280 feet). Using dividers,

you can find distance on a chart by one of
two ways:

1) The distance scale will be near the
   chart title block.
2a) The latitude scale on the chart pro-
    vides a means for measuring distance.
    One minute of latitude is equal to one
    nautical mile. Most coastal naviga-
    tion charts provide latitude scales in
    their left and right margins.
2b) You will find latitude scales on small-
    craft charts along certain meridians
    of longitude.

9 Always make distance measurements by using the latitude scale as close to the plotted
course line as possible; latitude scales on
most charts change as latitude changes.

10 When measuring short distances, open the
dividers to the exact distance being measured. Then move the dividers to either the
nautical mile scale, or the adjoining latitude
scale, and read the distance.

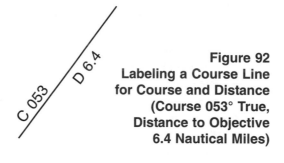

**Figure 91
Measuring Distance
on the Latitude Scale**

11 When measuring distances too long to be obtained in one spread of the dividers, preset
the dividers on the latitude scale to a convenient distance, (perhaps one or two nautical
miles). Then, starting at one end of the
course line you are measuring, walk the dividers along the line. If the last step goes

beyond the line, close the dividers to the remaining distance and return to the latitude
scale to find the additional distance.

12 Sample Problem: Please return to the sample
course line (G C "1" to RG "D") on the
Bowditch Bay practice chart. On the latitude scale just to the left of the course line,
preset your dividers to two nautical miles.

13 Starting at G C "1" walk your dividers along
the course line toward the RG "D" GONG.
You will be able to measure five full
"spreads" of the dividers (10 nm). The additional distance will measure 1.2 nautical
miles on the latitude scale. The total distance
is 11.2 nautical miles.

14 **Labeling Course Lines for Distance:** Label distance *under and near the middle of
the course line.* Show distance in nautical
miles to one decimal place. In this manner,
label your practice course line for distance
as measured above.

**Figure 92
Labeling a Course Line
for Course and Distance
(Course 053° True,
Distance to Objective
6.4 Nautical Miles)**

Speed

15 Always express speed in knots, (kn), to the
nearest one-tenth of a knot (such as 13.4 kn).
A knot is one nautical mile per hour.

16 **To Compute Speed (S).** Start by writing
the formula. Then fill in the information you
know. For example: If a boat ran 8 nm in 40
minutes, what speed did it travel?

Formula:	$60 \times D = S \times T$
Known information:	$60 \times 8 = S \times 40$
Multiply two numbers:	$480 = S \times 40$
Divide by other number:	$S = 12.0$ kn

17 If it took 50 minutes to run the 11.2 nm between G C "1" and RG "D", how fast were you traveling?

Formula:	$60 \times D = S \times T$
Known information:	$60 \times 11.2 = S \times 50$
Multiply two numbers:	$672 = S \times 50$
Divide by other number:	$S = 13.4$ kn

18 **Labeling Course Lines For Speed.** Label speed (S) *below the course line, under the course label.* Show it in knots to one decimal place (such as, "13.4").

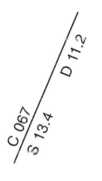

**Figure 93
Labeling a Course Line
for Course, Distance,
and Speed
(Course 067° True,
Speed 13.4 Knots,
Distance to Objective
11.2 Nautical Miles)**

19 **To Determine the Speed of Your Boat.** After plotting the course on a chart and determining the distance, the time required to complete the run may be calculated if the speed of the boat is known.

20 Charts for many areas show a measured mile or half-mile, which may be used to determine a boat's speed at various engine speeds (tachometer revolutions per minute), or to check the calibration of a speedometer.

21 Where a measured mile is not available, select a distance on a chart as close to a nautical mile as possible. Make the run in opposite directions, calculate the speed for

each run (60D = ST), and average the two speeds. This allows for wind or current that may affect the boat during the two runs.

Time

22 Always express time (T) in minutes, to the nearest whole minute (such as 17m). Time is figured in order to estimate elapsed time. *Elapsed time* is the time it takes you to go from one place to another. It can be used to determine the estimated time of arrival (ETA) at a given destination.

23 **To Compute Time (T).** Start by writing the formula. Then fill in the information you know. For example, if distance is 5 nm and speed is 10 kn:

Formula:	$60 \times D = S \times T$
Known information:	$60 \times 5 = 10 \times T$
Multiply two numbers:	$300 = 10 \times T$
Divide by other number:	$T = 30$ m

24 Sample Problem: How long will it take you to run your boat 11.2 nautical miles at a speed of 13.4 knots?

Formula:	$60 \times D = S \times T$
Known information:	$60 \times 11.2 = 13.4 \times T$
Multiply two numbers:	$672 = 13.4 \times T$
Divide by other number:	$T = 50$ m

25 **The 24-Hour Clock.** To simplify working with time in navigational problems, it is convenient to consider the day as one 24-hour period and to number the hours in series: 00 to 24. This is known as the *24-hour clock,* and is sometimes called *nautical time.*

26 Time of day is shown in four digits; the first two digits indicate the hour beginning at midnight, and the second two digits indicate the minutes past the hour. As an example: 2015 means 15 minutes past the 20th hour, or 8:15 P.M. Refer to this time as "twenty-fifteen."

Figure 94 24-Hour Clock

27 Always express nautical time simply in four digits. The terms "A.M." and "P.M." are not used, and the word "hours" is never used. Times such as 1000 and 2000 are correctly referred to as "ten hundred" and "twenty hundred," respectively.

28 Sample Problems:

1) What was the elapsed time if a boat left at 0912 and arrived at its destination at 1547?

Arrive:	15 47
Depart:	09 12
Elapsed Time:	06 35 (6h 35m)

2) A boat leaves at 1015 and runs 5 hours and 27 minutes. What time did it reach its destination?

Depart:	10 15
Elapsed Time:	05 27 (5h 27m)
Arrive:	15 42

3) What was the elapsed time if a boat left at 1047 and arrived at its destination at 1612?

Arrive:	16 12 (1572)
Depart:	10 47
Elapsed Time:	05 25 (5h 25 m)

29 (Note the change of 1612 to 1572. Subtract 1 hour and add 60 minutes to allow easy subtraction of minutes.)

4) A boat leaves at 1045 and travels 3 hours and 30 minutes. What time did it reach its destination?

Depart:	10 45
Elapsed Time:	03 30 (3h 30m)
Arrive:	13 75 (1415)

30 (Note the conversion of 1375 to 1415; by subtracting 60 minutes and adding 1 hour.)

Alternative Method of Using the 60 D STreet Formula

Figure 95 DST Formula Circle Diagram to Compute Distance

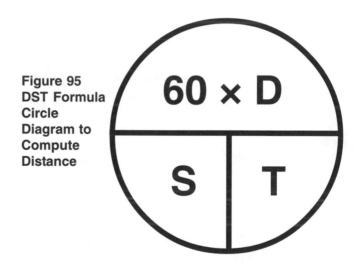

31 **To Compute Distance:**
 1. Cover the **60 × D** on the diagram
 2. The formula is **S × T**
 3. Divide result by 60

32 **To Compute Speed:**
 1. Cover the letter **S** on the diagram
 2. The formula is **60 × D ÷ T**

33 **To Compute Time:**
 1. Cover the letter **T** on the diagram
 2. The formula is **60 × D ÷ S**

Homework

Name: _____ **Date:** _____ **Group:** _____

1. The 60 D = STreet formula is a method of :
   a. estimating the draft of a boat when you know its length.
   b. computing distance, speed, or time, when any two of the values are known.
   c. establishing nautical time of day in daylight savings time.
   d. computing the difference between statute and nautical miles.

2. Distance in piloting is always expressed in :
   a. nautical or statute miles.
   b. knots.
   c. scope.
   d. boat lengths.

3. A nautical mile is:
   a. shorter than a statute mile.
   b. equal to one minute of longitude.
   c. equal to one minute of latitude.
   d. used along coastal highways.

4. The distance of a course line is always labeled:
   a. under and near the middle of the course line.
   b. on top and near the middle of the course line.
   c. on top of the course line near its origin.
   d. under the course line and below the course label.

For questions 5 and 6, refer to the course lines you drew on the "Bowditch Bay" practice chart:

5. The distance in nautical miles from R "6" to RW "OR" is:
   a. 1.8 nm.
   b. 5.6 nm.
   c. 9.3 nm.
   d. 11.1 nm.

6. The distance in nautical miles from RW "OR" to R N "2" is:
   a. 2.3 nm.
   b. 8.1 nm.
   c. 12.9 nm.
   d. 14.4 nm.

7. If you run your boat 46 minutes at a speed of 6.0 knots, how far will you go?
   a. 6.0 nm.
   b. 4.6 nm
   c. 7.8 nm.
   d. 46.0 nm.

8. If you run your boat 1 hr and 24 minutes at 11.4 knots, how far will you go?
   a. 8.1 nm.
   b. 12.3 nm.
   c. 16.0 nm.
   d. 24.4 nm.

9. A knot is defined as:
   a. something you should not do.
   b. one nautical mile per hour.
   c. speed of a boat when not affected by current.
   d. one statute mile per hour.

10. What is the speed of your boat if you
    travel 8.0 nautical miles in 48 minutes?
    a. 4.8 kn.
    b. 6.1 kn.
    c. 10.0 kn.
    d. 11.4 kn.

11. You left your marina at 1000. At 1130
    you determine that you have traveled
    12.5 nautical miles. What has been your
    speed?
    a. 8.3 kn.
    b. 9.2 kn.
    c. 12.5 kn.
    d. 15.0 kn.

12. When computing time in navigation, it is
    always expressed in:
    a. seconds to the nearest whole second.
    b. hours and tenths of hours.
    c. daylight saving time.
    d. minutes to the nearest whole minute.

13. What is the elapsed time if you depart at
    1327 and arrive at your destination at
    1601?
    a. 0h 34 m
    b. 1h 34 m
    c. 2h 34 m
    d. 3h 78 m

14. You plan a cruise of 21.0 nautical miles.
    If you leave port at 0830 and cruise at a
    speed of 12 knots, at what time will you
    arrive at your destination?
    a. 0930
    b. 1015
    c. 1030
    d. 1110

15. Nautical time is always expressed in
    _____ digits.
    a. three
    b. four
    c. six
    d. nine

16. In nautical time, 11:51 A.M. is:
    a. 1151 hours.
    b. 1151
    c. 2351
    d. 2351 hours.

17. In nautical time, 11:51 P.M. is described
    as:
    a. one thousand one hundred fifty-one.
    b. twenty-three fifty-one hours.
    c. eleven fifty-one.
    d. twenty-three fifty-one.

18. 2221 nautical time is the same as
    _____ conventional time.
    a. 2.22 P.M.
    b. 10:21 P.M.
    c. 11.21 P.M.
    d. 12.21 P.M.

19. Nautical time 47 minutes later than 11:51
    a.m. would be:
    a. 1104
    b. 1198
    c. 1228
    d. 1238

20. Nautical time 47 minutes later than 0044
    would be:
    a. 0091
    b. 0131
    c. 1331
    d. 2357

12

Navigation Rules

1 Every time a boat comes near another, there is a risk of collision. The Navigation Rules are traffic rules for boats and are designed to prevent collisions. The Rules tell us how to operate our boats when we are with other boats, and how to tell their skippers what we plan to do.

2 The Navigation Rules also apply to commercial vessels. They apply whether you operate a 10-foot personal watercraft, a 60-foot yacht, or a 200-foot tanker.

3 Upon completion of this chapter, you should:
   - understand the traffic rules that apply on the water
   - recognize the various navigational lights and know their meaning
   - properly equip your boat to satisfy the Navigation Rules in the waters in which you operate

Two Sets of Rules

4 There are two sets of Navigational Rules:
   1) International Rules
   2) Inland Rules

International Rules

5 International Navigation Rules apply to all vessels on the high seas outside established *navigational lines of demarcation.* You will see these magenta (purplish-red) dashed lines on coast and harbor charts-even for areas within the continental boundaries of the United States.

Inland Rules

6 Inland Navigation Rules apply inside the navigational lines of demarcation. They are special regulations that apply to busy harbors, rivers, lakes, and crowded waterways.

7 If you operate a boat over 39.4 feet (12m) in length, you must have a copy of the Inland Navigational Rules aboard. You may purchase the booklet, *Navigation Rules, International and Inland,* from the Superintendent of Documents, United States Government Printing Office, Washington, DC 20402; from GPO sales agents located in many cities; or by accessing their Internet site: http://www.access.gpo.gov/.

8 The International Rules and Inland Rules are similar but with some important differences. We will present them as one, pointing out significant differences where they exist.

General Rule of Responsibility

9 You, as a skipper, are responsible for complying with the Navigation Rules. However, since no one can write rules to cover every possible risk of collision, there is a General Rule of Responsibility.

10 This rule states that the owner, captain, and crew of any vessel must comply with the Rules. It also states that the owner, captain, and crew must take every precaution required by the "ordinary practice of good

seamanship" to avoid immediate danger, including collision. *Precaution* may include departing from the Rules.

11 In other words, common sense must prevail, even when it means *breaking* the Rules to avoid danger.

12 We will cover many of the practices of good seamanship in this course. Be alert at all times! If the Rules state that you are the stand-on vessel and must maintain your course and speed, and it looks as if the other vessel is not taking appropriate action to avoid collision, do whatever you must to get out of the way! There may be a reason the other vessel cannot stay clear of you!

Terms

13 Some of the basic terms necessary to understand the Navigation Rules follow, in alphabetical order.

14 **Give-Way Vessel.** A vessel required to stay out of another vessel's way, and take early and substantial action to do so by changing course and/or speed.

15 **Power-Driven Vessel.** A vessel propelled by machinery.

16 **Restricted Visibility.** A condition when vessel crews are unable to see each other due to fog, haze, mist, rain, sleet, snow, high seas, etc.

17 **Right-of-Way.** This term applies to vessels on the Great Lakes and Western Rivers. A power-driven vessel in a narrow channel or fairway proceeding downbound with a following current shall have the right-of-way over an upbound vessel. Vessels crossing rivers shall keep clear of vessels that are ascending or descending the river.

18 **Risk of Collision.** Every vessel shall use all available means appropriate to the prevailing conditions to determine if the risk of collision exists. If there is *any* doubt in your mind, then you must act as though the risk exists: take whatever evasive action is necessary to avoid a collision.

19 **Sailing Vessel.** A vessel under sail only. A sailing vessel underway with the engine running and the propeller engaged is a power-driven vessel and must abide by all of the rules for power-driven vessels, even if its sails are raised.

20 **Stand-On Vessel.** A vessel required, in normal conditions, to maintain its existing course and speed.

21 **Underway.** Afloat and not at anchor, aground, or made fast to shore. A vessel underway is not necessarily moving through the water.

22 **Vessel Engaged in Fishing.** A vessel restricted in maneuverability as a result of using nets, lines, or trawls. A vessel fishing by trolling (trailing a lure or baited line behind a slowly moving boat), or fishing with other apparatus which does not restrict maneuverability, has no special rights or privileges.

23 **Vessel Not Under Command.** A vessel unable to maneuver or keep out of the way of other vessels due to special circumstances. Examples are vessels without operable power, unable to steer, or those aground.

24 **Vessel Restricted in the Ability to Maneuver.** A vessel unable to keep out of the way of other vessels because the nature of its work may make maneuvering difficult. Examples are vessels dredging or engaged in diving operations and vessels towing.

25 **Whistle.** Any sound signaling device (including a horn) capable of producing a prescribed blast.

> *Prolonged Blast.* A whistle blast of four to six seconds duration.

> *Short Blast.* A whistle blast of about one second duration.

Steering & Sailing Rules

26 The steering and sailing rules are general rules of navigation that apply to the conduct of vessels operating in three general situations:
  1) in any condition of visibility
  2) in sight of one another
  3) in restricted visibility

Vessels in Any Condition of Visibility

27 **A proper lookout is a major factor in preventing collisions. According to Coast Guard statistics, improper lookout is the major cause of collisions. Maintain a lookout whenever you are underway. Be alert for the sight and sounds of other boats.**

28 **Safe Speed.** The Rules require that you proceed at a safe speed at all times. Safe speed is that speed that allows you to stop your boat in time to avoid collision. Visibility, wind, sea conditions, depth of water, the amount of vessel traffic, the ability to maneuver your boat, the proximity of navigational hazards-these are all factors entering into determining safe speed. Local and state regulations may regulate the speed of your boat, even in open waters.

29 **Narrow Channels.** When proceeding in a narrow channel, keep to the right and as close to the edge of the channel that lies to your starboard side as is safe and practicable. In a narrow channel, keep clear of large vessels whose movement is constrained because of their draft. Never cross in front of one of these vessels.

30 If you find it necessary to cross a narrow channel, cross it quickly. The fastest route is one at right angles to the centerline of the channel. Never impede the passage of a vessel that can only safely navigate within a narrow channel because of its depth. Never fish in a narrow channel and do not anchor in one unless you are in an emergency situation.

31 **Rounding a Bend.** Be alert and proceed with caution when nearing a channel bend where you cannot see vessels approaching from the other direction. Sound one prolonged blast of your whistle. Any vessel within hearing should answer with the same signal.

Table 17		
	Vessel Status	**Example**
1	Vessels not under command	No steerage, no power
2	Vessels restricted in ability to maneuver	Towing, diving, surveying, dredging
3	Vessels constrained by draft	Deep draft vessel in narrow channel
4	Fishing vessels or trawlers	Using lines, nets, trawls, but not trolling
5	Sailing vessels	Under sail, no power
6	Powerboats	(Last in ranking)

32 **Vessel Priority.** Except where specifically required otherwise (such as when in an overtaking situation or operating in a narrow channel), a priority of movement order exists. Vessels farther down the list in Table 17 (page 121) have the least priority and have to stay out of the way of all vessels higher in the list.

33 For example, a fishing vessel must stay out of the way of vessels constrained by draft, restricted in the ability to maneuver, or not under command; a powerboat must stay out of the way of all higher-listed vessels.

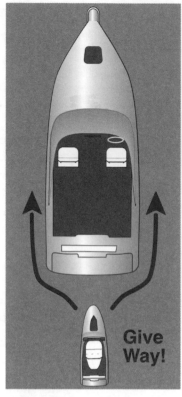

**Figure 96
Power Boat
Overtaking
Power Boat**

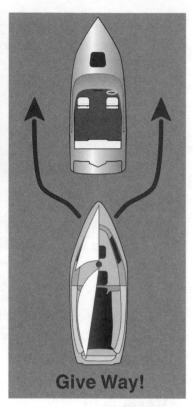

**Figure 97
Sailboat
Overtaking
Power Boat**

Vessels in Sight of One Another

34 These steering and sailing rules tell you how to operate your boat in three dangerous, close-approach situations that could involve collision:
  1) overtaking
  2) meeting
  3) crossing

35 **Vessels Overtaking-Inland Rules.** Any vessel, including a sailing vessel, overtaking another, is the give-way vessel: it must keep clear of the vessel being overtaken. The overtaken vessel must maintain course and speed. With the use of proper whistle signals, the overtaking vessel may pass on either side of the overtaken vessel, Figures 96 and 97. (See Sound Signals, page 125.)

**Figure 98
Power Boat
Meeting
Power Boat;
Passing
Port to Port**

**Figure 99
Power Boat
Meeting
Sailboat;
Passing
Port to Port**

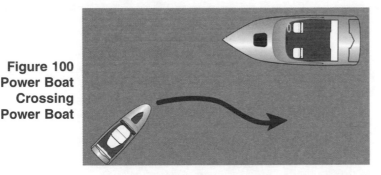

Figure 100 Power Boat Crossing Power Boat

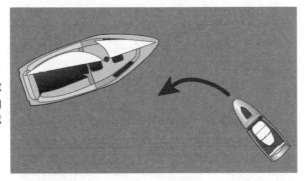

Figure 101 Power Boat Crossing Sailboat

36 **Vessels Overtaking-International Rules.** Sound signals for overtaking vessels in International Waters differ in that they are preceded by two prolonged blasts followed by the proper overtaking signal.

37 **Vessels Meeting.** When two power-driven vessels meet bow to bow, both must take action to stay out of the way of the other. Each should sound one short blast and turn to starboard, Figure 98, passing port to port. With the use of proper whistle signals, vessels may alternatively pass starboard to starboard. When a power-driven vessel and a sailing vessel meet bow to bow, the power-driven vessel must take action to stay out of the way of the sailboat; preference is for the power-driven vessel to alter course, Figure 99, passing port to port. (See Sound Signals, page 125.)

38 **On the Great Lakes and Western Rivers,** power-driven vessels in narrow channels or fairways, proceeding downbound with following current, have the right-of-way over upbound vessels. Downbound vessels give the sound signals first and choose the place of passing.

39 **Vessels Crossing.** When two power-driven vessels cross, the vessel with the other on its starboard side is the give-way vessel and must keep clear. It must take early action to change course, slow down, or back down, until the other vessel passes. The crossing vessel, as the stand-on vessel, must maintain course and speed until it is able to determine the intentions of the give-way vessel. If necessary, it must alter course and speed to avoid collision, Figure 100. When a power-driven vessel and a sailing vessel cross, the power-driven vessel is required to take action to stay out of the way of sailboat, Figure 101.

40 **Sailing Vessels Approaching One Another.** When two sailing vessels (not under power) approach one another, the position of the wind determines which vessel is the give-way vessel:

Figure 102   Sailboat Meeting Sailboat; Wind From Different Sides

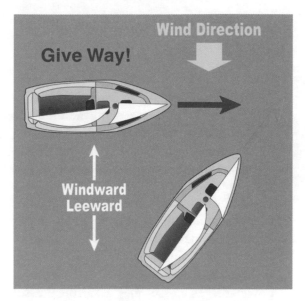

Figure 103   Sailboat Meeting Sailboat; Wind From Same Side

- If each vessel has the wind on a different side, the one with the wind on its port side keeps clear and gives way to the other, Figure 102 (page 123)
- If both have the wind on the same side, the vessel nearest to the direction of the wind keeps clear, Figure 103

Figure 104   Sailboat Overtaking Sailboat; Wind From Astern

- If both have the wind on the stern, the overtaking vessel must alter its course to starboard, Figure 104

Vessels in Restricted Visibility

41 Except for the General Rule of Responsibility, entirely different rules apply when vessels are in restricted visibility. These rules require you to:

- Proceed with utmost caution at a safe speed for the circumstances. A safe speed is one that allows you to stop in half the distance of visibility. Chances of collision are less if all vessels follow this rule.

Table 18: Sound Signals Meeting Other Vessels	
Meaning	**Signal**
I intend to pass you on my port side	1 short
I intend to pass you on my starboard side	2 short
I am operating with astern propulsion	3 short
I am departing from a dock, pier, or mooring	1 prolonged
I am approaching an intervening obstruction or channel bend	1 prolonged
There is danger in what you intend to do!	5 or more short
I am in doubt as to your intentions	5 or more short
I do not agree with your maneuver	5 or more short

- Display your running lights and sound the proper signals for your boat.
- Listen for signals from other vessels. Post a watch both bow and stern! If necessary, stop your boat to listen, but keep the engine running so that you will be ready for immediate action.
- Use all options to avoid collision, if more than two vessels meet in restricted visibility.

42 However, all vessels should avoid turning to port. With all vessels turning to starboard there is less risk of collision.

Sound Signals

43 Sound signals are important methods of signaling. The Inland Rules use *maneuvering* and *warning* signals to announce a skipper's intentions to other vessels and gain their agreement. In International Rules, sound signals announce an action being taken.

Table 19: Sound Signals Anchored in Restricted Visibility	
Vessel Length	**Signal Required**
Vessels under 39.4 feet (12 m)	Any efficient signal device sounded every 2 minutes
Vessels 39.4 feet and less than 328.1 feet (100 m)	Ring a bell rapidly 5 seconds of every minute
All vessels	May supplement bell ringing with 3 whistle blasts in succession—

Restricted visibility signals warn nearby vessels of another vessel's presence.

44 **Boats Less Than 39.4 Feet (12m)** may use any sound-producing mechanism that makes an efficient sound. Canister horns are popular for this purpose, but even a police whistle may be used.

45 **Boats Less Than 65.6 Feet (20m) and 39.4 Feet (12m) or More** must be equipped with a "whistle". *Whistle* means any sound signalling appliance capable of producing the prescribed blasts audible for one-half a nautical mile. A bell is no longer required.

46 **Boats 65.6 Feet (20m) or More** must be equipped with a bell and a whistle audible for one-half a nautical mile.

47 State regulations may differ.

Maneuvering and Warning Signals

48 These signals are required in Inland Waters, but are never used unless vessels are in sight of one another. Powerboats use them in the three dangerous, close-approach situations: *meeting*, *overtaking*, and *crossing*.

49 Sailing vessels (not under power) *are required* to use maneuvering and warning signals when overtaking, and *may* exchange them with other sailing vessels.

50 If the other vessel agrees with your maneuver, it returns the same signal. If it does not agree, it sounds the danger signal: five or more short and rapid blasts on the whistle. Pay attention if you hear a danger signal-*you* may be the one in danger. Never proceed until the situation is clear!

51 Whenever you make a course change, always make it obvious. In busy harbors, VHF

| Table 20
Sound Signals Underway
in Restricted Visibility ||
Vessel Type	Signal
Powerboats making way	1 prolonged blast every 2 minutes
Powerboats underway, but stopped	2 prolonged blasts every 2 minutes
Sailing vessels Vessels restricted in ability to maneuver Vessels not under command	1 prolonged blast, followed by 2 short blasts every 2 minutes

Channel 13 will be helpful for contacting vessels about close-approach situations.

52 In International Waters, a signal given indicates that the maneuver *is being carried out,* rather than merely *intended,* as in Inland Waters. Return signals are given only in overtaking situations in narrow channels or fairways, or where necessary when approaching other vessels.

Signals in Restricted Visibility

53 Whenever anchored or underway in restricted visibility, it is necessary to sound the proper sound signal for your type of boat and circumstance. It is important to be familiar with these signals so you can recognize the types and sizes of vessels you may encounter. (See Table 20 for signals by vessels underway.)

54 Boats less than 65.6 feet (20m) are not required to sound signals if anchored in a special anchorage area.

Navigation Lights

55 The Navigation Rules include lighting requirements for every description of watercraft. In this course we will concentrate on navigation lights that are of importance to recreational boaters operating boats less than 65.6 feet (20m) in length. You will find a more detailed account of these requirements in Appendix G of this manual.

Purpose of Lights

56 Navigation lights serve three purposes:
   1) to alert other boats of your presence and relative location
   2) to tell other boats something about your vessel's size, speed, course, and type (sail, power, etc.)
   3) to enable you to properly apply the Navigation Rules

57 If you operate your boat at night, learn what the various lights signify, especially those on tugs, barges, and large vessels. That knowledge could save your life.

58 You are required to equip your boat with the correct navigation lights and display them when operating between sunset and sunrise and during periods of reduced visibility. Lights that satisfy International Rules meet requirements of the Inland Rules.

Types of Navigation Lights

59 There are five basic types of vessel navigational lights, four of which are shown in Figure 105.

60 **Masthead Lights** are white lights placed forward over the centerline of a boat that shine 225 degrees forward (112.5 degrees on each side of the vessel). The name is a little misleading for they are seldom at the top of the mast, but partway down. They are used only when a vessel is under power.

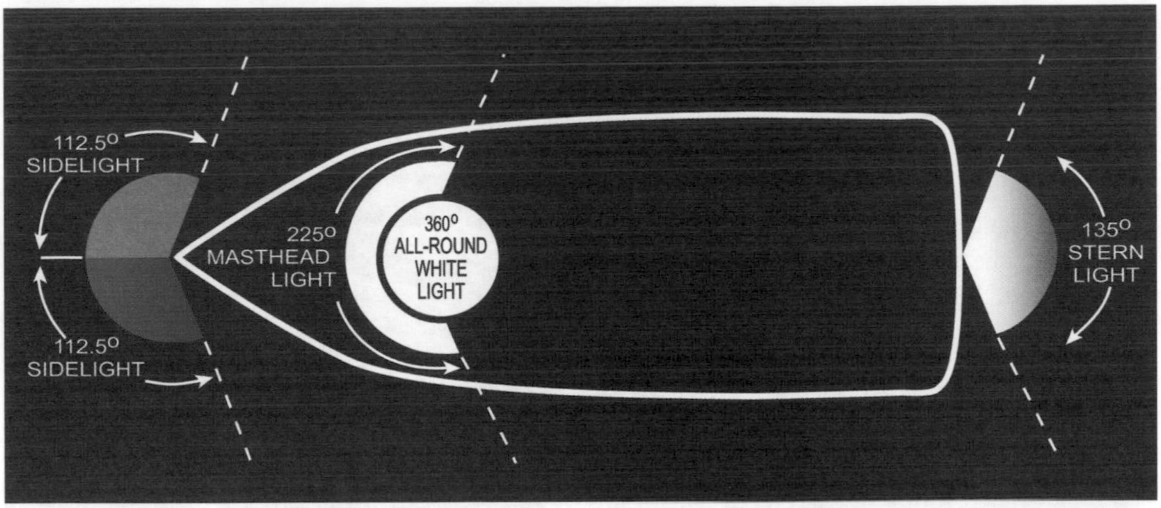

**Figure 105
Arcs
of a Vessel's
Navigation
Lights**

112.5°
SIDELIGHT

112.5°
SIDELIGHT

225°
MASTHEAD
LIGHT

360°
ALL-ROUND
WHITE
LIGHT

135°
STERN
LIGHT

61 **All-Around Lights** are visible 360 degrees around the horizon. They may be white, red, green, or yellow, depending on their function.

62 **Sidelights,** red on the port side and green on the starboard side. They shine 112.5 degrees on each side of the vessel from dead ahead.

63 **Stern Lights** are white lights that shine 135 degrees aft (67.5 degrees from directly astern and to each side of the vessel). When you see a stern light of another vessel, you will not see its sidelights or masthead light.

64 **Towing Lights** are yellow lights with the same characteristics as stern lights and are mounted at the stern on towing vessels. A towing vessel is a power-driven vessel towing astern, alongside, or pushing ahead.

Navigation Light Requirements

65 Navigation light requirements for various types and lengths of boats are listed below. (See also Appendix G of this manual.)

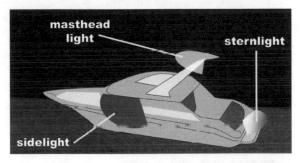

Figure 106   Powerboats Less Than 65.6 Feet, Separate Sidelights

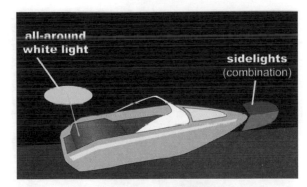

Figure 107   Powerboats Less Than 65.6 Feet, Combination Sidelights

Powerboats Less Than 65.6 Feet (20 Meters)

66 See Figures 106 and 107:
- white masthead light forward
- red and green sidelights (separate or combined)
- white stern light

Powerboats Less Than 39.4 Feet (12 Meters)

67 Powerboats and sailing vessels under power (Figures 108 and 109):

- red and green sidelights (separate or combined)
- masthead and stern lights may be combined into one all-round white light

Sailing Vessels Less Than 65.6 Feet (20 Meters)

68 Sailboats under power display the lights of powerboats shown above. Sailing vessels (not under power) do not display white masthead lights (see Figure 110).

- red and green sidelights (separate or combined)
- white stern light

69 Sailing vessels less than 65.6 feet may combine sidelights and stern lights into one tricolor light at the top of the mast. This provides better visibility when offshore.

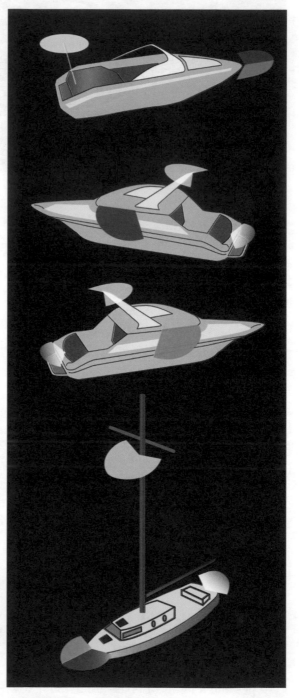

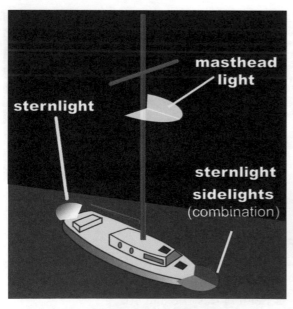

Figure 108   Navigation Lights of a Sailboat Under Power

Figure 109   Powerboats Less Than 39.4 Feet

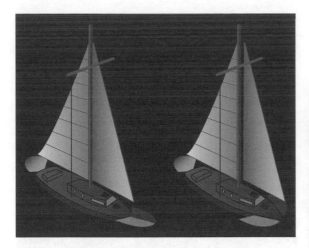

Figure 110   Sailboats Less than 65.6 Feet

Figure 111   Sailboat Less than 23 Feet

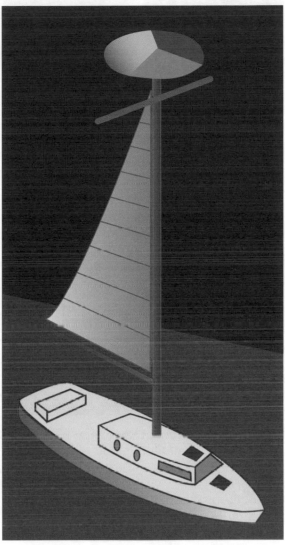

Figure 112   Sailboat Less than 23 Feet, Combined Masthead Light

Sailing Vessels Less Than 23 Feet (7 Meters) and Boats Propelled by Oars or Paddles

70 If it is not practical for sailing vessels less than 23 feet to display the lights shown in Figures 111 or 112, a single white light may be used (Figure 113, page 130). Boats propelled by oars may display the lights of

Figure 113   Sailboat Less than 23 Feet, Sail Illuminated by Flashlight

Figure 114   Rowboat With Flashlight

sailing vessels or, if not practicable, a single white light as prescribed above for sailing vessels less than 23 feet (Figure 114).

Vessels Restricted in the Ability to Maneuver

71 Vessels Towing Astern, in addition to red and green sidelights and white stern light, will display:
- two forward white masthead lights in a vertical line (tows over 650 feet require three masthead lights)
- a yellow towing light above the white stern light (towing lights also shine 135 degrees aft)

72 The vessel being towed will display red and green sidelights and white stern light. See Figure 115.

73 **Vessels Pushing Ahead or Towing Alongside,** in addition to standard red and green sidelights and masthead lights depicted above, display:
- In *International Waters,* a single stern light
- In *Inland Waters,* two yellow towing lights in place of a white stern light

74 On some Western Rivers, the two masthead lights are not required.

75 **Groups of Vessels** being pushed or towed alongside are lighted as a single vessel.

76 Those being pushed display red and green sidelights forward. Those being towed alongside display a white stern light in addition to the sidelights.

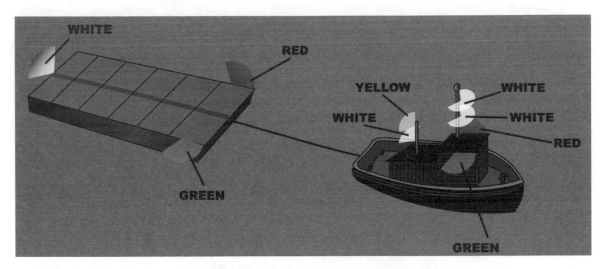

Figure 115   A Tug Towing a Barge Less Than 650 Feet In Length

77 In *Inland Waters,* a special flashing light is displayed forward on a vessel or group of vessels being pushed or towed alongside. A special flashing light is a yellow flashing light displayed forward. The arc of the light must be at least 180 degrees, but not more than 225 degrees. In other words, the light may be seen anywhere from dead ahead of the towing vessel to 22.5 degrees abaft the beam on either side of the vessel.

78 | Accidents often occur at night when vessels try to cross between vessels towing and vessels being towed. Tow lines are usually below the surface and very hazardous! If you see more than one white masthead light, or any lights you do not recognize, stay away until you determine what it is.

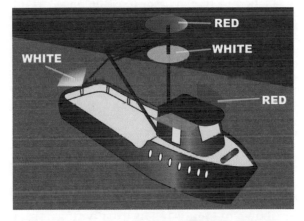

Figure 116   Fishing Vessel Using Nets or Lines, Not Trolling

79 **Vessels Engaged in Fishing** (Figures 116, 117) are often restricted in their ability to maneuver due to their fishing apparatus. A vessel engaged in fishing can be fishing or trawling. *Fishing* is using lines or nets (but not trolling). Fishing vessels display a red all-round light over a white all-round light, in addition to standard sidelights and stern light.

80 *Trawling* is dragging a net or scoop along the bottom. Trawlers display a green light

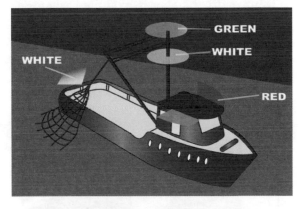

Figure 117   Fishing Vessel Trawling a Net Over the Bottom

over white. If a vessel engaged in fishing or trawling is not underway, it does not exhibit sidelights and stern light.

81 **Vessels Dredging or Diving** must display:
- the lights of a vessel restricted in ability to maneuver; three all-round lights, red over white, over red (ball over diamond, over ball day shapes in daylight)
- two vertical all-round red lights (or two day-shape balls) to show the side on which an obstruction exists
- two vertical all-round green lights (or two day-shape diamonds) to indicate the side where another vessel may pass

82 Vessels engaged in diving with divers attached to their vessel must display a rigid blue and white *International Code A* flag (Figure 118). In addition, they must exhibit the red and green lights required of vessels engaged in dredging and diving (see above).

83 If divers are free-swimming, the vessel is not restricted in its ability to maneuver. The well-known, "diver-below" flag (a red square with white diagonal stripe) is distinctive from the International Code "A" flag described above. The *diver-below* flag, also shown in Figure 118, is usually flown from a boat, raft, float, or buoy to indicate the location of free-swimming divers.

84 Neither diver's flag is exhibited when underway, or when divers are not in the water. Boaters should stay well clear of these activities, for divers often stray from the diving vessel. Many states have local regulations governing diving and underwater operations.

Figure 118   International Code Flag A (Left) and Diver-Below Flag (Right)

Vessels Not Under Command

85 Vessels that are unable to keep out of the way of other vessels must display two vertical red all-round lights. Examples are vessels aground or adrift without operable power or steering.

Boats at Anchor

86 Boats at anchor exhibit an all-round white light from sunset to sunrise where it can best be seen. Vessels over 164 feet in length will display two white anchor lights. However, anchor lights are not required in a specially designated anchorage area.

Law Enforcement Vessels

87 Law enforcement vessels may display a flashing blue light. Vessels engaged in government-sanctioned, public-safety activities (i.e., marine parades and regattas) may alternatively display a flashing red and yellow light signal.

Vessels in Distress

88 In Inland Waters, vessels in distress may display a high-intensity, flashing-white strobe light.

Day Shapes

89 Day shapes are objects of specific shape and size that serve the same purposes during the day that navigation lights serve at night. They are always black. They indicate special situations, such as vessels anchored, engaged in fishing, or sailboats with sails raised operating in International Waters under power. For example, an inverted cone is displayed on a vessel when propelled by both sail and power, as in Figure 119. (Not required on vessels less than 39.4 feet, 12 meters, long in Inland Waters).

Figure 119   A Typical Day Shape

Navigation Lights by Color (a Recap)

90 To operate safely after dark, you need to be able to recognize light configurations on any type of vessel you may encounter in your boating waters, especially lights on commercial vessels. The following is a recap of navigation lights, by color, that may help you in understanding them.

91 **White Lights** identify the type and size of boat you are encountering and the direction it is going. Approach white lights cautiously.

92 *White Masthead Lights.* Most powerboats (including sailboats under power) display a white masthead light. Large ships and vessels towing or pushing ahead require two white masthead lights. (Long tows over 650 feet will have three white masthead lights.)

93 *White All-Around Lights.* Some powerboats less than 39.4 feet will display a white all-round light as a substitute for a masthead light and stern light; they are also found on anchored boats, small sailboats, and boats under oars.

94 *Stern Lights* (always white) are seen on powerboats, sailing vessels, and vessels being towed.

95 **Red Lights** signify possible danger. When you see a red light, slow down and steer clear!

96 *Red Sidelights* off your starboard side identify a stand-on vessel. You are the give-way vessel and must keep clear! Maintain a proper lookout and make any changes necessary to avoid a collision.

97 *Red All-Around Lights.* Two red all-round lights indicate vessels not under command. (If you also see a white anchor light, the vessel is aground.) Dredges use two all-round red lights, one above the other, to indicate the side where it is dangerous to pass.

98 *A Red All-Around Light Over a Green All-Around Light* is occasionally seen on sailing vessels. Vessels fishing with nets or lines display a red all-round light over a white all-round light. Vessels restricted in their ability to maneuver exhibit two all-round red lights with a white all-round light in between.

99 **Green Lights** (as well as red) tell you the direction a vessel is headed. With other colored lights, they may alert you to a sailing vessel or fishing trawler. Exert caution when you see a green light, even if you do not have to give way, such as in a crossing situation.

100 *Green Sidelights* are found on the starboard side of all vessels. On some sailing vessels this green light may be at the top of the mast as part of a tri-color fixture.

101 *Green All-Around Lights.* Two green all-round lights, one above the other, are used by a dredge to indicate the safe side to use in passing.

102 *A Green All-Around Light Below a Red All-Around Light* is occasionally seen at the top of the mast of a sailing vessel. A green all-round light over a white all-round light is displayed on a fishing vessel trawling a net or scoop along the bottom.

103 **Yellow Lights.** When you see yellow lights, think "towing." (Remember: there's an "OW" in yellow and tow.) Give them a wide berth. In Inland Waters, one yellow light means one or more vessels being towed behind; two yellow lights means one or more vessels ahead of or alongside the towing boat.

104 *One Yellow Light Above a White Stern Light* is displayed by a vessel towing astern. When you see this light configuration, you are behind the towing vessel, and there is also a towed vessel behind it to avoid.

105 *Two Vertical Yellow Stern Lights Without a White Stern Light* reveals a vessel towing alongside or pushing ahead.

106 *A Flashing Yellow Light* means you are viewing the forward portion of a barge or vessel being pushed; look at their navigation lights to avoid getting into their path.

Homework

Name: _____ **Date:** _____ **Group:** _____

1. The purpose of the Navigation Rules is to:
   a. prevent collisions.
   b. be used with nautical charts.
   c. set standards for plotting courses.
   d. set limits for the size of vessels.

2. Navigational Lines of Demarcation define the boundaries of:
   a. inland waters and the three mile territorial limit.
   b. the high seas and the low seas.
   c. International Waters and Inland Waters.
   d. hazardous and non-hazardous areas.

3. The General Rule of Responsibility:
   a. is only applicable in International Waters.
   b. provides that you may break the Navigation Rules to avoid danger.
   c. prescribes the insurance you must carry on your boat.
   d. describes who is responsible for equipping vessels with proper lights.

4. A sailing vessel with sails raised and underway, under power is a:
   a. vessel not under command.
   b. vessel restricted in her ability to maneuver.
   c. fast vessel.
   d. power-driven vessel.

5. You are fishing by trolling a lure behind your slow-moving boat. According to the rules you have:
   a. special privileges, providing you show the lights of a vessel engaged in fishing.
   b. priority of movement over all other vessels.
   c. no special rights or privileges.
   d. special privileges, because you are restricted in maneuverability.

6. Generally speaking, in the priority of movement list, _____ have the least priority and have to stay out of the way of all vessels higher on the list.
   a. fishing vessels
   b. boats under oars
   c. sailing vessels
   d. powerboats

7. You are required to maintain a lookout at all times when underway. A proper lookout is a major factor in:
   a. finding lines of demarcation.
   b. pointing out an unmarked channel to the helmsman.
   c. determining the accuracy of the compass heading.
   d. preventing collisions.

8. You are required to proceed at safe speed at all times. Safe speed is the speed that will:
   a. get you home in a hurry when you are running out of fuel.
   b. not put strain on your engine or sail rigging.
   c. permit your boat to throw only a one or two foot wake in an anchorage.
   d. allow you to stop your boat in time to avoid collision.

9. When operating in a narrow channel, you must keep your vessel:
   a. as close to the center of the channel as is safe and practicable.
   b. as close to the edge of the channel that lies to your port side as is safe and practicable.
   c. as close to the edge of the channel that lies to your starboard side as is safe and practicable.
   d. with the wind and current on your stern for best control.

10. When a vessel overtakes another, the _____ is the stand-on vessel.
    a. vessel closest to the direction of the wind
    b. vessel capable of the most speed
    c. overtaking vessel
    d. vessel being overtaken

11. When two power-driven vessels meet bow to bow, _____ is the stand-on vessel.
    a. neither of the two vessels
    b. the one with the wind on its starboard side
    c. the one proceeding against the current
    d. the one that first signals

12. A powerboat observing another vessel crossing its course from off its starboard side must:
    a. speed up to pass ahead of the other vessel.
    b. maintain course and speed.
    c. take early action to keep clear.
    d. signal five short blasts on its whistle.

13. When two sailing vessels approach each other, each with the wind on a different side, the vessel _____ must keep clear.
    a. with the wind on its starboard side
    b. with the wind on its port side
    c. nearest to the direction of the wind
    d. with the greatest sail area

14. Sound signals have two purposes: 1) to announce your intentions to other vessels, and 2) to:
    a. alert slower boats, such as sailing vessels, that you are the stand-on vessel.
    b. reply to another vessel's crossing signals in international waters.
    c. alert other vessels of your presence in restricted visibility.
    d. announce your arrival at the club rendezvous.

15. The *doubt* or *danger* signal used to express disagreement with an intended maneuver is:
    a. 1 short blast of the whistle.
    b. 5 or more short and rapid blasts of the whistle.
    c. shouting "danger!" as loudly as possible.
    d. rapid and constant waving of the arms.

16. While operating in a thick fog, you hear
    1 prolonged blast every 2 minutes off
    your starboard bow. You proceed slowly
    and watch for a _____
    ahead of you.
    a. vessel not under command
    b. vessel engaged in fishing
    c. sailing vessel underway
    d. powerboat making way

17. Off your starboard side you see a boat
    with a white light over a red light
    approaching. You should take immediate
    precautions because you are meeting a:
    a. large vessel at anchor in a narrow
       channel.
    b. vessel engaged in diving.
    c. powerboat crossing in front of you
       from right to left.
    d. law enforcement vessel.

18. Navigation lights required on powerboats
    less than 65.6 feet are the same as those
    for sailing vessels except that a
    _____ is required.
    a. yellow all-round light
    b. red strobe light
    c. white masthead light forward
    d. white anchor light

19. Navigation lights most frequently found
    on sailing vessels under 65.6 feet include
    a white sternlight and:
    a. red and green sidelights.
    b. a white masthead light.
    c. a blue anchor light.
    d. a yellow sternlight.

20. If you see two white lights in a vertical
    line, take immediate caution because you
    are meeting a:
    a. surfaced submarine.
    b. large sport fisherman.
    c. vessel towing or pushing ahead.
    d. night-time sail race.

13

Piloting—Determining Position

1 As skipper, you need to be aware of your approximate chart position at all times. This information is essential to the safety of your vessel and crew. Basic to such knowledge is a technique of navigation known as dead reckoning.

Dead Reckoning

2 The term *dead reckoning* (DR) is a derivation of "deduced reckoning." It is the process of estimating a boat's position by applying course and distance traveled from a previously determined position.

3 Dead reckoning ignores external forces, such as wind and current, which may move a vessel off track. Advanced USPS courses, Piloting and Advanced Piloting, address methods to correct for those variable influences.

Dead Reckoning Track

4 A *dead reckoning track* (DR track) is the intended course line of a vessel as plotted on a chart.

5 Plotting a DR track is an essential measure in the safe operation of a vessel, especially when boating in large open bodies of water. It is the procedure that keeps you informed of the approximate position of your vessel.

6 You should not rely solely on electronic navigational equipment to guarantee the safety of your boat and crew. Global Positioning Systems (GPS), Loran, and Radar are of tremendous help, but electronic equipment is often subject to failure in a marine environment. Consider the sudden loss of use of electronic navigational equipment if you have not been keeping a DR plot. U.S. Navy ships, with their state-of-the-art navigational equipment and backup systems, still meticulously plot DR tracks.

7 Use electronic equipment to verify the results of DR calculations. This exercise will either instill confidence in your ability, or persuade you to take additional courses in navigation!

8 Dead reckoning tracks:
   • always start from a known position
   • are always true courses (*True* is the "language" of the chart)
   • show distance traveled and DR positions along the track; these are calculated by using run time and the estimated speed of the boat through the water

9 Note the DR track illustrated on the sample plotting sheet shown in Figure 120.

10 **Labeling a DR Track.** Always label a charted course line immediately. Chapter 11 demonstrated proper ways to label course lines for distance, speed, and time. You will find these labels illustrated again in Figure 121, Labeling Examples.

Dead Reckoning Position

11 A *dead reckoning position* (DR position) is a presumed position of a vessel on a DR track. Dead reckoning positions should be calculated and plotted:
   • every hour on the hour

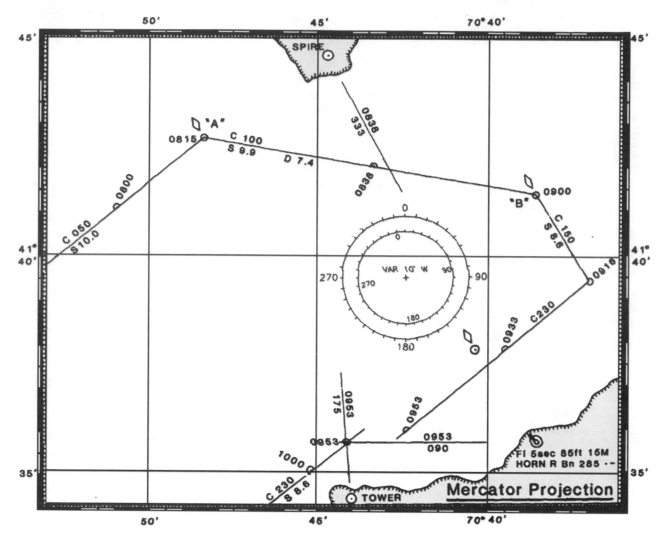

Figure 120   Sample Plotting Sheet

- every time there is a change in course or speed
- whenever making an observation or taking a bearing

12 Although a DR position is seldom the exact position of your vessel, it is highly useful when out of sight of land, in restricted visibility, or in an emergency situation.

13 **Labeling a Dead Reckoning Position.** The chart symbol for a DR position is a small half-circle placed on top of a course line around a dot of position. (Draw the semicircles using the template in the center of your USPS plotter.)

14 Label the time of a DR position in four digits at an angle to the DR track but not parallel to the bottom of a chart. In Figure 120, note DR positions plotted hourly at 0800 and 1000; at 0916, when a course change took place; and at 0838 and 0953, when bearings were taken.

Lines of Position

15 A *line of position* (LOP) is a line plotted on a chart along which the boat lies, as determined from a single observation. Lines of position are regularly used to determine position. The exact location of the vessel on a

line of position is not known. However, an LOP is valuable in that it tells you the vessel is somewhere on that line and not somewhere else. That information is useful in many situations.

Bearings

16 A *bearing* is the horizontal direction of an object from an observer and is expressed as an angle from true north or magnetic north. The angle is described in degrees as a three-digit number (such as 030°) and is always the direction of the object *from* the vessel. A bearing becomes a line of position when plotted on a chart.

17 **Magnetic Bearings.** A bearing taken by compass is a magnetic bearing. It is a magnetic bearing because it is referenced to magnetic north. (*Magnetic* is the "language" of the compass.)

18 The simplest type of compass bearing is the *bow-on bearing:* one taken directly ahead of your vessel. Turn your vessel toward the object and, after the compass has settled down, read the numbers on the compass. In this course we will assume that all compass bearings have been taken in this way.

19 **True Bearings.** Just as a compass course must be converted to a true course to plot it on a chart, a compass bearing must be converted to a true bearing to draw it as a line of position on a chart. (*True* is the "language" of the chart.) The difference between a magnetic compass bearing and a true bearing is the variation for the particular area.

20 In an area where variation is 10° W, a magnetic bearing of 055° would be corrected to a true bearing of 045°. This type of computation uses the same TVMDC formula used to convert true courses to magnetic courses, and vice versa. A true bearing is plotted on a chart by positioning the course plotter to

the desired bearing while aligning the edge of the plotter to the sighted object.

21 **Labeling a Bearing.** Label a bearing by showing the plotted time in four digits above the line, and the direction in three digits below the line. In Figure 120, note the line of position taken by the bearing at 0838. This line of position established the true direction of the spire from the boat. Your vessel is somewhere on that line.

Fixes

22 A *fix* is a relatively accurate position of your vessel at a given time that is determined without reference to a former position. Fixes are frequently established:
- when alongside known charted objects such as buoys, beacons, breakwaters, or other identifiable objects
- at the intersection of two plotted lines of position that were taken at approximately the same time

23 Lines of position are usually determined by taking bearings. A new course line always starts at a fix, for it is a known position.

24 **Labeling a Fix.** The chart symbol for a fix is a small circle around a dot of position or around the intersect point of two lines of position. (Use the circle template in the center of your USPS plotter to draw the circle.)

25 Label fixes only with time to the nearest minute, using a four-digit notation. The label should not lie on the line, but should be *parallel to the bottom of the chart.*

26 Note the fixes in Figure 120 at 0815 and 0900 taken close aboard two buoys. The 0953 fix was obtained by using two bearings to create lines of position; one taken on the lighthouse with the HORN and the other on the TOWER.

GPS-Reported Position

27 If you use a GPS receiver, it will report your current position continually as long as it is receiving signals from the satellites and is operating properly. Generally, the quality of the position reported by the GPS is quite high (typically within 50 feet). This is considered to be a fix.

28 In order to navigate, it is necessary to transcribe the GPS-reported position onto your chart. As previously identified, the GPS has no inherent knowledge of what is around you. To do this, you will need to transfer the coordinates provided by the GPS onto your chart and mark your current location.

29 It is possible the GPS may malfunction. You may have incorrectly entered the coordinates for a waypoint or inadvertently selected the wrong waypoint. Consequently, it is wise to cross-check your position. It is not wise to rely solely on one form of navigation for your and your crew's safety.

30 Periodically, you should compare your GPS position with that derived from a dead reckoning plot or by taking bearings to visible objects. Appendix A is an introduction to using digital charts along with a GPS unit. This material is optional.

Plotting Exercise

31 Use the Sample Plotting Sheet, Figure 120, to work through the following problems. Figure 120 is not to scale and may be dimensionally inaccurate. In the Plotting Exercise, use the provided answers (shown on the Sample Plotting Sheet and in parenthesis within the text of the Plotting Exercise) to continue solving the various parts of the exercise. Follow the labeling examples shown in Figure 121 when drawing course lines and lines of position.

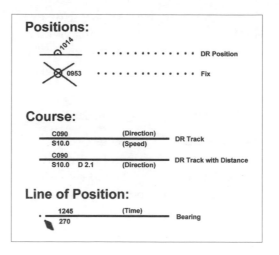

Figure 121   Labeling Examples

1. Beginning at the 0815 fix at buoy "**A**," head for buoy "**B**."

    a. What is the true course? (100°)

    b. What is the magnetic course if the variation is 10° W?
        | True course | 100° |
        | Variation | 10° W (+) |
        | Magnetic course | 110° |

    c. What is the distance of the run? (7.4 nm)

    d. Leaving buoy "A" at 0815, what speed is required to arrive at buoy "B" at 0900?
        $$60 \times D = S \times T$$
        $$60 \times 7.4 = S \times 45$$
        $$S = 9.9 \text{ kn}$$

2. At 0838, you decide to check your position. You stop the boat and turn it toward the spire to take a bow-on bearing. The compass shows a magnetic bearing of 343°. The compass rose shows a variation of 10° W.

    a. What is the true bearing?
        | True bearing | 333° |
        | Variation | 10° W (–) |
        | Magnetic bearing | 343° |

b. Plot and label this line of position.

c. Establish the 0838 DR position. Calculate the distance run from 0815 to 0838.
$$60 \times D = S \times T$$
$$60 \times D = 9.9 \times 23$$
$$D = 3.8 \text{ nm}$$

d. Measure 3.8 nm along the DR track from the 0815 fix and plot the 0838 DR position.

3. At 0900, at buoy "B," the course changes to 150° true and the speed changes to 8.6 knots. Draw the DR track.

4. At 0916, the course changes to 230° True. Speed remains at 8.6 kn. Draw the DR track.

a. Establish the 0916 DR position. Calculate the distance run from 0900 to 0916.
$$60 \times D = S \times T$$
$$60 \times D = 8.6 \times 16$$
$$D = 2.3 \text{ nm}$$

b. Measure 2.3 nm along the DR track from the 0900 fix and plot the 0916 DR position.

5. At 0953, you stop the boat and point it toward the lighthouse with the horn. The compass reads 100°.

a. What is the true bearing of the light?
True Bearing	090°
Variation	10° W (−)
Magnetic Bearing	100°

b. Plot and label this line of position.

6. At approximately the same time (0953), you turn the bow of the boat toward the tower on the point. The compass reads 185°.

a. What is the true bearing of this tower?
True Bearing	175°
Variation	10° W (−)
Magnetic Bearing	185°

b. Plot and label this line of position.

7. Establish the 0953 DR position and calculate the distance run from 0916 to 0953.
$$60 \times D = S \times T$$
$$60 D = 8.6 \times 37$$
$$D = 5.3 \text{ nm}$$

a. Measure 5.3 nm along the DR track from the 0916 DR position and plot the 0953 DR position.

8. Plot and label the 0953 fix. This is the point where the two lines of position established by bearings cross.

a. Draw a small circle around the intersection point of the two LOPs.

b. Label the time of the fix in four digits. This time label should be parallel to the bottom of the chart.

9. Note that the fix is not on the DR track. How far away were you from your estimated DR position? (1.4 nm)

a. Inaccurate steering, incorrect speed determination, wind, current, and other factors will affect the accuracy of a DR track. That is why it is so important to periodically check your position.

Homework

Name: _____ Date: _____ Group: _____

1. **Dead reckoning is the estimating of a boat's position by applying course and distance traveled from:**
   a. any location on a DR track.
   b. a previously determined position.
   c. any point on a depth curve.
   d. any estimated position.

2. A dead reckoning track is:
   a. a course line that is absolutely correct in its accuracy.
   b. the actual course of a vessel plotted over the bottom.
   c. a measured course used to practice navigational exercises.
   d. the intended course line of a vessel as plotted on a chart.

3. The value of plotting a DR track is that it will:
   a. keep a skipper informed of the approximate position of a vessel.
   b. provide instant information of marine facilities whenever needed.
   c. give an exact position of a vessel at any given time.
   d. always tell a skipper where to expect heavy seas.

4. Always label a DR position on a chart with:
   a. a small half-circle placed on top of a course line around a dot of position.
   b. the letters "DR" in italic capital letters alongside a dot of position.
   c. a magenta circle around a dot of position.
   d. a full circle around a dot of position on the course line.

5. A bow-on bearing is one taken:
   a. by setting the compass on the boat's bow.
   b. on the bow of another boat.
   c. directly ahead of the vessel.
   d. while a boat is right alongside a buoy.

6. To plot a compass bearing on a chart it must be:
   a. converted by using the 60 D Street formula.
   b. taken as the direction of the vessel from an object.
   c. converted to a true bearing.
   d. taken over the stern of the boat.

7. Label a bearing on a chart by showing the plotted time in four digits above the line and
   a. the direction in three digits alongside the time.
   b. no other labeling is necessary.
   c. the direction in three digits below the line.
   d. magnetic course on top of the line.

8. A relatively accurate position of a vessel at a given time that is determined without reference to a former position is called a:
   a. plot.
   b. bearing.
   c. DR position.
   d. fix.

9. A fix is frequently established when alongside known charted objects or:
    a. when two DR positions are plotted at the exact same time.
    b. at the intersection of two plotted lines of position which were taken at approximately the same time.
    c. when taking a single bow-on bearing.
    d. whenever estimating your position.

10. A fix is labeled on a chart with a small circle around a dot of position or:
    a. around the intersect point of two lines of position.
    b. around a triangle marking two lines of position.
    c. by writing the word FIX in capital letters next to a dot of position.
    d. the intersect point of two DR positions.

14

Adverse Conditions and Emergencies

1 Recreational boating is fun for the whole family. There is something for everyone; waterskiing, fishing, swimming, camping out. The possibilities of recreational boating are almost endless.

2 Every boater would prefer to be on the water in pleasant weather and ideal conditions. In spite of the best planning and preparation, you will at some point encounter the unexpected. Unfortunately, emergency situations or changes in weather are facts of life.

3 Many unusual situations encountered on the water can be avoided—and all can be better handled—with proper knowledge.

4 Upon completion of this chapter, you should know how to:
- plan your fuel needs in advance so that you will always have ample fuel
- handle your boat properly in bad weather, heavy seas, and restricted visibility
- respond in a capable manner to situations such as collision, grounding, falls overboard, fire, swamping, capsizing, towing, and certain medical emergencies
- decrease inconvenience and minimize difficulties by planning ahead, being alert, operating courteously, and knowledgeably handling your boat under almost any condition

Life Preservers
5 One message will be repeated throughout this chapter; the importance of wearing a life

preserver. Make sure everyone is wearing one at the first sign of bad weather or trouble. If life preservers are not being worn, they must be readily accessible. Without exception, everyone on board should wear a life jacket when underway at night.

6 Life preservers float; you don't! Most boating fatalities involve people not wearing life preservers. In eight out of ten fatalities, life preservers were available but not worn.

Running Out of Fuel
7 Running out of fuel can be inconvenient, sometimes dangerous, often expensive, and always embarrassing!

Prevention
8 Know your boat's maximum range with a full load of fuel. To determine this, you need to know the usable capacity of the tank and the boat's rate of fuel consumption.

9 Run your boat at various speeds or revolutions per minute (RPM) for a measured amounts of time; measure the amount of fuel consumed. Refer to this information to estimate the amount of fuel needed to run a course at a given speed.

10 Use the one-third rule: one third of the tank to get there, one third to get home, and one third for emergencies.

11 Always fill your tank before you leave port and try not to let it go below one-third full.

Plan for extra fuel if you expect bad weather or strong currents. Know the location of fuel stations in the area of your cruise. Carry any extra fuel in tanks designed for marine use. Gasoline weighs 6.1 pounds per gallon and will add considerable weight to your boat. Secure portable tanks so they will not move around in the boat.

Responding to a Fuel Shortage

12 If you run out of fuel, you can get into trouble drifting. Try to anchor if you are in a safe location. Be sure everyone on board is wearing a life preserver; with lack of power there is no way to reach a victim who falls overboard.

13 Help may be available from a fellow boater. Getting help may be more difficult if you are offshore or in a secluded cove.

14 You may ask the Coast Guard for help on VHF radio (Channel 16). They won't send one of their boats unless there is a life-threatening situation. However, they will contact a towing company for you. If you do not request a specific company, the Coast Guard will issue a general radio call to which any commercial tower in the area may respond. There will be a charge for service you receive from a private tower; towing insurance may be a worthwhile investment. You may bypass the Coast Guard and call a towing company yourself.

Grounding

15 Running aground is often more of a nuisance than a danger. Knowledge, fast work, and a little luck can often reduce the inconvenience to just a matter of minutes.

If You Run Aground

16 First check your hull! Rocks and stumps are hazards in many areas. Hitting an object at even a moderate speed can crack or puncture a hull. If you are taking on water, it is better to be aground than afloat, until you take corrective measures.

17 If you run aground on a rising tide, time will work with you. If it is a falling tide, you must work quickly, or you may be stranded for hours.

18 Small boats with shallow drafts are usually easy to free. Tilt outboard motors or stern drives to their full up position. Raise the centerboards or daggerboards on small sailboats.

19 Do not run your engines; you could pump sand or mud into them, especially if you try to back off at high speed. It may be possible to get afloat by shifting weight to the stern. You may be able to float the boat off by rocking it from side to side. Another boater running his shallow draft boat to create a wake might lift you free.

20 It may be possible to push the boat into deeper water. Before sending anyone into the water to try this, be sure they are wearing life preservers and are attached to safety lines. Always make sure in advance there is an easy way back into the boat.

21 Larger sailboats are more difficult to free. You may try several methods. Firmly set an anchor some distance from the boat, using a dinghy. The boat may come free by slowly winching in the rode.

22 *Heeling* (leaning) a sailboat over to one side may reduce draft enough to free the keel from the bottom. Move the crew to the low side. Place a heavy crew member at the end of the boom while holding it at right angles to the low side of the boat. If the wind is blowing towards deeper water, hoist the mainsail broadside to the wind; the wind may help push you off.

Figure 122   Healing a Sailboat to Free Its Keel

23 Another way to heel the boat is to rig a halyard to an anchor set off the beam. Slowly and carefully winching in the halyard may sufficiently reduce the draft.

24 If you call the Coast Guard or a commercial company for help, you will need to know your estimated position.

Towing or Being Towed

25 You may be asked sometime to take another vessel in tow. If the boat is in no danger, help them get professional assistance, and then stand by until it arrives. If there is an immediate danger to persons or property, and prompt action is necessary, act reasonably and prudently. Rendering assistance to others in distress is not only common courtesy, but required by law if it does not endanger your own boat or crew.

26 Federal law protects from liability a person who in good faith and acting "reasonably and prudently" renders assistance at the scene of an accident without objection of the person being assisted. (See Chapter 8, Boat Handling.)

Towing Procedures

27 Towing requires certain safety precautions with which you should be familiar:

- Each person in the towed vessel should put on a life preserver.
- Towlines must be strong. Nylon makes a good towline, because it stretches and absorbs shock. Braided nylon is preferable to twisted nylon; twisted nylon can be dangerous if it breaks, for it has a greater "snap-back" action. An adequate anchor line from the boat being towed often makes a good towline.
- Never tie to an improperly mounted cleat. Cleats used for towing should always be through-bolted with a backing block to spread the strain. Don't use a cleat if you cannot see how it is mounted. Bow eyebolts and transom eyebolts are usually through-bolted.
- Keep passengers out of direct line with a tow rope in case it breaks or a deck fitting pulls out of the deck. A piece of hardware at the end of a stretched nylon towline can be a lethal weapon.
- Fasten towlines securely to both boats in a position and manner that does not interfere with steering. You will find steering difficult if you fasten a towline to just one side of a boat. A better way is to form a bridle between eyebolts or cleats located on opposite sides of the transom. Attach the towline in the middle of the bridle.
- Keep outboard motors and stern drives on the towed boat down and centered to prevent yaw (swinging to one side and then the other).
- If a small sailboat does not have a bow eye or bow cleat, tow it by fastening a tow line to the mast at the deck (if the mast base is mounted on the keel).

Figure 123 Cleat with Backing Block

- Keep the towline centered by tying it to the headstay fitting. Raise the centerboard and fasten the tiller or wheel so the rudder remains centered. Make sure the sails are lowered.
- Adjust the length of the towline so the towed boat rides a minimum of three wave lengths behind the towing vessel. This will prevent the towed boat from running up on the tow boat.
- Shorten the towline when maneuvering in confined areas.
- Start up cautiously and tow slowly. Post lookouts to watch for hazards in the water and keep an eye on the towline so that it does not foul in the propeller of the towboat. See that the towed vessel rides properly in the water.

Man Overboard!

28 People fall overboard even when wind and seas are calm. A fall can be dangerous. Many people are not in good enough physical condition to withstand the shock of being tossed in the water. Imagine being in the water with no life jacket, being dragged down by the weight of water-soaked clothing, and trying to tread water. Couple this with the fact that you may not even be missed from the boat! Now add the possibility that you might be the only one capable of handling the boat to retrieve a person in the water. Wearing a life preserver can be your only source of survival.

Prevention

29 Do not allow passengers to stand in small boats underway or sit on foredecks, gunwales, engine boxes, seat backs, or transoms. Deck-gripping shoes are the best footwear; bare feet have poor traction.

30 Keep your weight low and close to the centerline when moving around in small boat.

31 Equip your sailboat with through-bolted lifeline stanchions. If there are children aboard, install safety netting. In bad weather, attach crew members to special safety lines with harnesses. It is difficult to find and recover a person lost overboard, especially in poor visibility.

32 Practice a procedure for recovering someone lost overboard. Toss a life jacket over the side while moving. See how long it takes to stop, turn, and retrieve it. What would you do if you were alone and fell overboard? Could you get back on board?

Recovery Procedures

33 The following procedures are recommended in man-overboard situations:
- Shout "Man Overboard!" immediately. Make sure your helmsman hears you. Toss a life preserver to the person overboard, even if he or she is wearing a life preserver and can swim. It will improve visiblity and provide something buoyant to grasp.
- Assign someone to constantly point at the person in the water and never let the victim out of sight.
- Stop the boat immediately; in sailboats, drop the sails and start the engine.
- To avoid running over the person in the water, approach against the wind

**Figure 124   Life Preserver to
                Overboard Victim**

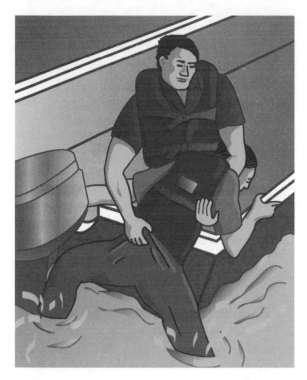

Figure 125   Boarding Over the Transom

and waves. Carefully come close aboard. Shift into reverse to stop forward motion.

- Turn off the engine in gear to keep the propeller from turning; propellers are sharp and can easily injure someone in the water. It is safer to trail a life preserver on a line astern and circle the person in the water until the victim can grasp it.
- In a boat with low freeboard, the best place to bring a person aboard is over the transom; but always be alert to the presence of hot outboard motors and exhaust pipes and carbon monoxide.
- In boats with high freeboard, use a swim platform or ladder. If these are not available, rig a sling, rope ladder, or even a knotted line. A strong swimmer can go over the side to help a weak person in the water, but should always wear a life preserver and safety line.
- In a sailing vessel with no power, sail toward the wind when approaching the

victim. If the boat has a centerboard or daggerboard, lower it all the way to stabilize the boat. In larger sailboats, try to pull the person into a sail lowered into the water. Use the sail as a sling and roll the person into the boat. If so equipped, a winch will make this task easier. There is special man-overboard retrieval equipment available that is especially effective for sailboats.

Figure 126   Recovering a Victim with a Sail

Restricted Visibility

34 Unexpected rain, fog, smog, hail, or snow can restrict visibility. Your primary concern in restricted visibility is to avoid collision. Make every effort to detect other boats and to make your presence known to them.

35 The following procedures are recommended in restricted visibility:

- Reduce speed; the Navigation Rules require it. You should be able to stop your boat in one-half the distance you can see. If an approaching boat is following the same precaution, collision is unlikely.
- Your crew should be wearing life preservers. A person in the water in a life preserver is more easily seen, especially when visibility is poor.

- Post lookouts; one on the bow and one on the stern. The helmsman must concentrate on the operation of the boat.
- Turn on your navigation lights.
- Sound the proper sound signals for your vessel. Powerboats sound 1 prolonged (4–6 seconds) blast every 2 minutes. Sailing vessels (not under power) sound 1 prolonged blast followed by 2 short blasts every 2 minutes.
- If necessary, briefly shut down your engine to listen for sounds of nearby boats and navigational aids. If you hear a signal, reply with your own signal, and proceed cautiously until you determine the position of the other boat. The direction of sound is difficult to determine in a fog.
- Determine your position as accurately as possible and plot the safest course to your destination. Try to run from one lighted navigational aid to another. Avoid a course that brings you close to hazards. Never take undue risks to get home!
- If lost, try to anchor and wait for conditions to improve. This will save fuel. Be sure to sound the proper signal; see Chapter 12, Navigation Rules, for vessel sound signals when anchored in restricted visibility.

Weather

36 Weather is a major concern to all boaters. Next to running out of fuel, bad weather spoils more boating days than anything else. Rain, cold, or heavy seas can turn a beautiful cruise into an unpleasant experience.

Avoid Severe Weather

37 Before setting out, check the weather forecast. If high waves or high winds are predicted, wait for a better day. Do not go into conditions that could be beyond your boating ability or the capabilities of your boat.

38 Listen to weather forecasts while on the water. Keep an eye to the west; weather usually changes from that direction. High, dark clouds or a change in wind direction or velocity often tell of threatening weather. Excessive static on an AM radio is caused by electrical activity in the air usually associated with thunderstorms.

39 If there are warnings of approaching bad weather, try to find a safe harbor as soon as possible. The approach of a storm should cause immediate concern for the safety of your craft and crew.

Severe Weather Procedures

40 Even a cautious skipper is caught in bad weather occasionally. If forced to ride out a storm, the following procedures are recommended:

- Have all passengers put on life preservers. If on a sailboat, fasten safety harnesses to a jackline or a sturdy through-bolted fitting. (A jackline is a stainless steel wire running from bow to stern at the middle of the deck.)
- Make sure your best helmsman is steering the boat. Meet the waves at the most advantageous speed and angle for your boat under existing conditions. Only experimentation will determine the correct crossing angle for your hull; the angle will vary with sea conditions. Take special care when you are required to take waves on the stern or broadside.

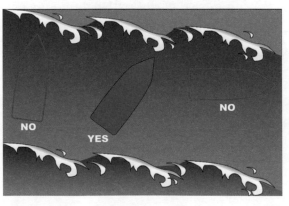

**Figure 127
Crossing
Waves
at an Angle**

- Find the best speed for controlling your boat. Reduced speed will decrease steering control. Selecting the correct speed requires practice and will vary with conditions.
- Batten down (secure) your boat. Close all hatches and ports. If you are in a sailboat, reduce the size of the sails. Fasten down all loose gear.
- In a small boat, seat your passengers in the bottom of the boat, as close to the centerline as possible.
- Check for water in the bilge—keep it dry; pump it as often as required. Water is heavy and affects boat stability.
- Know where you are and the location of the closest safe harbor. Choose the safest course-it may not be the shortest route! Always steer away from hazardous ground.
- It may be necessary to anchor. This will keep your bow headed into the waves. If the water is too deep to anchor, put out a sea anchor from the bow to keep your boat headed into the waves. You can make one from a bucket, ice chest, or tackle box.

Swamping and Capsizing

41 Swamping is when your boat fills with water. Capsizing is when your boat overturns. Capsizing is one of the major causes of boating fatalities.

42 *Stay with the boat* if you swamp or capsize!

43 A boat is easier to see than a person in the water. A swamped or capsized boat is itself a distress signal easily seen by passing vessels. Few people have the strength and endurance to swim more than a short distance, especially in cold water. Shore is always farther away than it looks. A person can hang on to a floating boat or object longer than

he or she can swim. Less heat is lost when a body is kept out of the water.

44 Persons in the water should always be wearing life preservers. Keep calm, and encourage others to do the same. You may be able to turn the boat right side up, bail it, and paddle towards shore. You can use hands for paddles, if necessary.

45 Boats less than 20 feet long, and built since 1973, are required to have built-in flotation. This flotation is to be sufficient to maintain the boat upright and keep it from capsizing. There must be enough buoyancy to keep the heads and shoulders of its crew out of the water.

46 Special techniques for recovery are often necessary when sailboats swamp or capsize.

Wind

47 The hull and superstructure of a boat act as a sail. Wind pressure on these areas affects steering. Powerboats have little hull below the waterline to resist the forces of wind. Wind from the side creates *leeway;* a sideways motion of a boat through the water. This is especially true when running slowly.

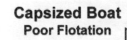

Swamped Boat
Good Flotation

Capsized Boat
Poor Flotation

Figure 128　Swamped Boat;
Capsized Boat

48 Over a period of time, leeway can have a large effect on the accuracy of your steering. Correct the problem by steering more toward the wind. You will need practice in making the necessary corrections to maintain your desired course.

Waves

49 Waves will affect both the forward movement of the boat and its steering. Seas striking the forward section of the boat tend to decrease its speed through the water. Waves coming up astern can increase speed in short bursts. A boat drifting without power will turn broadside to the waves. The helmsman must continually adjust steering to stay on course.

50 *Current* is horizontal movement of water relative to the bottom. It is often confused with *tide,* the vertical rise and fall of ocean water. Current, like wind, will affect the direction of the boat; it is necessary to make corrections for it. Determining and predicting current, its effect, and how to compensate for it are taught in the USPS Piloting and Advanced Piloting courses.

51 **Running Before the Waves** in a planing boat requires keeping the stern square to the waves and running on the back of a single wave. Use engine power to maintain a position about a third of the way back from the wave's crest. Be ready to adjust speed-faster or slower-to maintain steerage and control. In a slow displacement vessel, you may not be able to keep up with a single wave.

52 If you cannot keep up with a single wave, concentrate on keeping the boat centered with its stern square to the waves coming up behind you, allowing successive waves to pass under your keel.

53 **Running Parallel to the Waves** is often uncomfortable and dangerous. Even relatively small waves can start a pendulum motion in your boat if they strike you on the beam (from the side). In almost every case, your boat will handle better if you head into the waves rather than running parallel with them.

54 If the spacing between successive waves happens to coincide with the natural roll period of the boat, each successive wave can give an additional push, resulting in greater and greater roll until the boat actually rolls over. This is called *"broaching."* To avoid this, you may find it necessary to head into the waves in a direction somewhat away from your destination. By taking a course that is easier on the boat and on you, you may actually be able to travel faster and get there sooner (and less tired) than if you traveled the most direct route.

Crossing Large Wakes

55 Wakes are waves. Alert your crew when you see a wake approaching. Minimize the effect by reducing speed and turning into the waves at the proper angle for your boat.

Figure 129   Running Before Waves

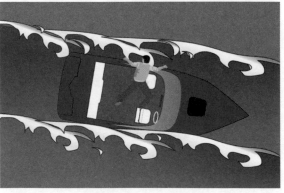

Figure 130   Broaching

An unexpected wave can toss people around—even overboard.

Stopping

56 Boats have no brakes. You must take the engine out of gear and let it coast to a stop, or put the engine in reverse to stop short. Practice with your boat to determine the stopping distance at various speeds. Always come to a stop gradually. This will allow your stern wave to subside, and avoid your being *swamped* or tossed against the pier or another boat.

Figure 131   Wakes Striking the Stern

Collision

57 Collision is the most frequent type of boating accident. Most boat collisions occur to experienced operators in daylight, around midday, on weekends. Visibility is generally excellent and weather is good.

58 Collisions occur because of high speed, and operators just not looking where they are going. Today's fast boats (including personal watercraft) cover a long distance in a short time. The distraction of an operator for just a few moments can cause a collision.

Reacting to a Collision

59 If involved in a collision, the actions you take depend on the severity of the accident:
- First, account for and check the condition of your crew and the occupants of the other boat. Immediately apply first aid if there is any serious injury.

- Get expert medical attention for seriously injured victims as soon as possible. Call the Coast Guard and nearby boats for help. (You learned how to place distress calls in Chapter 3, Marine Radiotelephone.) Try to have a good estimate of your position. This will save time and confusion when you place your call.
- Have all passengers put on PFDs.
- Determine the degree of damage to the vessels. Will they stay afloat? Check for hull damage and make necessary emergency repairs.

60 Remember, an operator involved in or observing any kind of boating accident must stop, offer identification, and render assistance to those in danger, providing he does not place his vessel or passengers at risk. If you act reasonably and prudently, in good faith, and without objection of the person being assisted, you will be protected by federal law.

61 After caring for all persons and property, the operators of both boats must file an accident report in accordance with local regulations in the area of the accident. The regulations designate where to make the report; usually the state boating law administrator.

Fire

62 Fire on a boat is a serious matter. On shore, a person can run away from a fire and call the fire department. On a boat, there is nowhere to go except into the water, and help may be far away.

Fire Prevention

63 Many fires are preventable. Correct at once any condition that may cause a fire.
- Inspect your boat's bilge frequently. Keep it free of grease, oil, and debris. Check your fuel system for leaks.

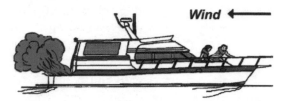

Figure 132   Keeping a Fire Downwind

- Regularly inspect electrical wiring. Repair any bare wires or loose electrical connections to prevent a spark from igniting fuel vapors.
- Use only marine-rated parts for repairs.
- Store dinghy fuel and propane so they have plenty of ventilation, preferably topside.
- Be careful if you carry charcoal on your boat; if allowed to get damp, it can ignite from spontaneous combustion.
- When fueling, ground your fuel line nozzle against the fill pipe to eliminate static sparks. See Chapter 8, Boat Handling, for fueling instructions.
- Ventilate your engine compartment after every fueling until you are sure there are no dangerous vapors. *Sniff for vapors.*

64 Most fires are caused by starting engines when there are gasoline vapors in the bilge. This type of fire starts with an explosion and spreads rapidly.

65 Diesel fuel will burn as fast as gasoline when ignited. The only difference is that the temperature at which diesel fumes ignite is higher.

66 Keep more than the required number and size of approved fire extinguishers readily accessible. Mount them properly where you can get at them quickly and easily. Have them checked annually to ensure they are fully charged and in working order.

67 Plan ahead. Know what you will do to combat fire in any section of your boat.

Responding to Fire

68 Follow these steps if fire breaks out while underway:

- Immediately notify the crew. Tell them the location of the fire. Be sure they are wearing life preservers. Instruct them to move to the unaffected portion of the boat, usually toward the wind.
- If you still have power, try to turn the boat to prevent the wind from blowing the fire into the occupied quarters.
- Turn off all fuel supplies; engine, galley stove, heaters. Disconnect all sources of electrical power.
- Find the source of the fire and try to put it out with your fire extinguishers. Point an extinguisher at the base of a fire. Use short bursts and sweep it from side to side until you use its entire contents. Know how to use your extinguishers in advance; do not try to read the label when a fire is in progress.
- Use water on an alcohol stove fire. Water will mix with alcohol and dilute it to the point that it cannot burn. Use your dry chemical extinguishers for all other fires.
- If you are unable to get the fire under control at once, place a distress call on VHF Channel 16 immediately. You can always notify the Coast Guard later if a Mayday situation no longer exists.
- Display a visual distress signal to attract local boats. It is always advantageous and comforting to have someone standing by to help.
- If there is the slightest doubt about whether you can put out the fire, don't even try.
- Immediately get the people off your boat and as far away as possible in case of an explosion.

Medical Emergencies on the Water

69 You are often far from medical help when an accident or injury occurs on the water. You must be self-sufficient. Be prepared by taking medical treatment courses such as life-saving, first-aid, and cardiopulmonary resuscitation (CPR) courses. They are offered by organizations such as the American Red Cross. This is particularly important if you are a serious boater who regularly sails out of range of immediate medical help. Keep a manual and well-equipped first-aid kit on board. (See the list of contents for a first-aid kit recommended by the Red Cross, below.)

70 Certain information on medical emergencies in this chapter has been extracted from the 1994 edition of *First Aid Fast*, a publication of the American Red Cross. This has been done through the courtesy of the American Red Cross (all rights reserved in all countries). The United States Power Squad-rons is grateful to the American Red Cross for their permission to use this information. Minor additions relative to on-the-water activities are noted in brackets ([ ]). *First Aid Fast* is an integral part of Red Cross training; but, by itself, does not constitute complete and comprehensive training. The book is designed to familiarize you with emergencies that can happen and prepare you to react before an emergency occurs. It is also a quick source for information in emergencies, guiding your actions in a step-by-step manner. The booklet is available from local chapters of the American Red Cross.

Heart Attacks, Cardiac Arrest, Drowning

71 The most important single factor in saving a victim who has stopped breathing is getting air into the lungs as soon as possible. Hopefully, someone on board will have had training in rescue breathing and cardiopulmonary resuscitation (CPR).

72 Rescue breathing is given to a victim who is unconscious and not breathing. CPR is given to a victim who is not breathing and does not have a pulse. Don't wait for an emergency to be convinced of the need for rescue breathing and CPR training.

73 Organizations such as the American Red Cross offer these courses. Take one now!

Table 21: First Aid Kit

Courtesy of the American Red Cross
All Rights Reserved in all Countries

Be prepared for an emergency. Keep a first aid kit in your home, in your automobile, and on your boat. Carry a first aid kit with you, or know where you can find one when you are participating in outdoor activities. Know the location of first aid kits where you work. A first aid kit should include the following:

Flashlight and batteries	Adhesive tape
Scissors and tweezers	Antiseptic ointment
Emergency blanket	Disposable gloves
Triangular bandages	Plastic bags
Antiseptic towelettes	Cold pack
Gauze pads	Syrup of Ipecac
Roller gauze	Activated charcoal
Band-Aids in assorted sizes	

Table 22: Breathing Emergencies
Not Breathing (Unconscious)

Signals
- Chest does not rise and fall
- Can't feel or hear breaths
- Skin appears pale or bluish

Care
- Check the scene and the victim
- Send someone to Call for an ambulance
- [On the water, radio for medical assistance on Channel 16]
- Tilt head all the way back and lift chin do not tilt a child's or infant's head back as far
- Look, listen, and feel for breathing for about 5 seconds

If victim is not breathing:
- Pinch the victim's nose shut, open your mouth wide, and make a tight seal around the victim's mouth For infant, cover both mouth and nose with your mouth
- Give 2 slow breaths, until the chest gently rises
- Check for a pulse at the groove beside the windpipe in the neck for about 5 to 10 seconds

If victim is not breathing and has a pulse:
- Give rescue breaths
    Adult: 1 breath about every 5 seconds
    Child or Infant: 1 breath about every 3 seconds
- Recheck pulse and breathing about every minute

Continue rescue breathing as long as a pulse is present but victim is not breathing.

If the victim vomits, turn the victim onto a side, wipe the mouth clean, and continue.

Drowning
Drowning often occurs to victims who never intended to get wet. Drowning can also happen in the home in as little water as a bowlful.

- Send someone to call an ambulance. [On the water, radio for medical assistance on CH 16.]

Once the victim is out of the water:
- Check the victim; care for any conditions you find
- Tilt the head back and check breathing; check the mouth for fluid or objects

If airway appears clear:
- Give 2 slow breaths

If breaths do not go in:
- Re-tilt the victim's head and re-attempt breaths
- If breaths still do not go in:
- Give up to five abdominal thrusts (Heimlich maneuver)
- Lift jaw and tongue and sweep out the mouth.
- Repeat breaths, thrusts, and sweeps, until breaths go in or victim breathes on his own.

**Figure 133
Rescue Breathing**

Adult:
With head tilted back, pinch nose shut, give 1 slow breath about every 5 seconds

Child/Infant: Give 1 slow breath about every 3 seconds

This information is courtesy of the American Red Cross. All rights reserved in all countries.

Table 23: Heat-Related Illness

Heat cramps and heat-related illness are progressive conditions caused by overexposure to heat. If recognized in the early stages, heat-related illness can usually be reversed. If not, it may progress to a life-threatening condition.

Heat Cramps Signals

- Painful muscle spasms, usually in the legs and abdomen.

Heat Cramps Care

- Have victim rest in a cool place
- Give cool water or a commercial sports drink
- Lightly stretch and massage the muscle
- Do Not Give Salt Tablets
- Watch for signals of heat illness

Heat Illness Signals

Early Stages:
- Cool, moist, pale, or flushed skin
- Headache, nausea, dizziness
- Weakness, exhaustion
- Heavy sweating

Late Stages:
- Red, hot, dry skin
- Changes in level of consciousness
- Vomiting

Heat Illness Care

- Move victim to a cool place
- Loosen tight clothing
- Remove perspiration-soaked cloth
- Apply cool, wet cloths to the skin
- Fan the victim
- If conscious, give cool water to drink
- If victim refuses water, vomits, or starts to lose consciousness:
- Send someone to Call for an ambulance. [On the water, radio for medical assistance on Ch 16.]
- Place victim on side.
- Continue to cool by placing ice or cold packs on victim's wrists, ankles, groin, neck, and in armpits.
- Continue to Check breathing and pulse

Table 24: Head and Spine Injuries

Although injuries to the head and spine account for only a small percentage of all injuries, they cause more than half of all injury-related deaths. Signals of a head or spine injury may be sometimes slow to develop and are not always noticeable at first.

Always Suspect a Head or Spine Injury in These Situations:

- A fall from a height greater than the victim's height
- Any diving mishap
- A victim found unconscious for unknown reasons
- Any injury involving severe blunt force to the head or trunk, such as from a motor vehicle [or a boom on a sailboat]
- Any incident involving a lightning strike

Injuries to Muscles, Bones, and Joints

Only a trained medical professional can tell the difference between a sprain, strain, fracture, or dislocation. You do not need to know what kind of injury it is to give the correct first aid.

Signals

- Pain
- Bruising and swelling

Care

- Check the scene and the victim
- Rest the injured part
- Apply ice or a cold pack to control swelling and reduce pain; place a towel or cloth between the source of cold and the skin
- Avoid any movement or activity that causes pain

If you suspect a serious injury:

- Immobilize the injured part to keep it from moving.
- Send someone to call an ambulance. [On the water, radio for medical assistance on Ch 16.]

Table 25: Cardiac (Heart) Emergencies

Cardiac (Heart) Emergencies here are two general types of cardiac emergencies: when the heart doesn't function properly, denying the heart muscle of much needed oxygen and causing chest pain, i.e., heart attack, and when the heart doesn't function at all (cardiac arrest).

Most people who die of heart attacks die within two hours after the first signals appear. Many lives are lost because people deny they are having a heart attack and delay calling for help.

Recognizing the signals of a heart attack, and calling for an ambulance before the heart stops, are critical steps to saving lives. [On the water, radio for medical assistance on CH 16.]

Chest Pain
Signals

- Chest pain or pressure; may range from discomfort to an unbearable crushing sensation; pain is not relieved by rest, changing position, or medication; may spread to shoulder, arm, or jaw.
- Trouble breathing; breathing is often faster than normal; victim feels short of breath
- Pulse may be faster or slower than normal or irregular
- Skin may be moist, pale, or bluish in appearance; victim may sweat more than normal

Care

- Have the victim stop activity and rest.
- Send someone to call for an ambulance. [On the water, radio for medical assistance on CH 16.]
- Help the victim rest in a comfortable position. A sitting position may make breathing easier. Loosen restrictive clothing.
- Assist with prescribed medication.
- Monitor breathing and pulse closely.
- Be prepared to provide CPR if victim loses consciousness and breathing and pulse stop.

Cardiac Arrest

A heart that stops beating effectively causes a victim to lose consciousness and the victim's breathing and pulse to stop. This condition can be caused by heart disease, severe injuries, or electrocution. CPR is given to a victim who is not breathing and does not have a pulse. It is a combination of chest compressions and rescue breathing.

Signals

- Unresponsive (unconscious)
- Not breathing and no pulse

Care
(Note differences if victim is a child or infant)

- Check the scene and the victim.
- Send someone to call for an ambulance [On the water, radio for medical assistance on CH 16.]
- Check for breathing.

If not breathing:

- Tilt head back, pinch nose, and give 2 slow breaths. Each breath should make the chest gently rise.
- Check for a pulse at the groove beside the windpipe in the neck (infant: between the shoulder and the elbow)

If no pulse, begin CPR.

- Find hand position in center of chest over breastbone (infant: use fingers)
- Position shoulders over hands (infant; hand over fingers); compress chest 15 times in about 10 seconds (child or infant: 5 times in 3 seconds)
- Give 2 slow breaths (child or infant: 1 slow breath)
- Do 3 more sets of 15 compressions and 2 breaths (child or infant: 3 more sets of 5 compressions and 1 breath)
- Recheck pulse and breathing. If there is no pulse, continue sets of 15 compressions and 2 breaths (child and infant: 5 compressions and 1 breath).

Cardiac Emergencies

Figure 134   CPR for Adults

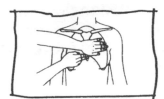

Find hand position

Position sholders over hands, compress chest 15 times

Give 2 slow breaths; recheck pulse and breathing. If no pulse, continue sets of 15 compressions and 2 breaths

Wounds

Figure 135 Wounds— Controlling Bleeding

Apply direct pressure and elevation

Apply a bandage

If bleeding doesn't stop,

Apply pressure to a nearby artery

arm, leg, and groin pressure shown here

Table 26: Wounds

A wound is an injury to the skin and the soft tissues beneath it. Damage to blood vessels causes bleeding. When caring for wounds it is important to take precautions to protect yourself against transmission of disease.

Follow these simple procedures:
- When possible, ask the injured victim to help you
- Wear latex gloves or place a barrier between yourself and the victim's blood
- Wash your hands with soap and water immediately before and after providing care

Signals
- Cuts, scrapes, punctures, or other breaks in the skin
- Bleeding, bruising; arca may swell

Care
- Check the scene for safety.
- If necessary send someone to call an ambulance. [On the water, radio for medical assistance on Ch 16.]
- Cover the wound with a sterile gauze pad and press firmly against the wound (use your bare hand to apply pressure only as a last resort).
- If a dressing becomes soaked with blood, do not remove it; apply additional dressings on top of it or them.
- Elevate the injured area above the level of the heart if you do not suspect broken bones
- Cover gauze dressings with a roller bandage to maintain pressure

If bleeding doesn't stop:
- Apply additional dressings and bandage
- Squeeze the nearby artery against the bone underneath
- Arm: Inside of the upper arm, between the shoulder and the elbow
- Leg: Crease at the front of the hip, in the groin

This information is courtesy of the American Red Cross. All rights reserved in all countries.

Table 27: Call for an Ambulance

[On the water, radio for medical assistance on Ch 16.]

- Deformity is present
- Feels or sounds like bones are rubbing together
- "Snap" or "pop" heard or felt at time of injury
- An open wound on or around the injury site; bone ends may or may not be visible
- Inability to move or use the affected part normally
- Injured area is cold and numb
- Injury involves the head, neck, or back
- Victim has trouble breathing
- Cause of the injury suggests that the injury may be severe

Table 28 Red Cross Health and Safety Programs

The Red Cross offers a variety of community programs that teach life saving skills and safety \information. Contact your local Red Cross chapter for information on these and other programs.

- American Red Cross Adult CPR*
- American Red Cross Basic Aid Training (for children)*
- American Red Cross Community CPR*
- American Red Cross Infant & Child CPR*
- American Red Cross Standard First Aid*
- American Red Cross 'Til Help Arrives
- American Red Cross Community Water Safety
- American Red Cross Learn to Swim Programs
- American Red Cross Longfellow's Whale Tales (for children)
- American Red Cross HIV/AIDS Programs

  * Available in Spanish

Table 29: Hypothermia

Signals
- Shivering, numbness, glassy stare
- Apathy, weakness, impaired judgment
- Loss of consciousness

Care
- Check the scene and the victim.
- Send someone to call for an ambulance. [On the water, radio for medical assistance on Ch 16.]
- Gently move the victim to a warm place
- Check breathing and pulse
- Give rescue breathing and CPR as necessary
- Remove any wet clothing and dry the victim
- Warm the victim Slowly by wrapping in blankets or by putting dry clothing on the victim
- Hot water bottles and chemical hot packs may be used when first wrapped in a towel or blanket before applying

Do not warm the victim too quickly, such as immersing him or her in warm water. Rapid warming can cause dangerous heart rhythms

Figure 136 *H.E.L.P.* **Position**

Hypothermia

74 *Hypothermia* is the abnormal lowering of the body's internal temperature due to exposure to cold air, wind, or water. It can occur even on a bright, sunny day. More victims of marine accidents lose their lives from hypothermia than from drowning. The use of alcohol can accelerate the onset of hypothermia.

75 To delay hypothermia, dress warmly, and stay dry and out of the wind. If you fall into the water and are wearing a life preserver, you can delay hypothermia by remaining inactive. A life preserver lessens the need to move around in the water and will help retain body heat.

76 Alone in the water, hold the inner side of your arms tightly against the side of your chest; press your thighs together and raise them to close off the groin region where blood vessels are close to the surface. This is the *H.E.L.P.* position (Heat Escape Lessening Posture).

77 When there is more than one victim in the water, the *Huddle* position is recommended. Victims huddle together as a group with chests side by side and arms around each other's shoulders to share body warmth.

Carbon Monoxide Poisoning

78 Carbon monoxide poisoning causes a startling number of boating fatalities. Often called the "silent killer," carbon monoxide is a colorless, odorless, and tasteless gas. It is the result of incomplete burning of any material containing carbon; such as, gasoline, diesel oil, alcohol, natural gas, or propane.

79 Extremely toxic even in small quantities, carbon monoxide can combine with the blood 250 times as readily as oxygen and will accumulate in the blood over a long period of time. It is very often impossible to detect carbon monoxide before it overcomes a victim, who is then too weak to escape or summon help.

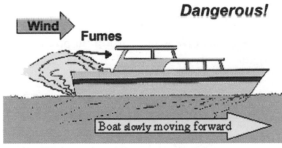

Figure 138   Exhaust Fumes Entering a Boat

80 Although carbon monoxide, in itself, has no telltale odor, it may mix with other gases that do have an odor. The odor of exhaust fumes almost guarantees the presence of carbon monoxide. However, carbon monoxide may accumulate in areas exclusive of exhaust fumes.

Figure 137 *Huddle* Position

81 Exhaust from engines, generators, cabin heaters, and galley stoves produce carbon monoxide. Breaks, cracks, or leaks in exhaust systems are the most frequent conditions leading to fatalities.

82 The exhaust from a boat's engines can be blown into a boat that is running ahead of the wind. The forward motion of the boat creates a backdraft at the stern that pulls the exhaust into the cockpit or cabin. When you detect this exhaust, open windshields and portholes to create a draft through the boat so fumes will exit. Introduce fresh air into the boat by making turns, or by zigzagging back and forth across the course.

Prevention

83 Regularly check your engine and generator exhaust systems, and the seals around your hatches and portholes for leaks. Check the ventilation of your alcohol stove. Maintain your generator meticulously. Carbon monoxide can leak from it without your knowing it. You may not want to run it while you are sleeping. It is a good idea to run your exhaust blower while using it.

84 Dangerous effects of carbon monoxide can occur when a boat is at a marina dock, anchored, or rafted up with other boats. With engines idling, or generators running to provide electricity, carbon monoxide can easily drift into your boat from nearby vessels, especially if your hatches or portholes are open.

85 Carbon monoxide detectors are available that feature not only a visual alert but also an audible alarm. The latter is most desirable for it will sound when carbon monoxide concentration in your boat becomes dangerous. You may want to consider one or more of these detectors as a vital part of your safety equipment.

86 The symptoms of mild carbon monoxide poisoning are nearly the same as seasickness, colds, and flu; nausea, weakness, dizziness, headache, watering of the eyes, ringing-in-the-ears. Severe poisoning can result in brain or heart damage or death. There is often a cherry-red coloring to the skin.

87 If you suspect carbon monoxide poisoning, get medical help at once! Treatment consists of immediately getting the victim to breathe large quantities of fresh air. Give supplementary oxygen if available. If breathing has stopped, start rescue breathing immediately. Watch for a relapse.

88 Victims often respond quickly, but collapse later because vital organs are damaged from lack of oxygen. Someone who has been exposed to carbon monoxide should have medical attention even if they feel they are all right.

Water Sports Safety

89 To be enjoyed safely, all water sports require certain knowledge and skills. Obtain the USPS Learning Guide entitled *Water Sports* for an extensive discussion of the safety issues of many water sports. All participants should be good swimmers, wearing approved life jackets whenever on the water.

Special Gear

90 Water sports such as waterskiing and riding a personal watercraft (PWC) involve high-speed falls. Wear a helmet and a high-impact life preserver when engaged in these sports. Protect yourself from the elements with appropriate clothing. Eat well, drink plenty of water, and avoid alcohol.

Know the Waters in Your Area

91 Falls in shallow water can result in injuries due to rocks, trash, and dangerous bottom conditions. Stay in safe waters, especially as you learn your water sport.

Night Activity

92 Local regulations often prohibit nighttime water sport activity due to the dangers of high speed travel in limited visibility.

What to Do in an Emergency

93 Never abandon your equipment in an emergency. Water skis, a sailboard, an ice chest, or an overturned boat will float you and provide a target in the water more easily seen than your head alone. Carry a whistle or horn to use if in need of help. Signal for help by slowly and repeatedly raising your arms outstretched to the sides.

Waterskiing

94 Waterskiing regulations vary; know the laws in your area relative to minimum age for participants, observer requirements, when you may water ski, etc.

95 Your ski boat operator must be a safety-conscious person, familiar with the ski boat and capable of good judgment. The boat should always be in first-class condition.

96 Safe waterskiing also depends on an alert observer. The observer keeps track of everything going on around the boat and alerts the operator to any safety-threatening situation and whenever the skier falls.

Fishing and Hunting

97 Victims who fish and hunt on the water have one of the highest boat fatality rates. Many consider their boats part of their hunting and fishing gear. The standard safety rules that apply to all boating also apply to hunters and fishermen. Check the weather before you go. Always wear a life preserver; don't stand in the boat; don't overload the boat; stow firearms and hunting knives properly.

98 Waders can be dangerous. If you fall overboard they can fill with water and make it impossible to get back into the boat or up an embankment. Assign shooting and casting areas to each person involved in hunting and/ or fishing to avoid accidents with others in the boat. Never use alcohol when boating!

Paddle Sports

99 Though paddling is a form of boating, paddlers have fewer rules to follow than captains of powerboats or sailboats. Since paddlers can go practically anywhere, unlike their boating big brothers, they will make more common-sense decisions. In navigating your small craft, it is necessary to understand you:
- may not be visible to the captain and crew of a larger vessel
- are more maneuverable than larger boats
- require less draft than larger crafts
- are not "under power"

100 As you paddle, a variety of situations will occur when you need to know where you are, where you should be, and what you can do to be safe. Below is a brief list of scenarios and what you can do to enhance your safety.

101 **Make Yourself More Visible:**
- travel close to shore or large stationary objects
- use bright colors on your boat and equipment
- use additional reflective tape on boat and equipment
- stay close to your paddling buddies

102 The basic rule of boating is: the craft under power has to yield to the boat not under power. Though this is true, the fact may be that those under power can't see you! This is why it is important to have bright colors and possibly some additional reflective tape

added to the sides of your vessel and other equipment. If the approaching vessel is larger and moving at a fast pace, there is even less time for the captain to notice you. Be proactive in assisting the captain of the vessel in noticing you.

103 Better yet, since you are more maneuverable, steer clear of larger vessels.

104 A good rule of thumb is to stay closer to the shoreline or large stationary objects, as larger vessels naturally avoid these areas. If shore is not close, stay within a few feet of other paddlers, thus making everyone more visible.

105 Traveling in groups ensures you are seen.

106 **Passing Other Vessels:**
  • oncoming vessel, pass to the right
  • both traveling in the same direction, pass on left as on U.S. highways
  • exaggerate the turn or change in direction
  • stay a safe distance away from other vessels

107 If you must pass a vessel coming toward you, pass to the right of that vessel. If the vessel is slower and you are both traveling in the same direction, go around the vessel on the left. (This is similar to driving on the roadways in the U.S.) If you must pass another vessel, when you turn either right or left depending on your situation, exaggerate the turn. This will ensure the other vessel recognizes you see them and lets them know your intention.

108 It is always wise to keep a safe distance from another craft; the larger the craft, the farther away you should stay.

109 **Large Ocean-Going Vessels:**
  • stay at least a mile away regardless of who has the right-of-way

110 If you see large cargo or ocean-going ships, stay a few miles away! These vessels, when entering or leaving a harbor or when traveling in narrow channels, are restricted by their draft and therefore must remain in the marked channel. Paddlers must give way to these vessels, even though they are a non-power boat.

111 The best rule here is to remember: they cannot stop or adjust course as fast as you when underway nor adjust course due to the depth they may require. Due to their height and size, it is even more difficult for them to see you.

112 Keep a distance of a mile or two behind ships as the water moving behind them is very forceful and dangerous. The general rule is: if the vessel is larger than you, it is best to stay out of their way regardless of who has the right-of-way.

113 **Channels:**
  • paddle outside of channels or to the far right
  • cross at the shortest distance across
  • cross as a group; stay close together

114 If you are near a channel or a channel marker, stay out of the channel or near the marker. Channels are designed for vessels that need deeper waters. If you must go out a channel, stay to the far right side as close to the marker line as possible or just outside the channel. The waters are perfect for you here (and safer), but not for larger craft.

115 If you must cross a channel, do it together, within 20 feet of other paddlers, when there is plenty of distance between you and an approaching vessel. This will make you more visible, and the large vessel (being less maneuverable) will not have to dodge multiple small craft in the same area.

Homework

Name: _____ **Date:** _____ **Group:** _____

1. To avoid running out of fuel, determine the usable capacity of your fuel tank and your boat's rate of fuel consumption, and then:
    a. bring extra fuel in easy-to-pour containers such as plastic milk jugs.
    b. plan to use one third of the tank to reach your destination, one third to get home, and one third for emergencies.
    c. plan on enough fuel to get to the next fuel dock.
    d. plan on one half of the tank to reach your destination and one half of the tank to get home.

2. If you run out of fuel, your first action should be to:
    a. try to anchor, if you are in a safe location.
    b. call the Coast Guard and request delivery of fuel by patrol boat.
    c. tie up to the nearest buoy and wait for help.
    d. check that you have all of your required equipment for when the Coast Guard arrives.

3. If you run aground, your first action should be to:
    a. put your boat in reverse gear and back off at high speed.
    b. quickly jump overboard and push your boat into deeper water.
    c. check the condition of your hull.
    d. move all passengers to the forward deck and try to back off.

4. If a victim falls overboard, one of your first actions should be to:
    a. stop the boat and immediately set off a visual distress flare.
    b. stop forward motion and back up quickly to retrieve the victim from the water.
    c. shout "Man Overboard" so that your helmsman hears you.
    d. approach from the direction of the wind and current, come close by, and toss the victim a line.

5. When encountering restricted visibility of any kind, your first reaction should be to:
    a. reduce speed so you will be able to stop in one-half the distance you can see.
    b. put on foul weather gear to keep from getting cold and wet.
    c. ring your ship's bell one short ring every second to advise other vessels of your presence.
    d. use your hailer every three minutes to announce that you are underway and ask that all other vessels keep clear.

6. To avoid going out in conditions beyond your boating ability or the capabilities of your boat:
    a. check the weather forecast before you leave.
    b. measure the height of the waves before leaving your dock.
    c. keep an eye to the east for white low-lying clouds moving westward.
    d. hold a wet finger up in the air to test humidity.

7. If your boat swamps or capsizes, the primary rule to remember is:
    a. immediately send someone over the side to swim for help.
    b. always stay with the boat.
    c. round up all passengers in the water into the H.E.L.P. position.
    d. fasten a line to the boat and ask all to help pull it ashore.

8. If involved in a collision, your first action is to:
    a. get the name, address, and insurance company of the operator of the other boat.
    b. check your VHF radio to see if it is damaged.
    c. place fenders between the two boats to eliminate further damage.
    d. account for and check the condition of your crew and the occupants of the other boat.

9. If fire breaks out on your boat, immediately notify your crew, have them put on life preservers, and:
    a. empty the contents of your fire extinguisher in the general area of the flame.
    b. instruct them to move to the unaffected portion of the boat.
    c. stay with the boat, even if the fire cannot be extinguished.
    d. turn the boat so the wind will fan the fire and help put it out.

10. Hypothermia is:
    a. excessive perspiration and thirst resulting from exposure to the sun for a long period of time.
    b. abnormal lowering of the body's internal temperature due to exposure to cold air, wind, or water.
    c. a hallucinating reaction resulting from excessive loss of moisture in brain tissue.
    d. abnormal raising of the body's internal temperature due to exposure to warm air, wind, or water.

11. Carbon monoxide poisoning is most frequently caused by exposure to:
    a. fumes from an overloaded holding tank.
    b. oil vapors emitted from a crankcase ventilation valve.
    c. exhaust from engines, generators, cabin heaters, and galley stoves.
    d. fumes from stale bait deteriorating in the bait well.

15

Trailering

1 Statistics show that 90% of all recreational boats in the United States today are trailerable. This translates into thousands of boat-trailer rigs sharing our busy highways with trucks, buses, campers, passenger vehicles, motorcycles, and other forms of modern-day transportation. These same trailer boaters must also share congested launching ramps and launching areas with their fellow boaters.

2 There are three major causes of trailering accidents: improper trailer maintenance, driver error, and improper loading of the boat on the trailer. If a trailer boater does not have proper knowledge, vacation plans can easily go awry, people can get hurt, and serious damage can occur to equipment.

3 Upon completion of this chapter, you should be aware of the important safety considerations of trailering your boat. For a more extensive discussion of this subject, obtain the USPS Learning Guide entitled *Trailer Boating*.

Boat Trailers

4 The large number of types and shapes of boats being manufactured today has resulted in trailer manufacturers producing a variety of trailers to properly support each of these different hulls. Choosing the right trailer for your boat, and setting it up properly, is very important. Skimping on a trailer is false economy.

5 Make sure the boat and trailer fit one another. The trailer must have sufficient weight-carrying ability to support the boat, motor, fuel, and all the gear you plan to add to it. A data plate on the left side of the trailer will display how much weight the trailer can carry and the size of the tires needed for the rated load.

6 For safety reasons, the capacity of the trailer should exceed the combined weight of the trailer, boat, motor, and gear by 15%. A larger trailer is always safer and easier to handle. Public scales used to weigh truckloads are a good place to weigh your trailer rig.

7 The trailer must support the hull so the load is evenly distributed and so the hull is not stressed and bent out of shape. There should be supports under the engine, fuel tanks, batteries, etc. Seek professional advice from your boat manufacturer and dealer to select the correct trailer for your boat.

Trailer Tires

8 Many boat trailers have small-diameter tires that turn at a higher speed than tires on the tow vehicle. These smaller tires usually require high pressure, sometimes as much as sixty pounds per square inch. Correct tire pressure is critical. Low pressure can lead to serious overheating and tire deterioration. Always check tire pressures when the tires are cold.

Wheel Bearing Protectors

9   The condition of wheel bearings is critical; many trailer wheels are small and turn at very high speeds. Bearing protectors hold waterproof grease under spring-loaded pressure. When installed properly, they help prevent water from entering wheel bearings. Take care when adding grease to bearing protectors; overfilling may cause seal failure.

Safety Chains

10   Motor vehicle laws require safety chains to keep the trailer from parting from the tow vehicle in case of coupler failure. They are installed between the trailer and the tow vehicle and should be crossed under the trailer tongue, as shown in Figure 139. They should be strong enough to hold the total weight of the entire trailer when loaded, and just long enough to support the coupler so it will not hit the ground if the ball hitch breaks. Allow enough slack in the chain to permit tight turns under normal driving circumstances.

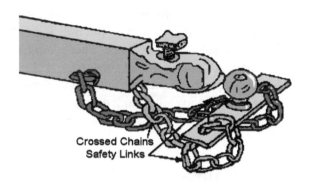

Figure 139   Safety Chains Crossed Under the Hitch Eye

11   Always install the connecting S hooks by inserting them into the hitch eye from the bottom up so they will not jump out of the hitch eyes. (See Figure 140.) Squeeze the openings of the hooks closed so they just barely clear the hitch eye rings.

12   Some states now require that S hooks be replaced with a secure form of connection that cannot accidentally become disconnected from the towing vehicle. Safety links, such as shown in Figure 139, fulfill this replacement requirement in most cases. Review your state's trailer law requirements, as well as those of states through which you will be driving.

Winches

13   To help load the boat, most trailers have a winch at the front with a cable or strap and a hook that can be attached to a strong fitting (the bow eye) on the stem of the boat. The strap or cable is under tremendous strain during loading, so make sure that it is in excellent condition with no kinks or frays.

14   Make sure no one is in direct line with the cable or strap. It could break and snap back. The hook can also break. Use steel cable winch lines for boats over 14 feet. If the winch is hand cranked, make certain the ratchet is engaged-a runaway winch handle can break bones. An electric winch and cable make it easy to draw a boat onto a trailer.

Wheel Jacks

15   A wheel jack is necessary to change a tire on most trailers. Be sure you have one that fits; most auto jacks will not lift trailers.

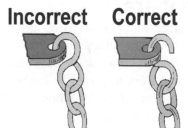

Incorrect   Correct

Figure 140   Installing Safety-Chain S Hooks in a Trailer-Hitch Eye

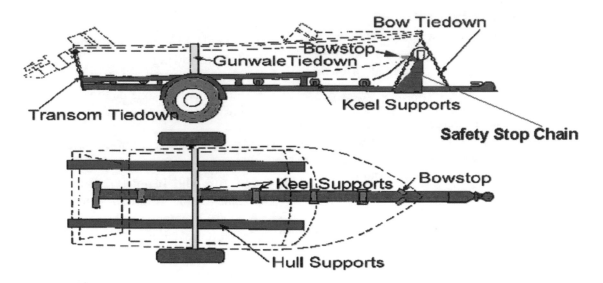

Figure 141   Trailer Arrangement Showing Supports and Tiedowns

Tie-Downs

16 Tie-downs keep a boat from shifting and sliding on a trailer during travel. Never use a winch cable for that purpose. Weld or bolt a special hook to the winch support. Use a chain and turnbuckle from this bolt (or hook) to the bow eye of the boat to keep the boat from sliding backward. Rig another chain from the boat toward the back of the trailer to keep the boat from sliding forward into the back of the tow vehicle in a sudden stop. Gunwale and transom tie-downs also prevent the boat from moving on the trailer. (See Figure 141.)

17 Tie down all equipment stored inside the boat so it will not shift around or fly out during trailering. This includes portable fuel tanks.

State Regulations

18 Most states require the registration of trailers. Additional regulations may call for extensive light, reflector, and turn-signal systems. Special braking and sway control systems may be required on larger trailers.

For the legal requirements, consult the authorities in your area and in each state in which you will be towing your boat.

The Tow Vehicle

19 A tow vehicle must have adequate power to tow the boat and trailer. The vehicle owner's manual will specify the maximum trailer gross weight and tongue weight acceptable for that vehicle.

20 Front wheel drive vehicles have limitations in their ability to tow heavy trailers. The weight of the trailer rig may lift the drive wheels off the ground. You may need special equipment even when pulling light-weight trailers with a front wheel drive car.

21 Modern frameless cars are often unable to support the hitches necessary for larger boats. Heavy-duty pickup trucks, vans, and utility vehicles, with their longer wheelbases, are often the choice for tow vehicles.

Tow Vehicle Equipment

22 How you equip your tow vehicle will depend upon the size and gross weight of your trailer rig. Special vehicle equipment often includes:

- larger engine
- oversized radiator
- heavy-duty battery and/or alternator
- heavy-duty brakes
- heavy-duty suspension systems
- heavy-duty flashers for expanded turn-signal systems
- nonslip differentials, special rear axle ratio
- heavy-duty transmissions with transmission coolers

23 Side-view mirrors, large enough to provide an unobstructed rear view, are desirable for safety reasons. Most vehicle manufacturers offer trailer towing packages that include the trailer hitch, coupler ball, and wiring harness, as well as much of the heavy-duty equipment mentioned above.

Hitching Systems

24 The total weight of the trailer rig must not exceed the load capacity of the trailer hitch. You will find the load capacity stamped on the hitch. The heavier your rig, the more critical the quality of the hitching system.

25 Leave the selection of a hitching system for your rig to a professional installer who will know the right type for your equipment.

26 **Tongue Weight** on the hitch should be approximately 10% of the weight of the rig when the coupler is parallel to the ground. Too much weight on the hitch will lower the rear of the tow vehicle, increase tire wear, make your vehicle difficult to steer, and reduce the effectiveness of the brakes. Too little weight and the trailer will fishtail. This may cause your trailer to overturn in extreme cases.

27 You can adjust tongue weight by changing any of the following:

- placement of gear in the boat
- location of the axle on the trailer frame
- position of the boat on the trailer

28 Highway weighing stations or moving company truck scales are good places to weigh your trailer rig. In many cases, you can check the tongue weight on your hitch with an ordinary 300-pound bathroom scale. Your trailer supplier should show you how to check the tongue weight and make the appropriate adjustments.

Before You Leave

29 Make a last-minute check to see that you have all required equipment and needed supplies. Use the following Pre-Trip Checklist

Table 30: Pre-Trip Checklist

- ☐ Emergency equipment: spare trailer tire, trailer jack, proper-sized lug wrench, wheel chocks, road flares, reflectors, extra bulbs, fuses, etc.
- ☐ Rear-view mirrors correctly positioned
- ☐ Equipment inside the boat tied down and secure
- ☐ Boat drained of all water; drain plug installed
- ☐ Coupler fully seated on ball and locked
- ☐ Safety chains installed correctly
- ☐ Electrical harness connected between vehicle and trailer; vehicle and trailer lights working
- ☐ Boat securely attached to trailer
- ☐ Tongue jack in full "up" position and locked
- ☐ Outboard motors/stern drives in up position
- ☐ Projections over the stern clearly marked with red flags or lights
- ☐ Masts, boat tops, antennas, and flags lowered and tied down, or removed
- ☐ Vehicle and trailer tires; correct air pressure
- ☐ Wheel lug nuts tight on all wheels

as a starting point for developing a check-list that is specific to your own boat, trailer, and tow vehicle.

Trailer Operation

30 If you have never towed a trailer, practice before venturing out on the highway. Driving with a trailer is not the same as driving the vehicle alone. The combination is longer and needs more space to turn. It is also heavier and requires more time to stop.

Backing

31 Find an empty parking lot and practice turning, parking, and backing. If possible, practice with an empty trailer first.

32 Mark out a target area and practice backing your trailer into it. A helpful hint when backing is to place your hand on the steering wheel at the bottom six o'clock position. When you want the trailer to go to the right, move your hand to the right. When you want the trailer to go to the left, move your hand to the left.

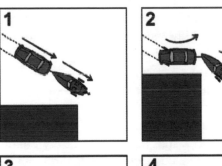

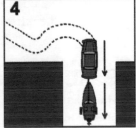

Figure 142 Backing a Trailer

33 The four steps required to back a trailer around a corner are illustrated in Figure 142.

Highway Operation

34 After completing your equipment check and driving practice, you are ready to take your trailer out on the highway. When operating your rig for the first time, choose ideal weather and a lightly traveled road. You will find acceleration slower and braking different with the added weight of a trailer.

35 On a clear stretch of road, practice gentle braking to get the feel. Swing a little wider when turning corners. It is a good safety practice to increase the distance between you and the car ahead.

36 You will need greater distance to pass other vehicles. Do not pass until you feel comfortable with the rig. Always be courteous. Signal your intentions well in advance to let surrounding vehicles know your intentions. Make it easy for faster moving vehicles to pass you. Keep to the right of the road and prepare to slow down if they need extra time to return to the proper lane.

37 Expect your trailer to sway when large trucks pass. Do not overreact and brake or steer to compensate. Keep to the right and relax and go with the flow; your car and trailer will withstand the pressure.

38 Never let anyone ride in the boat; it is not only dangerous but illegal in most states. Observe posted speed limits. Never forget that you have a boat behind you!

39 Be sensitive to unusual sounds or different handling. If something seems unusual, pull over in a safe spot and find out what it is. Make it a practice to stop periodically to perform a quick check. Inspect the coupler and ball, safety chains, electrical connections, lights, boat tie-downs, and the gear in your boat. Feel your wheel hubs to check

the temperature of the wheel bearings. Make sure the wheel lug nuts are tight and that tire pressures appear to be proper.

Launching Procedures

40 Always be considerate of others at the launch ramp. Make most of your preparations before entering the ramp and try to launch your boat in a reasonable time. Plan your launch in advance; visually inspect the launch ramp for hazards such as a steep drop-off, grease, or sharp objects. Observe current and wind as you would in docking your boat at a pier.

41 High-speed towing causes wheel bearings to get warm. If you immerse warm bearings in cold water, the contraction of air in the bearings will draw water in through the grease seals. If your trailer wheels do not have bearing protectors, wait until the bearings have cooled before launching. Unless absolutely necessary, keep wheel hubs out of the water.

42 Remove the tie-downs, but not the winch-cable hook, before backing into the water. Disconnect the trailer lights to prevent shorting out the electrical system or burning out a bulb. Never launch with the outboard or outdrive in the down position.

43 Attach bow and stern control lines in preparation for the launch. You can control the boat more easily with two lines.

44 If you plan to bring your boat alongside a pier, install fenders on the proper side. *Make sure that your hull drain plugs are in place and tightened securely!*

45 Back the boat slowly down the ramp. Keep the tow vehicle wheels out of the water: traction will be lost on wet surfaces. Be particularly cautious if using steep ramps with marine growth on their surfaces.

46 Shut off the engine, put the transmission in gear or park, set the emergency brake, and place chocks under the vehicle rear wheels. Have someone hold the bow and stern control lines before releasing the winch cable so you do not lose the boat.

47 When the boat is in the water, lower the outboard or stern drive and connect any necessary fuel lines. After sniffing for fumes, start the engine. Make sure the cooling system is working. If you are launching a sailboat with centerboard and rudder, lower them for stability when the water is sufficiently deep.

48 Clear the ramp as soon as practicable. Take the boat to a pier to finish loading and move your vehicle out of the ramp into the parking lot. If you are leaving your trailer on any kind of an incline, be sure to place chocks under the wheels so the trailer will not roll.

Hauling-Out Procedures

49 When returning to the boat ramp after a day on the water, drop your passengers off at the pier. Using bow and stern lines, guide the boat onto the trailer. Stay out of line with a winch cable; it can snap! Lock the winch after cranking the boat onto the trailer and secure the bow tie-down.

50 Pull away from the ramp as soon as possible and find a place in the parking lot to drain your boat. Secure your gear for traveling, and fasten tie-downs, safety chains, and electrical connections. Run through your Pre-Trip Checklist once more.

Sailboat Trailering

51 Many sailboats are trailered and launched in the same manner as powerboats. In fact, trailerable sailboats are often sold with a matching trailer.

52 Always trailer sailboats with the masts lowered and carried in a horizontal position. Some trailers and boats have special holders for the spars. Position the mast so it slopes upward at the rear of the boat to reduce danger to following vehicles. Use red flags or lights to alert drivers to the hazards of following too closely.

53 Always raise and lower your mast and install your rigging in the parking lot, not at the boat ramp. Take extra care when raising or lowering a mast; *look up!* Be certain there are no overhead electrical wires that can come close to or in contact with the mast or rigging. High-voltage electricity, especially in high humidity, can arc across a considerable distance, resulting in severe electrical shock or electrocution!

Trailer Maintenance

54 If you frequently immerse your trailer in the water, grease the bulbs and sockets regularly to prevent corrosion. Also, lubricate your winch and hitch coupler.

55 Inspect your trailer regularly for loose nuts, rusted frame, or deteriorated tires. If you find any part of the frame badly rusted, do not use the trailer until an expert examines it.

56 Deteriorated tires are the most frequent cause of trailer failure. Most trailer tires succumb to old age before they become worn. Sidewall cracks indicate the tire needs replacing. Tires will last longer if you remove the wheels when the boat is stored. Keep the tires inside away from the harmful rays of the sun.

57 Pump grease into the wheel bearings to force out water, being careful not to overfill and cause seal failure. On occasion, examine your trailer electrical system for chafed or bare wires or corroded terminals.

58 When storing your boat for any length of time, make sure drain plugs have been removed and the trailer tilted slightly to allow drainage. Remove any equipment that will be affected by dampness.

59 Support your boat evenly so you do not bend the trailer frame with uneven jacking. Tie down the boat cover in such a way that water does not collect in puddles. The weight of the water could stretch the cover and funnel water into the boat. Adjust the cover so it will not be caught and ripped by strong winds.

Homework

Name: _____ **Date:** _____ **Group:** _____

1. The capacity of the trailer should exceed the combined gross weight of trailer, boat, motor, and gear by _____:
   a. 5%
   b. 10%
   c. 15%
   d. 40%

2. Low tire pressure can lead to serious overheating and tire deterioration. Always check tire pressures when the tires are:
   a. warm.
   b. cold.
   c. just in off the road.
   d. jacked up off the ground.

3. Safety chains must be _____ the trailer tongue so that they will support the coupler in such a way that it will not hit the ground if the ball hitch breaks.
   a. crossed over
   b. hooked straight to
   c. crossed under
   d. directed around

4. The winch lines for boats over fourteen feet should be made of:
   a. polypropylene.
   b. nylon.
   c. manila.
   d. steel cable.

5. Trailer winch cables can snap. Be sure to:
   a. stand close by and watch the winch operation closely.
   b. tape up any winch cable that has broken strands.
   c. stay out of line with a winch cable.
   d. release the ratchet on the winch handle.

6. The _____ will specify the maximum trailer gross weight and tongue weight acceptable for the vehicle.
   a. vehicle owner's manual
   b. vehicle registration certificate
   c. trailer registration certificate
   d. trailer data plate

7. You can adjust tongue weight by changing any of the following:
   1) the placement of gear in the boat,
   2) the location of the axle on the trailer frame, or
   3) the
   a. position of the boat on the trailer.
   b. placement of the coupler ball.
   c. size of the trailer wheels.
   d. location of the trailer tongue.

8. A helpful hint when backing a trailer is to place your hand at the _____ of the steering wheel and move it in the direction you want the trailer to go.
   a. top
   b. left side
   c. right side
   d. bottom

9. Prepare your boat as much as possible before entering the launch ramp. Make sure that:
    a. your outboard or stern-drive unit is in the down position.
    b. all tie-downs are in place and fastened securely.
    c. your hull drain plugs are in place and tightened securely.
    d. you immerse your hot trailer hubs in cold water as soon as possible.

10. When raising or lowering a mast on a trailerable sailboat:
    a. be careful not to tip the boat off the trailer.
    b. wait until the boat is in the water.
    c. be certain that no overhead electrical wires come close to or in contact with the mast or rigging.
    d. take your time and do it correctly, even if you are tying up the ramp.

16

Personal Watercraft Operation

1 Personal WaterCraft (PWC) are also known as waterbikes, Jet Skis®, and sea sleds. Riding PWCs is one of the newer types of water sport. Getting the most out of a PWC calls for training and experience.

2 It is the owner's responsibility to see that a personal watercraft is operated safely. Instruct anyone driving or riding on one in its proper operation. In order to "ride safe and ride smart," an operator must develop skills and knowledge to avoid accidents.

It's a Boat

3 A PWC is not a toy, but a full-fledged boat! Anyone who operates a PWC is a skipper with the same responsibilities as the operator of a 40-foot yacht. Operators must adhere to many of the same rules and regulations as larger boats.

4 The Coast Guard considers personal watercraft to be Class A (less than 16 feet in length) inboard boats. The Personal Watercraft Industry Association further defines a PWC as an inboard vessel less than 13 feet in length that uses an internal combustion engine powering a water-jet pump as its primary source of propulsion. It has no open load-carrying area that could retain water. The vessel is designed to be operated by a person or persons positioned on, rather than within, the confines of the hull.

5 Some states consider PWCs to be a special type of boat because of their different operating characteristics and have special regulations for them.

Types of PWC

6 There are many types of personal watercraft (two of which are shown in Figure 143): challenging, spirited models; more sedate models for slow-speed maneuverability; cruising models for exploring; and models specifically designed to get you wet! Choose one that will match the use you intend, and the age, physical condition, and personal skill level of the person who will be using it.

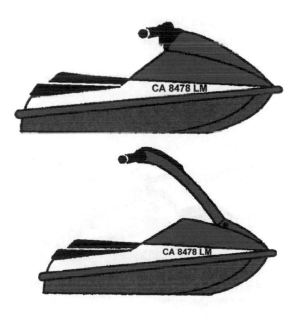

Figure 143   **Sit-Down Model PWC (top)**
Stand-Up Model PWC (bottom)

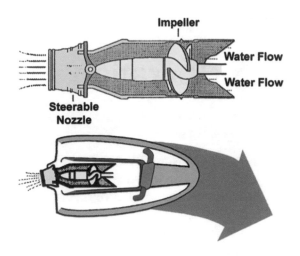

Figure 144   PWC Jet Drive and Steering Nozzle

7 Each type of PWC operates and handles differently from others. Always thoroughly read the owner's manual for a craft that is new to you.

How a PWC Works

8 A water-jet pump (Figure 144) draws water in through an underwater grate and forces it out the rear of the craft under high pressure. This pushes the boat through the water. At idle speed, the craft will move very slowly. As the engine speed increases, it will go faster.

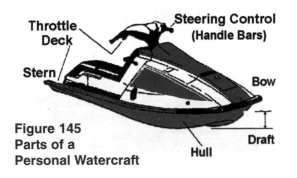

**Figure 145
Parts of a
Personal Watercraft**

Steering

9 Handlebars turn a movable nozzle that directs the high-pressure stream of water either right or left, turning the boat to one side or the other.

10 It is important to know that a PWC will turn only when the jet pump is operating and pushing a stream of water out of the stern of the craft and creating thrust. If you release the throttle to avoid collision while operating at high speed, your PWC will not turn. It will probably continue in the direction you were moving, often into the object that you were trying to avoid.

Operator Controls

11 Be well acquainted with your PWC before you ride. Read and understand the owner's manual. It is best to have a qualified person give you instruction in its operation. Understand the function of all controls, where they are located, and how to use them. The controls are the same for most PWCs, although you may find them in different places. You will usually find the engine and jet drive under the passenger seat; the fuel tank under the forward hood.

12 **Start and Stop Controls.** PWCs do not have ignition keys like an automobile. You push a button or switch on the handlebar or console to start and stop the engine. A manual choke control helps start a cold engine.

13 **Throttle Controls** are usually on the right handlebar grip. They can either be a *thumbpush* type or a *finger-pull* type.

14 **Fall-Off Controls** are an aid to reboarding your craft when you fall off. Some PWCs have an *auto-circle control* that slows the engine to idle speed and allows the craft to circle slowly. This permits you to swim to your PWC and reboard. If you have this type of control, be sure to set your idle speed correctly.

15 Other PWCs have a *lanyard cut-off switch* (sometimes called a *lifeline*) which, when fastened to your wrist, will stop the engine when you fall off. The engine will not re-start without it. This important topic is addressed again within this chapter in the section titled "Operate Your PWC Safely, Falling Off," page 188.

16 **Fuel Selector Switches** usually have three positions: an "off" position for use when not riding, an "on" position to use when riding; and a "reserve" position to use to head straight for a fuel supply when fuel runs out in the "on" position. Fuel and oil gauges are standard equipment on some of the larger PWCs.

17 **Reverse Levers** on some PWCs place a "clamshell" device over the steering nozzle to allow slow reverse operation. Never use the reverse lever as a brake or at high speeds-you could be thrown off the PWC and easily injured!

Government Regulations

18 Since your PWC is a boat, almost all governmental boating laws, regulations, and safety standards apply.

Federal Regulations

19 The following federal regulations and safety standards pertaining to the operation and equipping of Class A boats are of particular importance to the operator of a PWC.

20 **Registration and Numbering.** You must register and number a PWC. The hull design of a PWC requires that registration numbers be placed high on the bow in a prominent position. The rules for size of letters and numbers and contrasting color are the same as for all other boats. See Chapter 10 of this manual.

21 The registration certificate must always be aboard when underway. Laminate your certificate so it will not get wet. If your state requires boating safety education, also carry proof of your operator's qualification.

22 **Hull Identification Number (HIN).** Review the description of hull identification numbers in Chapter 10, Government Regulations. Make a note of your PWC's hull identification number and keep it handy. You will find it on the starboard side of the transom and in another hidden location. It is against the law to remove or alter this number. It is also a good idea to inscribe your driver's license number in some concealed location on your PWC.

Figure 146   Registration Number Placement

23 **Maximum Capacity.** Personal watercrafts are exempt from the USCG standard requiring capacity plates on small boats. However, manufacturers often make recommendations as to the number of persons and the weight their craft can safely accommodate. You will find this information on labels on their craft and in their owner's manuals. Never exceed these recommendations. However, the total combined weight of the people and equipment may limit the number of riders to less than the number of seats! No vessel should be overloaded, including a PWC.

24 An overloaded PWC will be unstable in the water, and you will not be able to operate it safely to avoid collisions. You can be cited

for reckless operation if you overload your craft and operate it dangerously.

25 **Life Preservers (Personal Flotation Devices)** for the operator and all passengers must be on board while underway. They must be a wearable type that is USCG approved and have a legible label. A Type III inherently buoyant flotation aid is usually the most comfortable, although this type of preserver will not turn an unconscious victim face up in the water.

26 PFDs should have an impact rating of at least 50 miles per hour—preferably in excess of the maximum speed of your craft. PWC riders should always wear bright colored life jackets-orange or yellow are the best colors.

27 Do not use an inflatable life preserver while using a PWC or in any other activity where you expect water impact at a high rate of speed (such as waterskiing). Wet suits provide protection from bodily injury as well as hypothermia, but are not a substitute for a life preserver unless they have a Coast Guard approval label. Review the section on life preservers in Government Regulations, Chapter 10.

28 When you ride a personal watercraft, you expect to spend a lot of time in the water. The Coast Guard recommends that all operators and passengers wear life preservers whenever the vessel is in use. Many states have regulations that require this.

29 **Fire Extinguisher.** A USCG-approved, marine-type fire extinguisher is required equipment. A size B-I is appropriate. (See Chapter 10, Government Regulations.) The bouncing, pounding, jarring movement of the PWC requires that it be stowed in a bracket. Some PWCs are equipped with a container or bracket to hold a fire extinguisher. However, mount your fire extinguisher in the bracket furnished

by the extinguisher manufacturer. Mount it in the same location as the PWC bracket.

30 Make sure your extinguisher is readily accessible. Stow it in a compartment that cannot become corroded shut. Do not mount it in the engine compartment where fires are most likely to occur. Check your extinguisher regularly to ensure it is at full pressure and the locking pin and sealing wire are in place. Most extinguishers have a pressure gauge that must point to the "green" area. Others have a green pressure button that pops back out when pressed, indicating proper internal pressure.

31 **Sound Producing Device.** You must have a way of making an efficient sound signal. The Navigation Rules require that all boats exchange sound signals under certain conditions. (See Chapter 12, Navigation Rules.) Due to the wet environment, a small mouth-operated whistle is best for use on a PWC. A good way to carry it is to attach it to the operator's life jacket.

32 **Visual Distress Signals (VDS)** are not required under federal regulations for Class A boats, although some state and local authorities include them as required equipment. If you go offshore, any farther than someone can see you waving for help (one-half mile is suggested), it is a good idea to carry day-type VDSs.

33 Orange distress flags (black square and ball displayed against an orange background), orange distress dye markers, and reflective mirrors make good signals for use on your PWC. Night distress signals are not necessary. In most cases it is illegal to use your PWC at night and, thus, it is not equipped with lights for night operation.

34 The international distress signal of slowly and repeatedly raising outstretched arms to each side is a simple attention-getter. (Do

not wave your arms over your head; it looks like a greeting.)

35 **Accident Reporting.** Chapter 10, Government Regulations, describes the federal requirements for accident reporting. Local regulations often differ. Always check for the requirements in your locale.

Vessel Safety Check Program

36 The United States Power Squadrons has joined with the U.S. Coast Guard Auxiliary in conducting free Vessel Safety Checks (VSCs) of pleasure boats. This program of checking and discussing the safety equipment on board your PWC is designed to make your boating activities safer for you, your family and friends, and fellow boaters. No report of your PWC is ever made to any law enforcement agency.

37 If your PWC meets VSC requirements, the award of the VSC decal is your assurance your boat is properly equipped and meets the minimum Federal Equipment Requirements. A properly equipped PWC is a safer boat.

The Navigation Rules

38 The purpose of the Navigation Rules is to prevent collisions between vessels and they apply to personal watercraft. Review the description of these rules in Chapter 12.

39 The speed and quick movement of a personal watercraft requires an operator's constant attention to his surroundings to avoid collision. This is even more important when operating with other personal watercraft. Operators must know the Navigation Rules in order to make split-second decisions to avoid collision. Rules of particular importance to PWC operators are:

40 **Lookout.** You must maintain a lookout at all times which includes looking ahead, to both sides, and in back of you.

41 **Safe Speed.** You must operate at a safe speed; that speed in which you will have time to react and avoid a collision. This means that if you are involved in a collision, you were going faster than you should have been going.

42 **Sound Signals.** You must use sound signals prescribed for powerboats. You should be able to recognize the meaning of these sound signals when you hear them, and be prepared to give them when necessary. Review these signals in Chapter 10, Government Regulations.

43 **Risk of Collision Situations.** Since a PWC is a motorboat, almost all other boats have priority in movement over a PWC. Review the Vessel Priority Table in Chapter 12, Navigation Rules.

44 **Navigation Steering Rules.** PWC operators must also obey the navigation steering rules:
  - If you are overtaking another boat, you must keep out of the way. Always signal your intention as to the side that you intend to pass.
  - When you meet another powerboat head-on, both boats must keep clear—both must take action to avoid collision. Whenever possible, pass port to port.
  - Yield to any vessel approaching you from the right. Looking straight ahead, turn your head to the right as far as you can without moving your shoulders. You must stay out of the way of any boat that you can see.

45 **Diver Below.** Many states have local regulations governing diving and underwater operations. Because divers often stray from their diving vessel, PWC operators should stay well clear of these activities. Chapter 12,

Navigation Rules, describes and identifies the two types of dive vessels.

46 **Responsibility.** As the skipper of a PWC, you are responsible for your own safety, the safety of your passengers and your watercraft, and any damage to persons or property caused by your wake.

State and Local Regulations

47 State and local governments often have stricter and more comprehensive regulations for the use of PWCs than those of the federal government. As a boat operator, you must be aware of and abide by all laws governing the use of personal watercraft in your area. The laws apply to anyone operating a PWC, not just the owner. Most states provide guides describing their boating regulations.

48 You have received instruction in this course in local and state regulations that differ from federal regulations. If your state requests that the course examination include questions relative to their regulations, your course instructor will cooperate with this request.

49 **Regulated Activities** often include restrictions on:
- nighttime use of PWCs
- wake jumping
- operating close to persons or other boats in the water
- locations where personal watercraft may be operated

50 Dangerous and discourteous operation of personal watercraft has resulted in many laws regulating operator age and conduct. If PWC owners do not operate their craft safely and prudently, authorities will pass additional restrictive laws. Awareness, good judgment, and consideration for others are most important.

51 **Additional Safety Equipment** is often required. In many states, you must wear a life preserver whenever aboard a PWC. Some states require day-type visual distress signals. Always check your local regulations for their requirements.

52 **Minimum Age and Education.** Safely operating a PWC on crowded waterways requires physical capability and maturity of judgment. For this reason, local regulations frequently have minimum age limits for PWC operators. Many require successful completion of a special course in PWC operation. The Personal Watercraft Industry Association recommends a minimum operator's age of 16.

53 Parents should insist that youth operating personal watercraft are of legal age, receive proper instruction in both boating safety and PWC operation, and operate their PWCs in a safe, considerate, and responsible manner.

Law Enforcement

54 The Coast Guard and most law enforcement officials may stop you anytime you are underway to conduct a safety inspection, or examine your certificates, decals, documents, etc. If hailed by a law enforcement vessel, stop your boat and allow the boarding officer to come alongside. Avoid penalties by following the Navigation Rules and all federal, state and local regulations.

Prepare to Get Underway

55 Safely operating a personal watercraft requires knowledge and skill in its use. Read the owner's manual. Understand the function of all controls; know where to find them and how to use them. Try to find a qualified person to instruct you in the use of your PWC.

56 Run your PWC slowly when first starting out. Check out its controls-especially the throttle-to make sure the craft is running properly.

Table 31: Equipment Checklist

- ☐ Operator's certificate or license (if required)
- ☐ Registration certificate
- ☐ Life preserver for each person
- ☐ Fire extinguisher; fully charged
- ☐ Visual distress signals
- ☐ Whistle or horn
- ☐ Compass
- ☐ Tool kit and spare parts (spark plugs, etc.)
- ☐ Spare oil
- ☐ Spare lanyard
- ☐ Gas funnel (to minimize spillage)
- ☐ Tow line

Systems Checklist

- ☐ Bilge free of fumes and water
- ☐ Fuel tank full; adequate lubricating oil
- ☐ Fuel tank and fuel lines free of leaks
- ☐ Battery charge and fluid level satisfactory
- ☐ Gauges and indicator lights working
- ☐ Steering operating properly
- ☐ Throttle operating smoothly
- ☐ Jet pump and water inlet free of debris
- ☐ Stop button tested: (start engine, press button)
- ☐ Lanyard cut-off switch tested: (start engine, pull lanyard)

Fuel Safely

57 PWCs are not stable craft, especially in wind and waves. For this reason, fuel them out of the water before launching. Make sure your PWC is level and fill your tanks slowly-do not overfill them. Do maintenance work on your PWC on shore for the same reasons.

58 If you must fuel your PWC in the water, make sure all passengers are off the craft and that it is level in the water. Tie it to the fuel pier with two dock lines. Turn off the engine and all electrical devices. Add fuel slowly and listen to the sound of air escaping from the tank. You will learn to recognize when the tank is almost full. Avoid spilling gasoline in the water at all costs!

59 PWCs have two-cycle motors that require mixing a correct amount of special oil with the gasoline. Most have separate oil tanks and mixing is done automatically. Always mix fuel properly or mechanical failure is certain to occur while underway.

60 After fueling, open the engine compartment to allow gasoline fumes to escape. Visually inspect the compartment for any sign of fuel leaks. The most important step is to sniff for fuel fumes before getting underway! Like any boat, gasoline fumes in a closed compartment are very dangerous. If you smell gasoline, be sure to correct the problem immediately! Refer to Chapter 8, Boat Handling, for a review of proper fueling methods.

Check Equipment and Systems

61 The checklists on this page will help you in making sure your PWC is in good condition and fully equipped before using it. Make copies of them.

Know the Weather

62 Before using your PWC, check the weather forecast. Is it safe to go? Your PWC is not a very stable platform from which to experience rough weather.

Know Your Waters

63 Check your charts and know what to expect in the waters where you will be operating your PWC.

64 Rocks, trash, or shallow water can injure you if you fall. Adverse currents can take you way off course.

Select Your Passengers

65 All passengers should be good swimmers. Make it a practice to never travel farther from shore than you and your passengers are able to swim. All persons aboard should be wearing life preservers and sitting down at all times. Never overload your PWC!

Optional Personal Equipment

66 Falling off a PWC at high speed can be dangerous. For bodily protection consider special equipment such as:
  * sunblock for protection from the sun's rays
  * strap-on floating sun glasses or goggles for eye protection
  * gloves to better grip the steering controls
  * footwear to protect your feet while in the water
  * wet suits to reduce the possibility of hypothermia and to protect the body from abrasion and injury

Boarding a PWC

67 Because some PWCs are unstable in the water, it is important to board them carefully. Place one foot on the side deck closest to the pier. Get a secure grip on the handlebars or passenger seat and swing your other foot over the seat to the opposite deck. This will distribute your weight across the centerline of the craft.

Operate Your PWC Safely

68 PWC operators must always be alert and vigilant when riding their craft. There are many things to think about when operating a craft that is so fast in speed and quick in response.

When Starting Out

69 If your PWC has a lanyard cut-off switch, make sure it is fastened to the operator's wrist. The Coast Guard recommends fastening it to the left wrist. If the right hand releases the throttle, the engine stops. The left wrist will do the same thing if the rider's hand moves far enough to impair balance, watchfulness, etc.

70 The water should always be at least waist deep-do not operate in shallow water. When operating at high speeds, your PWC can suck objects off the bottom when the water is six feet deep! Not only can those objects cause damage to the jet drive, debris being ejected with great force by the jet pump can injure bystanders and even passengers on your PWC.

71 Make sure the path ahead of you is clear. Proceed slowly using just enough power to maintain steering control.

Where to Operate

72 Find a non-congested area free of people and other boats when learning to use a personal watercraft. Stay close to shore, especially as you learn to use your personal watercraft. Never ride a PWC near a dam.

Hours of Operations

73 Many areas, especially on small lakes, have regulations governing hours of operation. These rules may apply to all boats or only to certain types of boats such as power driven or PWCs. The purpose of these rules is to improve boating safety or to reduce noise during certain hours.

Safe Speed

74 A PWC is fast and sensitive and, under certain conditions, unstable. Don't dart about. Always operate at a speed at which you will have time to react and avoid a collision. Many states have laws limiting the speed of a boat when near shore.

75 Maintain only minimum speed necessary to maintain steerageway when near shore, launch areas, swimming areas, docks, and anchored boats. No wake and slow speed zones are usually designated with markers. Observe them carefully. The speed limit in these restricted areas is often 5 mph or less.

Stopping

76 Since a PWC has no brakes, you must allow adequate distance in order to make a safe stop. The best way to stop is to "spin" your PWC — turn it in a tight circle.

Keep a Lookout

77 Operators of PWCs are often so intent on operating their craft and having fun they fail to maintain a lookout. Operating at high speed, they tend to focus their attention on the waves immediately ahead, disregarding what is to each side and to the rear. This tunnel vision prevents them from seeing approaching boats, swimmers in the water, and hazards to navigation.

78 Stay at least 100 feet away from boats, people, and objects in the water at all times.

Observe Aids to Navigation

79 The marks of the U.S. Aids to Navigation System and the Uniform State Waterway Marking System are the street signs and caution signs that guide PWC operators in safe boating. Review the buoys, beacons, sound signals, and regulatory and informa-

Figure 147   Observe Aids to Navigation

tion marks of these two systems. See Chapter 6, Aids to Navigation.

Steering

80 Remember, if there is no thrust of water from the jet pump, you have no steering! When the engine is running at idle speed, you will be able to turn slowly. When it is running at high speed, you will have excellent steering. However, if you release the throttle at high speed, you will have no steering! You will continue to glide ahead until you lose speed.

Turning

81 Just as you would with any boat, keep an eye on the stern of your PWC so you do not hit anything when turning in close quarters. See Chapter 8, Boat Handling.

Backing

82 Some PWCs have reverse levers that place a clamshell device over the steering nozzle to allow slow reverse operation. Never try to use reverse as a brake or use it at high speeds-you may be thrown off the PWC and be injured!

Jumping Wakes

83 Part of the fun of operating a PWC is jumping waves. However, cutting close to the sterns of other boats and jumping their wakes

is dangerous and often illegal. It is also a distraction to persons in the other boats.

84 When jumping a boat's wake, stay at least 100 feet behind the boat. This should allow you sufficient room to observe traffic conditions in all directions. Avoid jumping wakes in areas of heavy boat traffic. If you fall, you may not be seen in the water, and an approaching boat may injure you. Avoid cutting in front of other boats for the same reasons. Never follow closely behind another PWC when jumping wakes. If the other operator falls, you may hit him or her!

85 Always watch for traffic coming from in front of or behind other vessels. Visibility is very poor behind a moving boat. As a PWC operator, you cannot see approaching boats and they cannot see you. Visibility is also poor when you throw up a sheet of water when jumping a wake. Remember: a PWC out of the water has no steering because of loss of pump suction.

86 Trick maneuvers are dangerous. They require skill and common sense and often result in neglecting to pay attention to surroundings. Accidents and injuries are often the result.

Falling Off

87 You should expect to fall off! However, it will not be dangerous if you follow the manufacturer's safety guidelines. There are no rudders or propellers on the outside of the hull to cause injury. If you fall, push away from the PWC.

88 **Use of Lanyard:** Most PWCs being built today are equipped with a *Lanyard Cut-Off Switch* for the purpose of stopping the engine if the operator falls off the craft. This lanyard is a cord with a short strap that is attached to the operator's wrist or life jacket (PFD), and the other end is inserted into a cut-off switch plug. If the op-

erator falls off the vessel, the cord is pulled out of the cut-off plug and the PWC's engine turns off. The operator can then swim to the PWC and reboard.

Righting an Overturned PWC

89 If your craft rolls over and floats upside down, roll it back to the upright position according to the manufacturer's recommendations. Look for a decal at the rear of the craft for these instructions. If there is no decal, check your owner's manual. Turning it the wrong way could get water into the engine.

Figure 148   Falling Off a PWC

Reboarding

90 Some PWCs will circle and come back to you. Others will stop when the stop lanyard is pulled free. It is important to practice getting back aboard. Follow the manufacturer's instructions in your operation manual.

91 You may find it difficult to reboard when you are tired. Always practice reboarding in deep water. If you find it difficult, you may not want to ride alone.

92 Be cautious when riding in areas of strong current and when it is windy. You may have difficulty getting back to your craft under these conditions.

93 Never overestimate your ability. Be certain your skills and physical condition are sufficient to handle any wind, wave, or distance-to-shore conditions you may encounter.

Water-Skiers

94 Before towing water-skiers with your PWC, check with state and local authorities to see if it is permissible to do so. If you tow skiers, you must have a personal watercraft with capacity to carry three persons:
 • the operator
 • the observer
 • the skier and the skis when going to and returning from the ski area

95 Always keep a distance from water-skiers; never follow them or cross between them and the tow boat. Both you and the skier could have serious accidents.

Meeting Large Vessels

96 Just as the operator of a 40-foot yacht would stay clear of a large ship, PWC operators should stay clear of larger boats. The operators of large vessels often cannot see you and many cannot stop even if they want to.

Be Aware of Your Physical Condition

97 It is good practice to schedule a 10-minute break on the beach for every 30 minutes of riding. Fatigue is a major consideration when riding a PWC. If you become fatigued or start to feel cold, head for home. Your body is telling you that you are either running out of energy or there is an abnormal lowering of your body's internal temperature due to exposure to cold air, wind, or water. This can lead to hypothermia. See the discussion of hypothermia in Chapter 14, Adverse Conditions.

Boat Smart! Don't Drink or Use Drugs!

98 This is especially good advice when operating a fast-moving, extremely maneuverable PWC.

Figure 149   Key to Responsible Boating: Drinking—Don't Do It!

99 About four hours (often less) of exposure to noise, vibrations, sun, glare, wind, and other motion on the water produces boater's fatigue. It can slow reaction time almost as much as if you are legally drunk. Adding alcohol or drugs to these factors multiplies the risk of accidents.

Watch Your Fuel Supply

100 Make sure you have enough fuel to get back to shore. If you have to switch on the reserve tank, head straight for home or other fuel source.

Keep an Eye on the Weather

101 Pay attention to darkening skies, increasing wind, change in wind direction, and approaching thunderstorms. If bad weather threatens, head for shore right away. If caught in inclement weather, try to take the waves on an angle. See Chapter 8, Boat Handling.

Restricted Visibility

102 Do not operate a PWC after dark or in restricted visibility. Many state laws specifically prohibit the use of PWCs in the dark.

103 Know what to do if you find yourself in a sudden fog while operating your PWC. Review this subject under Adverse Conditions in Chapter 14.

Fire Onboard

104 If a fire occurs, stop your PWC immediately. Most fires occur in the engine compartment. Never open a closed engine compartment that contains a fire! It will introduce oxygen in the air that will fuel the fire. The best reaction to a fire in your PWC is to leave your craft and swim as far away from it as possible. Save your fire extinguisher to help other boaters.

105 If you have passengers, encourage them to stay together until help arrives. They should all be wearing life jackets. Never try to swim long distances to shore; it is always farther than you think!

Returning to Shore

106 When returning, approach your dock or launch ramp area slowly. Shut off the engine when you reach shallow water. Then get off and push your PWC to shore.

107 If possible, hose your PWC down with fresh water, especially if you operate in salt water. This will reduce rusting and corrosion.

Considerate, Responsible Operation

108 Being aware, using good judgment, and having consideration for others are most important in operating a boat of any kind. Always think of the effect that you have on others as you operate your PWC.

Consider the Environment

109 Be a responsible citizen and work toward the preservation of our fragile environment. There are certain things you can do in the operation of your PWC to accomplish this:
- Never throw trash or spill fuel or oil into the water.
- Try to operate in deep water as much as possible. When operating at high speeds, your PWC can disturb the delicate bottom in water six feet deep. Running through bottom vegetation can also foul your water intake.
- Keep wake at a minimum when close to shore; it can contribute to shoreline erosion.
- Operating near the shoreline can disturb wildlife. Excessive noise disturbs birds as well as other boaters and shoreline residents.

Operate Quietly

110 Try not to operate continuously in one area. Local ordinances frequently limit the noise level of boat engines. Making excessive noise is one of the quickest ways to make PWCs unpopular with other water users, as well as people on shore. It creates pressure to regulate PWC activity. Avoid residential areas, camping areas, and waterfronts-areas where people go to be quiet. Your PWC must be equipped with an effective muffling device. Altered mufflers are never permitted.

Maintain Your PWC

111 Always keep your PWC in first-class operating condition. Keep the hull free of damage and clean of algae and slime. Keep the engine tuned and free of grease and oil buildup. Check the battery fluid regularly and make sure all electrical connections are clean and tight. Make sure all cables operate properly. Check for loose nuts, bolts, and screws. Your PWC operates in a stressful environment!

112 Altering your engine or drive components could overpower your PWC, voiding its warranty and making it unstable in operation and hard to control at high speeds.

Breakdowns and Repairs

113 Due to the possibility of mechanical breakdown, fires, and other emergencies, it is advisable to travel with other PWC operators. You will be able to make very few repairs on the water. Opening your engine compartment in high wave conditions can swamp and sink your boat. However, in shallow protected water you may be able to perform simple tasks that will get you home. Carry a few tools and spare parts in your storage compartment. Examples are clean, gapped, spark plugs; spark plug wrench; pliers; adjustable wrench; screwdriver; and electrical tape.

114 Debris such as plastic bags and seaweed can be sucked against the water intake grate. You will note a severe reduction in thrust and speed. Never attempt to clear obstructions such as this with the engine running! Try rocking the craft back and forth. If this does not work, you may have to roll the craft over and remove the debris with your hands. Keep hands, feet, hair, and clothing away from the water intake whenever the engine is running. If you don't, the results could be deadly!

115 If you cannot repair your PWC on the water, you will need a tow to shore. Carry a towline in your equipment locker. Always tow a personal watercraft slowly. Once again, always stay with your boat until help arrives. Never try to swim ashore.

Security

116 Try not to leave your PWC unattended. If you leave it for any time, remove the stop-lanyard and carry it with you. Try to lock your craft to some immovable object with a chain and padlock. If you leave it on a trailer, add a trailer hitch lock. There are also special locks that fasten PWCs to their trailers, both underneath and at the bow eye. Removing one of the trailer wheels is another good theft deterrent.

Homework

Name: _____ **Date:** _____ **Group:** _____

1. Since the Coast Guard recognizes personal watercraft as full-fledged boats:
    a. operators must adhere to the same rules and regulations as larger boats.
    b. a PWC must show its navigation lights when used after dark.
    c. a PWC usually has priority of movement in meeting and crossing situations.
    d. PWCs are exempt from rules and regulations applying to larger boats.

2. Steering a PWC involves turning a movable nozzle that directs a high-pressure stream of water either right or left, which turns the boat to one side or the other. It is important to know that a PWC will turn only when the:
    a. engine is turning at least 4000 rpm.
    b. jet pump is operating and pushing a stream of water.
    c. two rudders are in contact with the water.
    d. special steering pump is activated.

3. A PWC lanyard cut-off switch when fastened to your left wrist will:
    a. keep your signal whistle where it can be found.
    b. alert you when you are running too fast.
    c. stop the engine when you fall off.
    d. remind you to always wear your life preserver.

4. Most PWCs have a fuel selector switch. Use the *Off* position when not riding, the *On* position while riding, and the *Reserve* position to:
    a. head straight for a fuel supply when fuel runs out in the "on" position.
    b. retain a supply of fuel for another day on the water.
    c. switch to super high-octane fuel when challenged to a race.
    d. use any leftover fuel in the bottom of the tank.

5. It is important not to exceed the manufacturer's recommendations as to the:
    a. number of cylinders allowed in your engine.
    b. number of electronic devices you install.
    c. size of fuel tank allowed for your craft.
    d. number of persons and weight your craft can safely accommodate.

6. A life preserver (personal flotation device):
    a. is only needed by PWC users who are weak swimmers.
    b. should be worn at all times by anyone using a PWC.
    c. may not be necessary if riders are careful not to fall off.
    d. need not be approved by the Coast Guard.

7. A USCG-approved, marine-type fire extinguisher is required equipment on a PWC and:
    a. can be color-matched to the boat.
    b. should be stowed on top of life preservers to cushion wave action.
    c. should be mounted on the PWC in a bracket furnished by the extinguisher manufacturer.
    d. should be ready for action with locking pin and sealing wire removed.

8. Due to the wet environment, a _____ is the best sound signal for use on a PWC.
    a. large canister horn
    b. small air horn attached to the handlebars
    c. small mouth-operated whistle attached to the operator's life jacket
    d. good chromed electric horn fastened to the fuel compartment hood

9. It is a good idea to carry day-type visual distress signals if you:
    a. go offshore any farther than someone can see you waving for help.
    b. operate in crowded narrow channels.
    c. want to abide by the Navigation Rules.
    d. run your PWC in anchorages and along beachfronts.

10. When operating a PWC, consider the following special personal equipment:
    a. foul weather gear, contact lenses, and ear plugs.
    b. goggles, gloves, and footwear.
    c. ski belts, tanning lotion, and wide-brim hats.
    d. dry suits, Gatorade®, and inflatable life preservers.

11. Which of the following statements is true?
    a. It is legal to operate your PWC at night if visibility is clear.
    b. If your PWC stalls on the water, abandon it and swim to shore.
    c. A PWC operator is responsible for damage created by the wake of his or her craft.
    d. PWCs cannot hurt divers for their propeller is enclosed.

12. State and local governments often have stricter and more comprehensive regulations for the use of PWCs than those of the federal government. As a PWC owner or operator you are required to:
    a. carry a copy of the rules of the special PWC Rules Commission aboard.
    b. know the special Navigation Rules that apply only to PWCs.
    c. follow the rules established by the National Boating Association.
    d. be aware of and abide by all laws governing the use of personal watercraft in your area.

13. The most important step in safe fueling of a PWC is to:
    a. purchase gasoline with added antioxidants.
    b. sniff the engine compartment before getting underway.
    c. open the engine compartment cover while fueling.
    d. always fuel your PWC when it is in the water.

14. One of the first steps you should take before using your PWC is to:
    a. supply your beverage cooler.
    b. make sure there is an anchor aboard.
    c. check the weather forecast.
    d. install LORAN waypoints for your trip.

15. A PWC should not be operated in shallow water because of possible harm to its jet drive and:
    a. propeller.
    b. electronics.
    c. bystanders.
    d. swim platform.

16. Due to an effect called tunnel vision, PWC operators focus their attention on the waves immediately ahead and do not see:
    a. approaching funnel clouds.
    b. law enforcement patrol boats.
    c. boats, swimmers, and hazards in the water.
    d. navigational lights ahead.

17. Safe speed is that speed that allows you to:
    a. reach home in a hurry without breaking the speed limit.
    b. have time to react to avoid collision.
    c. observe wake limits in narrow channels and anchorages.
    d. miss swimmers in the water when operating at high speed.

18. When operating a PWC near shore, launch areas, swimming areas, docks, and anchored boats:
    a. take extreme care when jumping wakes in these restricted areas.
    b. run at minimum speed necessary to maintain steerageway.
    c. don't throw a wake more than three feet high.
    d. operate with the wind and current on your transom for better control.

19. Operators of PWCs should stay away from large vessels that:
    a. toss up wakes too high for a PWC to handle.
    b. may not be able to see small boats in the water.
    c. often tack back and forth across busy channels.
    d. do not like to come to a quick stop.

20. Cutting close to the sterns of other boats and jumping their wakes is dangerous and often illegal. Not only are such activities a distraction to the occupants of other boats, but:
    a. they can strain your PWC's outboard motor.
    b. smooth water in the wake of boats could make you lose control of your PWC.
    c. you could place yourself in danger of collision with approaching boats.
    d. PWCs are not designed for this type of activity.

21. If it is legal to tow skiers in your area, your PWC is required to:
    a. be equipped with a tow bar.
    b. have the capacity to hold two persons; the operator and the observer.
    c. have a minimum beam of 8 feet and length of 18 feet.
    d. have the capacity to carry the skis and three persons: the operator, the observer, the skier.

22. Which of the following statements is true?
    a. PWCs do not disturb the ecology of the water bottom.
    b. Wake from PWCs will not contribute to shoreline erosion.
    c. Noise from PWCs never disturbs bird life.
    d. Excessive noise from PWCs creates pressure to regulate PWC activity.

A

Using Digital Charts

1 The Global Positioning System (GPS) has changed the way boaters navigate. Digital Charts help make your GPS unit more practical by minimizing errors and easing the tasks of planning and managing your waypoints and routes. This chapter addresses different types of digital charts and explains your CD-ROM.

2 GPS provides continuous, accurate information on your position—a three-dimensional point in space. This is converted in your GPS receiver (also referred to as GPS) into a set of coordinates—latitude and longitude—you can use to locate yourself on the earth. It is imperative you recognize that GPS has no inherent understanding of what is around you at this location. That information must come from charts or maps and your personal observations.

3 You need to plot your latitude and longitude, as reported by your GPS, on a chart or map so you can see where you are and get a reference for proceeding with your navigation. This is a necessary skill; but, coordinates are just numbers, so it is easy to make a mistake and incorrectly plot your position.

4 Moreover, in order to navigate, you need to identify the coordinates of your destination and enter them into the GPS as a waypoint. Your paths on the water generally encompass a number of straight-line segments around obstacles to get you from one place to a final destination. Each of these line segments is called a *leg* and is identified by the points at each end—called *waypoints*. The coordinates for all of these waypoints then are stored in the GPS.

5 First, the legs are plotted on a chart. You need to scan along each leg on the chart to ensure the paths are free of obstacles and have sufficient depth to accommodate your boat. Then, you will use your dividers to measure the latitude and longitude of each waypoint and record these values for insertion into the GPS. Next, you will manually enter the name and the coordinates for each waypoint using the buttons on the GPS. Finally, you will select the waypoints, one at a time, for the paths you intend to navigate. By staying on these prequalified paths, you will be reasonably assured you should not encounter underwater obstacles while you focus your attention to watching what is around you above the water.

6 This is the basic procedure for navigation using a GPS. However, while the GPS may be extremely accurate, there are a number of chances to make an error that could lead you into peril. Many of those are related to working with waypoints. For example, you might misread the coordinates from the chart. You might incorrectly enter the waypoint coordinates into your GPS. And, once you have entered a number of waypoints into your GPS, there is the risk of selecting the wrong one and attempting navigation on an incorrect path.

Digital Charts

7 Digital charts greatly simplify the process of planning for your GPS, because your selections are communicated directly to the GPS using special software. In addition, this digital charting software computes a wealth of information about your plotted courses including: course direction, distance, total trip distance, and more.

8 At the heart of digital charting is the calibrated representation of a chart or map. There are two basic types of digital charts: raster and vector. The CD-ROM provided with the course uses raster charts.

9 What's the difference? *Raster charts* are created by scanning real charts and carefully calibrating them to provide accurate coordinates. Most boaters are comfortable with these charts because their appearance matches the paper charts they represent. However, the scanning process takes quite a bit of storage space; these charts generally are delivered on CD-ROMs.

10 *Vector charts* are created using the same paper charts by tracing the lines on a computer. The traced lines represent a large number of straight-line segments, but only the end points are stored (instead of the lines). This saves storage space, so these charts can be delivered on chart chips that work with chart plotters. Generally, these charts are not as feature-rich as raster charts, but the critical data is there. Typically, a chart chip will work only with chart plotters designed for that particular type of chip.

USPS Digital Chart CD-ROM

11 The CD-ROM provided with this course is based on the NOAA-certified raster digital charts provided by Maptech, Inc. The format of these charts is the format most widely used and can be used with most major charting programs.

12 You can work with these charts with the included Chart Navigator software program. This computer program is designed to work on PCs with Windows® 98, ME, NT4.0, 2000, or XP operating systems. You will be able to read all of the included charts as well as plot courses and waypoints.

13 Chart Navigator is designed to interface with most popular GPS receiver models so data can be uploaded to the GPS or downloaded into the program. The software provides a capable GPS route and waypoint editor. This software is designed as a planning tool: it does *not* provide real-time GPS positioning on the screen. A number of chart plotting programs can do that, and most of them use the same digital charts provided on the CD-ROM.

14 Over one hundred charts are included on the CD-ROM. Two of the charts correspond to training charts used in USPS courses. One is Bowditch Bay—a fictitious chart you will use with your coursework. A paper copy of this chart is included in the back of this course book and is the chart you will use with this Digital Charting supplement. Another training chart, the 1210tr, covers the region around Buzzards Bay, Massachusetts. This chart is used in USPS advanced courses.

15 In addition, the CD-ROM includes a wide selection of other charts. These all are real charts; however, *these charts are not intended for navigation!* To be accurate, you need to use the most recent editions of navigation charts, appropriately annotated with the latest changes as reported in the Local Notice to Mariners published by the United States Coast Guard.

16 The CD-ROM and digital charts included with this course are not updated and, therefore, are not current. Repeat:

These charts are not
intended for navigation!

Installing Your Software

17 The USPS Digital Chart Program is provided on a CD-ROM. You will need to install the Maptech Chart Navigator program on your computer to use the included charts. This chapter explains how to do that.

18 The CD-ROM contains the Maptech Chart Navigator program and a substantial selection of charts. You must install the program on your computer in order to use the charts. It is not necessary for you to install the charts to use the program. These can be run directly from the CD. This is recommended since *these charts are not for navigation,* and they require a substantial amount of hard-drive space. You will be able to transfer any or all of the included charts onto your hard drive at a later time if you choose to do so. You will need a PC using Windows® 98, ME, NT4.0, 2000, or XP operating system, and your computer should have at least 64 megabytes (MB) of random access memory (RAM) and 100MB of free disk space to install the Chart Navigator program. Installation of the software is quite easy and is explained below.

Installing Chart Navigator

19 Insert the Digital Chart CD-ROM in the CD drive on your computer. It should automatically start. An opening menu will appear. Select the option Install Chart Navigator which will take you through a self-explanatory sequence of menus.

20 **File Locations.** You will be prompted to Choose Destination Location. The default is C:\Program Files\Maptech\Chart Navigator\. If this is satisfactory, click Next. You then will be prompted to Choose Destination Location for the charts. The default is: C:\Chartkit\. If this is satisfactory, click Next.

21 **Install Charts.** You then will be prompted with Install Charts. If you click Yes, all of the charts will be installed on your hard drive. It is recommended you click No. You will be able to access these charts from your CD drive.

22 **GPS Setup.** If you have a GPS you're planning to use with Chart Navigator, the GPS Setup Wizard can show you how to configure your GPS unit for successful communication. You have the choice of setting up the GPS now or later. Click Yes if you want to enable it at this time. Clicking No will proceed with the installation, but you will be able to configure your GPS later. The menu has a button for setting up the GPS. When you choose to perform the setup, you will need your GPS and a cable to connect it to the computer's serial port.

23 Once your GPS has been set up with the Chart Navigator software, you will be able to exchange waypoints, routes, and tracks (some models) between the GPS and the Chart Navigator.

24 **Read Me.** This file provides an overview of the Chart Navigator program. You will be able to access this file and manuals for the program at a later time through the menu.

25 **Setup Complete.** The final menu indicates that Chart Navigator setup is complete and provides a default option to run the program immediately. The GPS Mark button sometimes is provided as a unique button. On other units, Mark is a second function on another button such as the ENTER button. Pressing the MARK button brings up the waypoint screen with the coordinates of your position at the time you pressed the button. You can store this point into the GPS, as described below, by pressing ENTER. If Mark is a second function, it will be labeled next to the button. To use Mark on these units, press the key while underway using the Map page.

26 If the CD does not autostart for any reason, go to My Computer in Windows and right-click on the icon for your CD drive. From the drop-down menu, select Open and double-click Setup to start the menu process.

Using Chart Navigator

27 This program will allow you to plan a boating cruise or voyage directly on the digital charts provided with your USPS CD-ROM, or any other Maptech charts. You will be able to upload your plans into your GPS and to download waypoints, routes, and tracks (some GPS models) from your GPS into Chart Navigator for viewing and editing.

28 Using Chart Navigator is quite easy and intuitive. Most planning software available on the market performs similar functions. This program will read any Maptech charts, as will most other navigation software. Chart Navigator will not read chart CDs of other formats.

29 This chapter provides the highlights of using the program—a *Quick Start* guide for the exercises included with this supplement. The full instructions for using Chart Navigator are on the CD.

Navigating the Screen

30 Chart Navigator displays a row of icons along the top of the screen. These icons can be used to access almost all of the functions you will use on the software. Two other ways to access these functions are:
    1) Use the right-click button on your mouse to get a drop-down menu
    2) Use the drop-down menus at the very top of the screen

31 **Cursor.** The default cursor you move around the screen is a small hand with crosshairs on the back. You can move the chart across the screen by pressing and holding the left

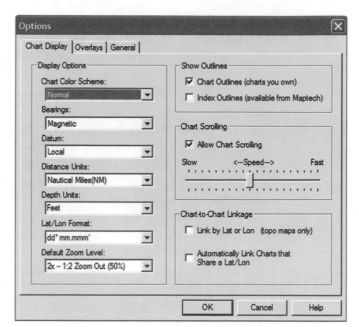

Figure 150   Chart Navigator Options Dialog Box

mouse button while you move the mouse. The chart will follow the hand. Alternatively, if you move to a corner or side of the chart, the hand is replaced by an arrow symbol. By clicking when the arrow is displayed, you will find the chart scrolls to provide you with a view in that direction.

32 Other cursor configurations are based on the function you are performing and are selected by the icon buttons described below.

Setup

33 The drop-down menu at the top of the screen under View, called Options, will help you set up the Chart Navigator for your personal preferences.

34 **Bearings.** The Bearings may be reported in Magnetic or True directions. Generally, you may find magnetic more convenient since you will steer with your compass.

35 **Distance Units.** You can set the distance units to nautical miles (recommended for

Bowditch Bay and coastal charts), statute miles (Great Lakes), or kilometers.

36 **Lat/Lon Format.** You can set the way latitude and longitude are expressed to: degrees-minutes-tenths (recommended for Bowditch Bay and coastal charts), degrees-minutes-seconds, and other formats.

37 **Overlays.** This separate tab accesses the options you prefer displayed on your screen.

Icons

38 The most frequently used icon functions will be described here. When you scroll the mouse over a Chart Navigator icon, a pop-up box will appear informing you of the function of the icon. The Hand icon is the most commonly used icon (default cursor) and is used to scroll about the chart. The other icons each have specific functions you will use when planning a trip.

39 **Hand Symbol.** This button is located in the middle of the icon row. It is used to return to the hand symbol (default cursor) if you have activated another function and want the hand back.

40 **Chart List.** This button brings up a complete list of available charts. When the program starts, it auto-detects all available charts—including those on your CD drive. These will be listed by clicking on this icon.

41 The table of Available Charts is sorted by Chart ID (number). You can sort by Chart Name or Type by clicking on the title at the top of the list. You will be using the Bowditch Bay chart which is numbered as BB001–1 for the exercises in this supplement.

42 Any chart can be opened by highlighting the appropriate line and selecting the Open Chart button to the right of the list.

43 You will note other pages on this screen by their tabs at the top of the window. For example, by clicking on the tab Copy Charts to Hard Drive, you will see the complete list in the left pane. You can highlight as many as you want and click Copy to add them to the right pane for copying to your hard drive.

44 **Charts at This Location.** This button will switch to other charts available at this location. Alternatively, by right-clicking the mouse, you will be presented with the complete available selection of charts at that specific location.

Figure 151   Chart Navigator Icons

45 **Scale.** There are two buttons that control scale—one for In and one for Out. These buttons change to the chart with the next larger or smaller scale at this location. You learned that charts are created with different scales. These scales are a ratio between a measure on a paper chart to the corresponding real world. Typical harbor charts may have scales of 1:10,000 or 1:20,000. This means that one inch on the paper chart corresponds with 10,000 (or 20,000) inches in the real world. Using these buttons, you switch to other charts with different scales.

46 **Zoom.** These two buttons (located toward the right of the button row) are represented by a magnifying glass symbol with either a + or – sign. The cursor becomes a magnifying glass with the plus or minus sign. These buttons do not change scale, but zoom in or out on the current chart displayed on the screen about the location of the cursor. This function is very useful since many of the charts represented may be four-feet across in their paper form, but your screen may be only a foot or so. Beware, over-zooming on a chart does not make it more accurate, only bigger. Charts' accuracy standards, used by NOAA and other hydrographic offices, are based on the scale of the chart. A small-scale chart (large area) is not as accurate as a harbor chart in regard to the specific location of objects. The other thing you will notice is the chart becomes blocky when you zoom in or hard to read when you zoom out, just as it would if you were using a magnifying glass on the paper chart.

47 **A2B.** This button, a line with a small square on each end, provides one of the handiest, navigation-assist tools available on the program. This tool is used for measurements rather than creating waypoints. Pressing the icon changes the cursor to a cross with A B printed on either side. Move this cursor to a position of your choice to begin the process of creating a single-leg range on the digital chart. When you left-click on the mouse, a red square with a letter A is placed on the screen. Now move to another position of your choice and click again. Another red box with a letter B is placed at the second location, and a blue line is drawn between the A and the B.

48 Next, move the cursor to either box—it turns into an arrow. Right-click and you are presented with some choices. First, the date and time of the A–B selection are shown for reference, and the line below is called Properties. Move the arrow over either of these fields and click to bring up a window with detailed properties about the cursor.

49 The A2B Properties window provides the coordinates of both Point A and Point B as well at the distance between them and the bearings from A to B and B to >.

50 **Create Route.** This icon button (lines at right angles with arrows) is used to create a route on the chart. The route tool is the most powerful tool available on digital charts. This enables you to plan your paths on the water, from point-to-point, avoiding obstacles and moving toward your destination. When the route is complete, it consists of a sequence of waypoints representing each turn between the straight-line route segments. Chart Navigator computes the courses and distances for each leg of the route and the total route distance.

51 These waypoints and the route can be uploaded into your GPS and navigated by selecting that route. Once selected, the route will direct you through the same sequence of waypoints on the GPS screen.

52 Upon clicking on this button, the cursor changes to crosshairs with an arrow symbol to the left. You move to the location of the first point you want to start your route and left-click. A circle is placed at that location

annotated with the number 1. Move to the next point and click. A second circle is placed with a number 2, and so on until you are finished. A line is drawn from each point (waypoint) to the next.

53 When you have reached the final point in the route sequence, right-click. The cursor changes to an arrow. Scroll down the menu to the first item called Save, and your route is saved—named with the date and time it was created. The entire route is saved as the sequence of waypoints.

54 **Create Mark.** There are times you will want to mark a spot that otherwise may be uncharted. This could be a wreck you discovered or a favorite fishing spot. You do this by selecting the Mark icon (a flag)—your cursor turns into crosshairs with Mark below it. By selecting the place for the mark and left-clicking, a menu box comes up and asks for Enter Mark Name. Selecting OK stores the mark with that name and an X is placed on the chart.

55 **Annotate Chart.** By clicking on the A icon, you can annotate the digital chart with notes of your choosing. The cursor converts to a line with ABC below. Move the cursor to the place where you want the notes to be placed and left-click. A pop-up box provides a window to enter your notes. You can select the font, color, and alignment of the notes. These notes will stay with your digital chart, but will not be uploaded into the GPS.

56 **Maptech "M".** By clicking this Maptech "M" logo, you will be redirected to the Maptech, MapServer via the Internet. This site displays the whole host of charts Maptech has on their server, so you can scroll around and look at alternative charts that are available.

57 **Chart Window.** You have a choice of three configurations for multiple charts. The most useful is two charts side-by-side. This al-

lows you to have two different charts for the same area. For example, you can observe a large-scale chart in one window and a larger-area, small-scale chart next to it. Alternatively, you can view a chart and photo chart next to it.

Other Chart Navigator Menu Features

58 There are a number of other features available on the Chart Navigator screen. The drop-down menus from the top line of the screen allow you to access far more functions than described under buttons.

59 **Help.** You can access instructions for the use of the program through the help menu. You also can access a host of data and publications of value to navigators. Included are:

    a. *Chart Symbols.* This provides access to the entire range of symbols and terminology used on charts, both on NOAA NOS charts and the NIMA international symbols

    b. *Coast Pilot.* This menu item provides access to the entire text of the *United States Coast Pilots 1* and *2*

    c. *Current or Tide Stations.* The current or tide stations for the active chart are displayed; this is equivalent to having the latest complete current and tide tables at your fingertips

    c. *Light List.* The light list for the active chart is displayed

60 **Locate.** This drop-down menu enables you to locate numerous features including:

    a. *Lat/Lon.* This menu will take you to a set of coordinates indicated by a bold arrow

    b. *Routes, Marks, Named Waypoints, A2Bs.* These menu items will pop-up lists of those stored items corresponding to the selection

    c. *Current and Tide Stations.* These menu items provide a list of all tide and current stations on the charts by number, coordinates, and features

   d. *Place Name, Marine Facilities.* These menus provide lists of all the place names and marine facilities available with the charts

61 **GPS.** This set of drop-down menus can be used to set up your GPS and start upload or download between the GPS and the computer.

Navigation Panel (Bottom of Screen)

62 The navigation panel provides a number of useful tools to help you work with charts.

63 **Colored Bars.** An array of colored bars are shown across the bottom of the screen. Each bar represents a different chart you have accessed or opened. By scrolling the cursor over each chart, you can read its number and name in the panes below. By clicking on the color bar, that chart will be placed on the screen.

64 **Coordinates.** The coordinates of the current cursor location are displayed in a window toward the right side of the navigation panel.

65 **Buttons for +/−.** These two buttons offer a quick way to zoom the chart in or out. They perform the same function as the + and − icons on the toolbar at the top of the screen, but without selecting those icons.

Working with Digital Charts

66 The real power of digital charts lies in the flexibility to create and adjust courses to suit your needs, and then upload that information directly into your GPS for navigation.

67 Now that you know how to push the buttons on the Chart Navigator, it's time to dive into

the best features of the program. The principal charting techniques described above are:
   A2B. Point-to-point measurements
   Mark. Waypoints for navigation
   Route. Routes for navigation

68 These features help you with navigation planning. Also, you can upload the marks and routes into your GPS for navigation.

69 The principal advantage to working with digital charts is that you plan directly on real charts with no need to manually transcribe your work to a GPS receiver. In this way, you enhance your planning with ease and then upload your results directly into the GPS for navigation.

70 When you plan and prequalify your paths on charts, you simplify your navigation on the water. By staying on those prequalified paths, you have a reasonable level of confidence you will not encounter charted underwater objects or shoals. Then you can concentrate your attention to those hazards and activities above the water.

71 You always should carry paper charts corresponding to your boating waters, appropriately annotated with the names of your waypoints and your routes. In fact, using digital charting programs such as Chart Navigator, you can print your own charts, along with all of the information you have plotted on them.

Planning and Charts

72 The chart is your security blanket. On it, you will find most of the key information you need to plan and execute safe navigation. Of course, use local knowledge and personal observations to enhance your navigation since charts are not infallible.

73 **Chart Information.** It is essential you have the latest versions of the charts for the area in which you intend to navigate. You also

should access the Notice to Mariners published by the U.S. Coast Guard to determine any changes since the publication date of the chart. The date of the chart can be found on the chart, usually near the Chart Number on the edge of the chart. Many commercial charts or chart books, such as those supplied by Maptech, are updated on a regular basis incorporating the latest Notice to Mariners information. The Title Block also provides critical information you will need to use. The chart projection and datum are provided, and the settings in the GPS must match the chart to use it for navigation. The Title Block also indicates the units for the Soundings of depth and the depth reference, such as Mean Lower Low Water (MLLW).

74 **Depths and Hazards.** The charts provide locations of harbors, channels, navigation aids, landmarks, and many other items. They also show depth soundings that are critical to planning your paths. These soundings are based on a reference datum such as MLLW. This means the depth of the water at that spot is marked with its value for the mean (close to average) depth at the lowest of the two low tides for that spot for each day.

75 If you know the tide level for a particular time, you can adjust the value up or down for when you plan to travel across that spot. Generally, it's prudent to assume that depth for your planning and not venture into areas where the draft of your boat nears that of the chart sounding, unless you have better local knowledge.

76 The chart shows locations of wrecks, prominent rocks, and other hazards—usually with their depths identified. The type of bottom is indicated in many locations. This is important if you choose to anchor. It also affects how your depth sounder works. You may wish to avoid rocky bottoms if you have a deep-draft boat.

A2B

77 This is a planning technique used for measurements rather than creating waypoints. The A2B marks are not uploaded into a GPS, but reside on the Chart Navigator screen for reference. This tool temporarily marks two points: A and B, and provides information about the location (coordinates) and relative position of each with respect to the other

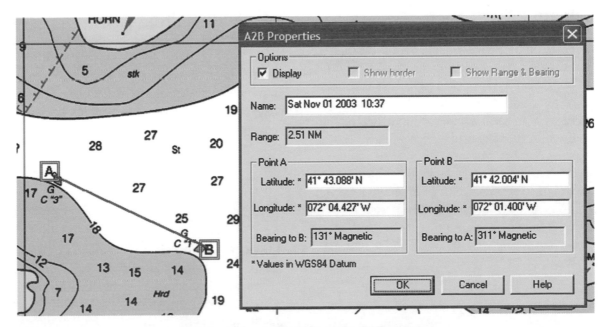

Figure 152   A2B Properties Dialog Box

(bearing and distance). It can be used to quickly measure a distance or to establish a bearing. This is particularly useful in establishing a Range for navigation or for measuring the bearing to a landmark.

78 A range is made by any two charted landmarks, the alignment of which can be used as a visual reference line on the water. Some are designed as navigation aids and are labeled. Others are the self- created for the boater's own convenience.

79 As explained in the previous chapter, you select the A2B icon, which changes the cursor to crosshairs. You simply place the cursor at the first point and click; then the second point and click. The first point is labeled A and the second point is labeled B; a line is drawn between them. You are not limited in the number of A2Bs you use on your chart.

80 The A2B Properties window provides the coordinates of both Point A and Point B, as well at the distance between them and the bearings from A to B and B to A.

Mark

81 Marks are convenient reference points you place on the chart. You have a choice of symbols you can attach to the marks. The default mark symbol is a red X. This is a means of annotating the chart with particular features or hazards you have identified and are not otherwise charted.

82 Each mark is shown on the chart and is stored in a Mark List by name and location. You can upload the marks into your GPS for reference as well. Simply right-click while the cursor is over the mark and select Send to GPS.

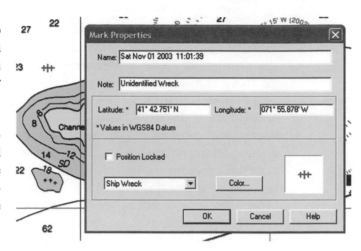

Figure 153   Chart Navigator Mark Properties Dialog Box

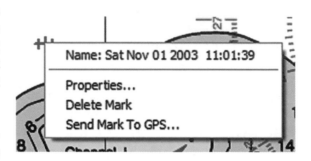

Figure 154   Command Selection to Send Mark to GPS

Route Planning

83 The digital chart has revolutionized the way you create routes. Simply stated, a route is a sequence of straight-line segments you navigate to get from one place on the water to another while avoiding obstacles, hazards, and shallow water.

84 There are two ways to create a route: a) linear, and b) quick. The techniques are similar. Which way you choose depends on your personal preference.

85 **Linear Route Planning.** As the name suggests, linear route planning starts at one place; and you decide, leg-by-leg, the paths you will take from start to destination. The technique is simply click and scroll until you

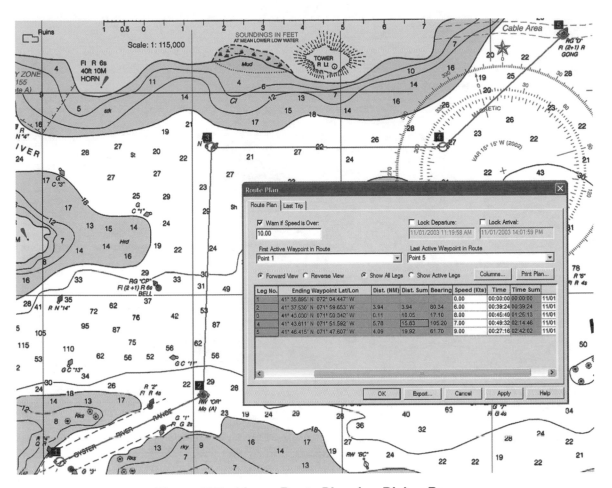

Figure 155   Linear Route Planning Dialog Box

have reached your destination. This is analogous to how you plan using paper charts, plotting tools, and a pencil.

86 If you decide to change or adjust that route, you can do so easily with the editing tools available on the Chart Navigator described below. This is far easier than using an eraser.

87 **Quick Route Planning.** Quick route planning makes maximum use of the editing tools described below. You start by creating a two-point route which includes only your starting point and destination. The straight-line path between the two is unlikely to be navigable, so you will edit to tune the route to your needs. The advantage to this technique is the initial, straight-line path represents the

shortest distance. Through editing, you will vary from that optimum path; but your baseline was the shortest distance. As a result, your completed route should be nearly the shortest path you could take.

88 **Editing.** Above and beyond the ease of plotting routes using digital charts, you will find editing even easier. Any point placed on the digital chart can be moved, and points can be added at the beginning, end, or in the middle of an existing route by simple mouse clicks. Then the resultant edited route can be uploaded into your GPS for navigation.

89 **Moving Waypoints, Marks, A2Bs.** You can move any waypoint (or mark) on the screen.

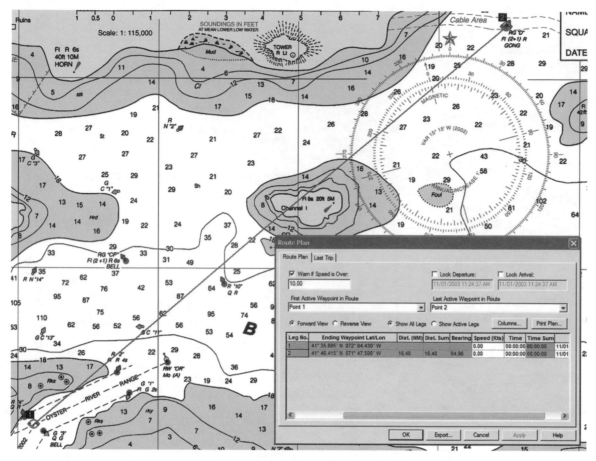

Figure 156   Quick Route Planning Dialog Box

Simply move the cursor to the circle marking the waypoint. It will turn into a crossed-arrow symbol. Then, hold down the left button on the mouse and drag it to where you want it moved.

90 If you want to move a mark (indicated by an X), the steps are the same. Move over the X and the cursor changes into crossed-arrows as above. Move it to the new location using the same click, drag, and drop method.

91 If you want to move the A or B in an A2B, do exactly the same thing.

92 All attendant information associated with these routes, marks, and A2Bs are immediately updated to reflect the changes.

93 **Editing Marks.** Marks are edited or deleted by right-clicking while on the mark. The coordinates are modified by changing the data fields, the chosen symbol edited from the default to a number of alternatives, and the color changed for each mark.

94 **Adding or Deleting Waypoints in a Route.** You can easily add or delete waypoints in an existing route as part of your editing task. Simply place the cursor over the route line between waypoints until the crossed-arrow symbol appears. Next, right-click using the mouse.

95 You will be presented with a menu of choices which include:

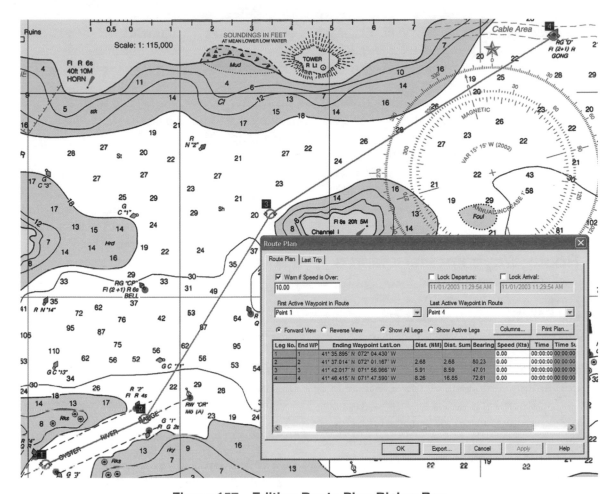

Figure 157   Editing Route Plan Dialog Box

96 *Insert Waypoint at Beginning (of Route).* Clicking on this option turns the cursor into crosshairs surrounded by a large black circle. A line extends from this cursor back to the original, first waypoint. You can add as many points as you choose in advance of the old, first waypoint. All of the waypoints are renumbered as you go. When you are finished, right-click and select Done.

97 *Insert Waypoint at End.* Clicking on this option provides the same crosshair and circle with the line now extending from the former end waypoint. You add as many additional waypoints as required and finish with Done.

98 *Insert Waypoint in Line.* Place the cursor, now crossed-arrows, on the line where you want to add the waypoint. Right-click and

select this choice. A new waypoint will be placed at the location of the cursor, and the waypoints will be renumbered. You can re-locate this new waypoint to suit your needs using the moving techniques outlined above.

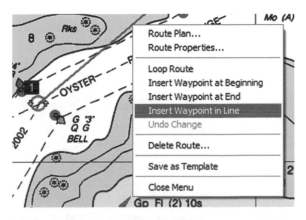

Figure 158   Insert Waypoint Command Line

99 *Replace with Named Waypoint.* Place the cursor over a waypoint in the route. Right-click and select this menu item. A list of your named waypoints will appear. Select the named waypoint and your route will be adjusted to use that waypoint.

100 *Delete.* Place the cursor over the waypoint you want to delete. Right-click and select Delete this Point on the menu. The point will be deleted.

Route, Waypoint Lists, Marks

101 Each route, waypoint, and mark can be reviewed and edited in a tabular format. In addition, the lists provide extensive information about your routes.

102 You can access this information by placing the cursor over a route on the screen and selecting Route Plan. Alternatively, you can use the drop-down menu at the top of the screen labeled Routes and select Route List. The route list is a complete list of your routes, independent of what appears on the screen.

103 **Route Plan.** The route plan shows all of the legs of your route beginning with the first waypoint. The coordinates of each waypoint are shown in the same format you selected in the setup. The following information is provided:
1. Leg Number
2. Starting and Ending Waypoint Coordinates
3. Leg Distance
4. Cumulative Route Distance
5. Bearing for Leg
6. Speed (you can enter values for this for each leg)
7. Time (leg time will be computed)
8. Time Sum (cumulative time for the route will be computed)

104 The route can be presented in the forward or reverse sequence, printed for reference, and completed routes uploaded into the GPS.

105 **Marks.** A list of your marks is found under the drop-down menu for Locate. By clicking on Marks, you will be presented with a tabular list of all marks by name and coordinates. Marks can be deleted from this menu or by right-clicking on the mark and selecting Delete Mark.

106 Marks are uploaded into the GPS by right-clicking on the mark and selecting Send Mark to GPS. This brings up a menu that allows you to assign the mark a short name (used as the waypoint name in the GPS) and a long name (which usually is stored in the GPS comment field).

Exercises with Digital Charts

107 Now that you understand how to use digital charts, it's time to use them.

Checking Boating Course Exercises

108 The best place to start with digital charts is by repeating some of the homework questions and exercises you answered using paper charts.

109 **Chapter 5, Charts.** Homework question number 5 asks for the LAT/LON coordinates of the beacon on Channel Island in the center of the Bowditch Bay chart.

110 Go to the Chart List (the leftmost icon button on the button bar under the drop-down menus) and select Chart Number BB001-1, Bowditch Bay.

111 Mark that location and read its properties. Compare with your answer to homework question 5 of Chapter 5.

112 **Chapter 7, Piloting—Plotting a Course.** Homework questions 8 and 9 ask you to plot

two courses and determine the true course for each.

113 First, go into your Chart Navigator software; under the View menu at the top of the window, click Options. Under the item Bearings, select True. Under Distance Units, select Nautical Miles.

114 Now, using the A2B tool (icon with a line ending with small squares):
   a) Plot a course from R "6" Fl R 4s buoy (chart center right) to RW "OR" safe-water buoy at the entrance to Oyster River. The true course is _____. Compare this result with your answer to question 8 of Chapter 5.
   b) Plot a course from RW "OR" to RN "2" at the entrance to Perkins Cove. The true course is _____. Compare this result with your answer to question 9 of Chapter 5.

115 **Chapter 9, Piloting—The Mariner's Compass.** Homework questions 9 and 10 ask for the compass course for each of the true courses in the above two questions (Chapter 4, questions 8 and 9). Since the deviation is assumed to be zero in each case, the magnetic course and the compass course will be identical.

116 Go into the View drop-down menu, then the Options submenu, and change Bearing to magnetic.
   a) Go to the A2B plot for R "6" Fl R 4s to RW "OR" and read the properties to determine the magnetic course. Compare this result with your answer to question 9 of Chapter 9.
   b) Go to the RW "OR" to RN "2" A2B plot on Bowditch Bay and ready the properties to determine this magnetic course. Compare the result with your answer to question 10 of Chapter 9. What is the reciprocal course when you return?

117 **Chapter 11, Piloting—Distance, Speed, Time.** Homework questions 5 and 6 ask for the distances in the two plots on Bowditch Bay you did for Chapter 7. Using the A2B function, answer the following questions:
   a) Go to the A2B plot for R "6" Fl R 4s to RW "OR", read the properties to determine the distance. Compare this result with your answer to Chapter 11, question 5.
   b) Go to the RW "OR" to RN "2" A2B plot on Bowditch Bay and ready the properties to determine the distance. Compare this result with your answer to Chapter 11, question 6.

118 Now, delete the two A2B plots on your chart using the right-click while your cursor is on either the A or the B for each plot.

119 Next, using the Create Route icon (to the right of the hand icon), create a route from the two plots you just erased (1st leg: R "6" Fl R 4s to RW "OR"; 2nd leg: RW "OR" to RN "2").

120 Now, call up the Route Plan (right-click on the cursor when it's over one of the waypoints). Compare the magnetic headings for the two legs with your answers to the two questions in Chapter 9.

121 Next, scroll across the route window until you see the column named Speed (Kts). Go to the 2nd box down (corresponding with the row with the first distance—the 1st leg).
   a) Enter 8.0 knots in the box corresponding to Leg 2 (your 2nd waypoint) under Speed. Click on any part of the gray area and observe the time field. How long did it take you to get to RW "OR"?
   b) Enter 9.0 knots in the box corresponding to Leg 3 (your 3rd waypoint). How long did it take you to get to Perkins Cove from RW "OR"? What was the total time for the trip?
   c) Calculate and compare the estimated time enroute for the two legs using $60 D = S \times T$.

Piloting Exercise

122 The cruise at the end of this appendix will provide you with the opportunity to get some experience with your charting software. It was originally created as a manual exercise to be plotted as you go along. In this exercise, you will plan the cruise in advance. Since Chart Navigator is a planning tool, it does not assign starting times, so you will need to work some of the problems by hand while you cruise.

123 Of course, you can convert between magnetic and true in the software by changing the setup in Chart Navigator. But, we recommend that you conduct the cruise with magnetic bearings. Then, go back later, change the setup to true, and check your manual computations.

A Day's Cruise Exercise

Name: _____ **Date:** _____ **Group:** _____

1. You have invited some friends for a day of cruising on Bowditch Bay. You depart the marina and head down the Oyster River to begin your cruise. At 0815, you pass close aboard buoy R "2" Fl 4s (this becomes a fix and is your starting point for the plotting). You turn onto a course to the FL R 6s 40ft light on the north shore of the Shark River at a speed of 8.5kn.

   At 0845, you take a bearing on the light at Chapman Point (FL 6s 126ft) of 295° using your hand-bearing compass (assume there is no deviation in this compass and the correction for variation is 15°W). At the same time, you take a 010° reading on your hand-bearing compass of the beacon FL R 6s.

   a) What is your compass course?
T (measured)	_____°
V (given)	15°W
M	_____
D (given)	0°
C (the answer)	_____

   b) What is the true bearing to Chapman Point Light? What is the true bearing to the beacon FL R 6s?

	Chapman Lt	Beacon
T (plotted)	_____	_____
V (given)	_____	_____
M	_____	_____
D (given)	_____	_____
C (measured)	_____	_____

   c) What is your 0845 DR position?
   DR 0845
   <u> 0815</u>
   30 Min
   Distance = Speed × Time ÷ 60
   = _____ × 30 ÷ 60
   = _____
   L = _____
   Lo = _____

   d) What is your 0845 Fix position?
   L = _____
   Lo = _____

2. You change course for the green can G "3" off Chapman Point on the Shark River. You maintain a speed of 8.5kn. You arrive at the buoy at 0900.

   a) What is your new true course?
   _____

   b) What course do you steer on your compass?
T	_____
V	_____
M	_____
D	_____
C	_____

   c) How fast were you actually going?
   Distance (measured) = _____
   S = 60 × D ÷ T   = _____

3. From G "3", looking at your chart, you decide to head east on a true course of 090° and speed of 10.0 knots. At 0942, you notice the tower R Lt on the hill is abeam to port and the beacon on Duttons Island is dead ahead.

    a) What course do you steer on your compass?

        T _____
        V _____
        M _____
        D _____
        C _____

    b) What is your DR?
        DR 0942
        _____0900
            42
        $D = S \times T \div 60$

        L   _____
        Lo _____

    c) What is your present position (fix)?
        L   _____
        Lo _____

    d) Are you on course?
        _____

    e) If not, how far from your DR are you?
        _____

4. From your 0942 position, you decide to change course and head for buoy RG "D" Fl R (2+1) GONG.

    a) What time do you expect to arrive at RG "D"?
        Distance   = _____ (measured)
        $T = 60 \times D \div S$ = _____

        ETA = 0942 + T = _____

    b) What course do you steer on your compass?
        T (measured)   _____
        V (given)   _____
        M   _____
        D (given)   _____
        C   _____

    c) What is the depth of the shallowest water you will cross?
        _____

5. You arrive at RG "D" at 1020 and decide you would like to visit Perkins Cove. You steer a course for the beacon Fl R 6s 24ft at the entrance to the cove. You set your speed at 9.0 knots.

    a) What is your true course to Perkins Cove?
        _____

    b) What course do you steer on your compass?
        _____

    c) At what time do you expect the beacon on Duttons Island (Fl 8s 42ft) to be abeam?
        _____

6. At 1125, you become concerned you may not be on course for Perkins Cove and decide to take a fix with your handheld GPS set. At 1127, you read GPS coordinates of 41°37.8′N and 71°15.0′W. You discover it is later than you expected, and you want to be back at the marina before mid-afternoon; so, you decide to head directly back to the RW "OR" Mo (A) at the mouth of the Oyster River.

    a) What is your 1127 DR position?
        L   _____
        Lo _____

b) Are you on course? If not, how far are you from your DR and in which direction have you been pushed off course?

_____

_____

c) Would it be wise to go directly back to RW "OR"?

_____

d) What concerns do you have?

_____

_____

7. You decide a more prudent approach would be to go from buoy to buoy back to Oyster Bay. You steer a course for C "7" Fl G 4s north of the chimney, to the west of Haven Bluff. Concerned, you proceed at a speed of 5.0 knots.

a) What is the true course to C "7"?

_____

b) What course do you steer on your compass?

_____

c) Are you comfortable with this course?

_____

d) What actions could you take to assure a safer passage?

_____

_____

8. You arrive at C "7" at 1240 and change course for G "9" Fl G 4s. You are more comfortable and increase your speed to 10.0 knots. You arrive on time at G "9" and adjust your course directly for RW "OR" at the mouth of the Oyster River. You then proceed into the Oyster River along the range and arrive at your marina at 1430.

a) What is your compass course to C "7"?

_____

b) What time do you expect to arrive at C "7"?

_____

c) What is your compass course to G "9"?

_____

d) What time do you expect to arrive at G "9"?

_____

e) What is your compass course to RW "OR"?

_____

f) At what time do you arrive at RW "OR"?

_____

g) What is the function of the range on the Oyster River?

_____

_____

Answers to the Day's Cruise Exercise

1. You have invited some friends for a day of cruising on Bowditch Bay. You depart the marina and head down the Oyster River to begin your cruise. At 0815, you pass close aboard buoy R "2" Fl 4s (this becomes a fix and is your starting point for the plotting). You turn onto a course to the FL R 6s 40ft light on the north shore of the Shark River at a speed of 8.5kn.

At 0845, you take a bearing on the light at Chapman Point (FL 6s 126ft) of 295° using your hand-bearing compass (assume there is no deviation in this compass and the correction for variation is 15°W). At the same time, you take a 010° reading on your hand-bearing compass of the beacon FL R 6s.

a) What is your compass course?

T (measured)	351°
V (given)	15°W
M	006°
D (given)	0°
C (the answer)	006°

b) What is the true bearing to Chapman Point Light? What is the true bearing to the beacon FL R 6s?

	Chapman Lt	Beacon
T (plotted)	280°	355°
V (given)	15°W	15°W
M	295°	101°
D (given)	0°	0°
C (measured)	295°	010°

c) What is your 0845 DR position?

DR 0845
 0815
 30 Min

Distance = Speed × Time ÷ 60
　　　　 = 8.5 × 30 ÷ 60
　　　　 = 4.25 = 4.3nm
L　= 40° 41.5′ N
Lo = 71° 31.8′ W

d) What is your 0845 Fix position?
L　= 41° 41.0′ N
Lo = 71° 32.1′ W

2. You change course for the green can G "3" off Chapman Point on the Shark River. You maintain a speed of 8.5kn. You arrive at the buoy at 0900.

a) What is your new true course?
T	327°

b) What course do you steer on your compass?

T	327°
V (given)	15°W
M	324°
D (given)	0°
C	342°

c) How fast were you actually going?
DR 0900 − 0845 = 15min
Distance (measured) 　= 2.5NM
S = 60 × D ÷ T 　　= 60 × 2.5 ÷ 15
S = 10.0kn

3. From G "3", looking at your chart, you decide to head east on a true course of 090° and speed of 10.0 knots. At 0942, you notice the tower R Lt on the hill is abeam to port and the beacon on Duttons Island is dead ahead.

   a) What course do you steer on your compass?

T	090°
V	15°W
M	105°
D	0°
C	105°

   b) What is your DR?

      DR 0942
          0900
      ─────────
           42

      $D = S \times T \div 60 = 10.0 \times 42 \div 60$
      D = 7.0nm
      L   41° 43.1′ N
      Lo 70° 26.0′ W

   c) What is your present position (fix)?
      L   41° 44.0′ N
      Lo 71° 25.7′ W

   d) Are you on course?
      No

   e) If not, how far from your DR are you?
      0.9nm

4. From your 0942 position, you decide to change course and head for buoy RG "D" Fl R (2+1) GONG.

   a) What time do you expect to arrive at RG "D"?
      D = 6.1nm (measured)
      $T = 60 \times D \div S = 60 \times 6.1 \div 10.0$
      T = 37min
      ETA = 0942 + 37 = 1019

   b) What course do you steer on your compass?

T (measured)	067°
V (given)	15°W
M	082°
D (given)	0°
C	082°

   c) What is the depth of the shallowest water you will cross?
                    14–15ft

5. You arrive at RG "D" at 1020 and decide you would like to visit Perkins Cove. You steer a course for the beacon Fl R 6s 24ft at the entrance to the cove. You set your speed at 9.0 knots.

   a) What is your true course to Perkins Cove?
                    158°

   b) What course do you steer on your compass?

T (measured)	158°
V (given)	15°W
M	173°
D (given)	0°
C	173°

   c) At what time do you expect the beacon on Duttons Island (Fl 8s 42ft) to be abeam?
      D = 3.2nm (measured)
      $T = 60 \times D \div S = 60 \times 3.2 \div 9.0$
      T = 21min
      ETA = 1020 + 21 = 1041

6. At 1125, you become concerned you may not be on course for Perkins Cove and decide to take a fix with your handheld GPS set. At 1127, you read GPS coordinates of 41°37.8′N and 71°15.0′W. You discover it is later than you expected, and you want to be back at the marina before mid-afternoon; so, you decide to head directly back to the RW "OR" Mo (A) at the mouth of the Oyster River.

a) What is your 1127 DR position?
DR 1127
$\underline{\quad 1020 \quad}$
107 = 67min
D = S × T ÷ 60 = 9.0 × 67 × 60
D = 10.1nm
L   41° 37.1′ N
Lo 71° 15.6′ W

b) Are you on course? If not, how far are you from your DR and in which direction have you been pushed off course?

No; 0.9nm, to the NE

c) Would it be wise to go directly back to RW "OR"?

No

d) What concerns do you have?

Rocks to the south of G"5" are along that course.

7. You decide a more prudent approach would be to go from buoy to buoy back to Oyster Bay. You steer a course for C "7" Fl G 4s north of the chimney, to the west of Haven Bluff. Concerned, you proceed at a speed of 5.0 knots.

a) What is the true course to C "7"?
266°

b) What course do you steer on your compass?

T (measured)	266°
V (given)	15°W
M	281°
D (given)	0°
C	281°

c) Are you comfortable with this course?

Somewhat

d) What actions could you take to assure a safer passage?
Take one of the following options:
1) Set a danger bearing* on C "7" of NLT 260°
2) Lay in a course to RW "BC", then a course directly for RW "OR"
3) Set a course further to the south until clear of the rocks

*Danger bearings and related advanced topics are taught in the Piloting course, which all USPS members are entitled to take without charge for instruction.

8. You arrive at C "7" at 1240 and change course for G "9" Fl G 4s. You are more comfortable and increase your speed to 10.0 knots. You arrive on time at G "9" and adjust your course directly for RW "OR" at the mouth of the Oyster River. You then proceed into the Oyster River along the range and arrive at your marina at 1430.

a) What is your compass course to C "7"?

T	265°
V (given)	15°W
M	280°
D (given)	0°
C	280°

b) What time do you expect to arrive at C "7"?

D = 6.1nm (measured)

$T = 60 \times D \div S = 60 \times 6.1 \div 5.0$

T = 73.2min

ETA = 1127 + 73 = 1240

c) What is your compass course to G "9"?

T	272°
V (given)	15°W
M	287°
D (given)	0°
C	287°

d) What time do you expect to arrive at G "9"?

D = 3.7nm (measured)

$T = 60 \times D \div S = 60 \times 3.7 \div 10$

T = 22.2min

ETA = 1240 + 22 = 1262 = 1302

e) What is your compass course to RW "OR"?

T	270°
V (given)	15°W
M	285°
D (given)	0°
C	285°

f) At what time do you arrive at RW "OR"?

D = 3.5nm (measured)

$T = 60 \times D \div S = 60 \times 3.5 \div 10$

T = 21.0min

ETA = 1302 + 21 = 1323

g) What is the function of the range on the Oyster River?

To keep you in the center of the channel.

B

Coastal Boating

1 Along the Atlantic and Pacific Oceans and the Gulf of Mexico are thousands of miles of coastal waters, including many sounds, bays, and estuaries. This section will discuss topics of importance that will enhance the coastal boater's enjoyment of these waters.

Tides

2 *Tide* is the *vertical rise and fall* of ocean water, often confused with *current,* which is the *horizontal movement* of water over the bottom. Most noticeable in coastal regions, tide results mainly from gravitational effects of the moon and sun. The sun's effect is less than that of the moon because it is farther from the earth. Tide affects safe passage in shallow water and under low bridges, and it is an important factor to consider when tying a boat to a pier, or anchoring.

Tide Predictions

3 There is a regular relationship between the tides and the movements of the sun, moon, and earth. On average, tides occur approximately 50 minutes later each day because of the moon's daily movement around the earth. As a result, times and heights of tides are predictable for any date at a given place.

4 The National Ocean Service develops tidal predictions annually and makes them available to commercial printers who supply tide tables to marine book and supply stores. These tables contain the predicted times and heights of high and low waters for each day

at *reference stations* along the coast. Additional tables provide corrections to these tables so that a skipper can determine tide information at many adjacent *subordinate stations.*

High and Low Tides

5 Although tidal action originates in the open oceans, it is most noticeable close to shore and in other tidewater areas such as the narrow stretches of rivers. Ocean levels usually rise and fall twice a day, but there are exceptions such as the Gulf of Mexico where, due to its geographic location, there is only one tide a day.

6 The extremes of these vertical fluctuations are called high and low tides. *High tide* is the maximum height reached by each rising tide, and *low tide* is the minimum height reached by each falling tide. Many newspapers, television stations, and radio stations give the times of high and low tides along with their weather reports. There are additional sources of tidal information on many modern-day computer programs.

Height of Tide

7 Charts show water depths at *mean lower low water,* the average of the lowest water levels over a long period of time. Since *charted depths are averages*, there will be times when the water depth will be even less than that indicated. You should allow for a margin of error.

Boston, Mass., 1996

Times and Heights of High and Low Waters

January

Day	Time (h m)	Height (ft)	Height (cm)	Day	Time (h m)	Height (ft)	Height (cm)
1 M	0125	1.0	30	16 Tu	0029	0.5	15
	0750	9.9	302		0643	10.4	317
	1412	0.6	18		1311	0.0	0
	2025	8.8	268		1920	9.2	280
2 Tu	0217	1.1	34	17 W	0127	0.3	9
	0839	10.0	305		0741	10.8	329
	1502	0.4	12		1410	-0.6	-18
	2115	8.8	268		2020	9.6	293
3 W	0305	1.1	34	18 Th	0224	-0.1	-3
	0924	10.1	308		0838	11.4	347
	1547	0.2	6		1507	-1.2	-37
	2200	8.9	271		2118	10.0	305
4 Th	0349	1.0	30	19 F	0321	-0.5	-15
	1006	10.2	311		0934	11.8	360
	1627	0.1	3		1601	-1.7	-52
	2241	9.0	274		2214	10.4	317
5 F ○	0430	0.9	27	20 Sa ●	0416	-0.9	-27
	1046	10.2	311		1029	12.1	369
	1706	0.0	0		1654	-2.1	-64
	2320	9.1	277		2308	10.8	329

February

Day	Time (h m)	Height (ft)	Height (cm)	Day	Time (h m)	Height (ft)	Height (cm)
1 Th	0237	1.4	43	16 F	0205	0.0	0
	0858	9.6	293		0821	11.1	338
	1521	0.6	18		1448	-1.0	-30
	2134	8.6	262		2101	10.0	305
2 F	0323	1.2	37	17 Sa	0304	-0.5	-15
	0942	9.8	299		0920	11.5	351
	1602	0.4	12		1543	-1.5	-46
	2216	8.9	271		2158	10.5	320
3 Sa	0406	0.9	27	18 Su ●	0400	-1.0	-30
	1023	10.0	305		1016	11.8	360
	1641	0.1	3		1636	-1.8	-55
	2255	9.1	277		2250	10.9	332
4 Su ○	0447	0.7	21	19 M	0454	-1.3	-40
	1102	10.1	308		1109	11.9	363
	1718	0.0	0		1726	-1.9	-58
	2332	9.3	283		2341	11.2	341
5 M	0527	0.5	15	20 Tu	0546	-1.5	-46
	1140	10.2	311		1200	11.8	360
	1754	-0.2	-6		1814	-1.8	-55

March

Day	Time (h m)	Height (ft)	Height (cm)	Day	Time (h m)	Height (ft)	Height (cm)
1 F	0204	1.6	49	16 Sa	0150	0.1	3
	0825	9.3	283		0807	10.7	326
	1446	0.9	27		1429	-0.7	-21
	2101	8.6	262		2046	10.1	308
2 Sa	0254	1.3	40	17 Su	0250	-0.4	-12
	0913	9.6	293		0907	11.0	335
	1529	0.6	18		1524	-1.0	-30
	2144	8.9	271		2141	10.6	323
3 Su	0339	0.9	27	18 M	0346	-0.9	-27
	0956	9.8	299		1002	11.3	344
	1609	0.3	9		1616	-1.2	-37
	2224	9.3	283		2231	11.1	338
4 M	0421	0.6	18	19 Tu ●	0438	-1.2	-37
	1036	10.0	305		1054	11.3	344
	1647	0.1	3		1704	-1.3	-40
	2301	9.6	293		2319	11.3	344
5 Tu ○	0501	0.2	6	20 W	0528	-1.4	-43
	1114	10.2	311		1143	11.2	341
	1724	-0.1	-3		1750	-1.2	-37
	2337	9.9	302				

Figure 159   Typical Page of a Tide Table for the Reference Station at Boston Harbor

8 The *Height of Tide* column in a tide table tells how much higher or lower the water will be above or below these average depths shown on charts. Add or subtract the height of tide to or from the charted water data to estimate the depth of water you can expect in a given area.

9 The height of tide varies from less than a foot at some places to as much as 50 feet at others. Figure 159 is an excerpt from a tide table for the reference station at Boston, Massachusetts.

10 As an example: at the Boston reference station on Thursday 18 January 1996, high tides would occur at 0838 and 2118. The height of tide at 0838 would be 11.4 feet (347 cm) more than the charted depth; at 2118, 10.0 feet (305 cm) more. Low tides would occur at 0224 and 1507. The height of tide at 0224 would be 0.1 feet (3 cm) less than the charted depth; at 1507, 1.2 feet (37 cm) less.

11 If you were at a location other than Boston, you would consult the Tidal Differences table in the tide tables book and apply the differences shown for your location to the above information.

Tidal Range

12 In areas where tidal range (difference in depth between high and low tide) is considerable, you may need to estimate the depth at a particular stage between high and low tides. Where there are two tides a day, the time between high and low (and low to high) is about 6 hours. However, the tide does not rise and fall at an even rate. The greatest change in depth will be during the middle $1/3$ of the range. Estimate heights at intermediate times as follows:
   - During the first $1/3$ of the cycle, the water level will change $1/4$ of the range
   - During the second $1/3$ of the cycle, the water level will change an additional $1/2$ of the range

- During the last ⅓ of the cycle, the water level will change an additional ¼ of the range

13 Using tide tables and the calculations above, you can easily convert charted depth to actual depth. Knowing the depth of the water, you can determine whether safe passage over a shoal is possible. Always leave a margin for safety.

14 Not every point on a chart has been measured, so rocks may exist between charted depths. Shoals may have formed since the last survey, improvement projects may have altered channels, etc. In addition, factors such as wind, barometric pressure, and amount of water flowing from a watershed can affect height of tide. Prolonged winds from one direction can also offset tide table predictions, as can heavy rains and extended droughts.

Current

15 Current is the horizontal movement of water. Tidal current is caused by the difference in tidal heights between two points but currents are also the result of other forces. Sustained wind blowing across the sea will force surface water to move. Water flowing from a higher level to a lower level, such as in some canals and rivers, produces current. This is the case in the Cape Cod Canal where current is the result of water flowing between Massachusetts Bay and Buzzard's Bay.

Flood and Ebb Currents

16 The movement of tidal water is called flood current when the flow is towards land and ebb current when the flow is toward the sea.

Slack Water

17 *Slack water* is the time at which there is little or no tidal current—the time at which the current has stopped running in one direction and is about to begin running in the opposite direction. Tidal current velocity at slack water will be zero. In most cases, tidal currents reverse direction nearly 180 degrees with each tidal cycle, and there will be four periods of slack water each day. Note that the times of slack water do not necessarily coincide with the times of high and low tides (when the vertical rise and fall of water has stopped).

Current Speed and Direction

18 Tidal currents can vary significantly—from a speed of less than half a knot to 6 knots or more. A current of even a knot or two will make your passage faster or slower. Currents will be stronger when tidal ranges are greatest (at the times of new and full moons). Maximum tidal current velocity will occur during the middle ⅓ of the ebb and flood cycles. Currents vary in direction and can cause the actual path of a vessel over the bottom to be quite different from the course steered. Be careful; current can move you off course, possibly into dangerous areas.

Current Predictions

19 There is a regular relationship between current and tidal height, so that times, speeds, and directions of currents are predictable for any date at a given place. Commercial printers using National Ocean Service predictions make current tables available to the general public.

20 Current tables predict the times of daily slack water and times of maximum current (ebb and flood) for a number of reference stations. Additional tables provide corrections to the reference station tables so that a skipper can determine information on current at many adjacent subordinate stations.

21 Figure 160 is an excerpt from a current table for the reference station at Boston Harbor.

Boston Harbor (Deer Island Light), Massachusetts, 1996

F—Flood, Dir. 254° True   E—Ebb, Dir. 111° True

	January								February								March						
	Slack	Maximum			Slack	Maximum			Slack	Maximum			Slack	Maximum			Slack	Maximum			Slack	Maximum	
	h m	h m	knots		h m	h m	knots		h m	h m	knots		h m	h m	knots		h m	h m	knots		h m	h m	knots
1 M	0129 0727 1404 2006	0452 1141 1721	1.2F 1.5E 1.2F	**16 Tu**	0040 0627 1317 1858	0255 0955 1533 2233	1.3F 1.3E 1.2F 1.2E	**1 Th**	0242 0838 1513 2118	0031 0604 1255 1831	1.3E 1.2F 1.4E 1.2F	**16 F**	0210 0757 1443 2032	0516 1219 1759	1.3F 1.4E 1.3F	**1 F**	0211 0801 1441 2040	0003 0534 1226 1801	1.2E 1.1F 1.3E 1.1F	**16 Sa**	0151 0736 1422 2013	0511 1205 1746	1.2F 1.4E 1.3F
2 Tu	0220 0820 1453 2059	0006 0542 1231 1810	1.4E 1.2F 1.5E 1.2F	**17 W**	0137 0723 1411 1956	0358 1129 1659	1.4F 1.4E 1.3F	**2 F**	0329 0921 1557 2153	0118 0650 1340 1916	1.3E 1.2F 1.4E 1.2F	**17 Sa**	0306 0854 1537 2126	0048 0621 1311 1855	1.4E 1.4F 1.5E 1.5F	**2 Sa**	0259 0848 1525 2121	0051 0621 1312 1846	1.3E 1.1F 1.4E 1.2F	**17 Su**	0249 0835 1517 2109	0033 0610 1257 1839	1.4E 1.3F 1.5E 1.4F
3 W	0308 0905 1539 2139	0055 0629 1318 1856	1.4E 1.2F 1.5E 1.2F	**18 Th**	0230 0819 1504 2052	0001 0510 1227 1809	1.3E 1.4F 1.5E 1.4F	**3 Sa**	0411 1000 1636 2228	0203 0733 1423 1957	1.3E 1.2F 1.4E 1.3F	**18 Su** ●	0400 0949 1628 2221	0139 0716 1401 1946	1.5E 1.5F 1.6E 1.5F	**3 Su**	0343 0930 1606 2158	0135 0705 1355 1928	1.3E 1.2F 1.3E 1.3F	**18 M**	0342 0931 1608 2202	0124 0703 1346 1929	1.5E 1.4F 1.6E 1.5F
4 Th	0351 0946 1621 2216	0142 0714 1404 1940	1.4E 1.3F 1.5E 1.2F	**19 F**	0324 0913 1557 2146	0056 0622 1319 1905	1.4E 1.5F 1.5E 1.5F	**4 Su** ○	0451 1037 1714 2303	0245 0813 1502 2035	1.3E 1.2F 1.3E 1.3F	**19 M**	0451 1041 1718 2312	0229 0807 1451 2035	1.6E 1.5F 1.6E 1.6F	**4 M**	0425 1010 1645 2234	0217 0745 1434 2006	1.3E 1.2F 1.3E 1.3F	**19 Tu** ●	0434 1023 1657 2252	0213 0753 1435 2017	1.6E 1.5F 1.6E 1.6F
5 F ○	0434 1024 1701 2252	0226 0756 1447 2021	1.3E 1.2F 1.4E 1.2F	**20 Sa** ●	0418 1007 1648 2239	0148 0720 1410 1957	1.4E 1.5F 1.6E 1.5F	**5 M**	0531 1113 1751 2338	0323 0848 1537 2107	1.2E 1.2F 1.2E 1.3F	**20 Tu**	0543 1132 1807	0319 0858 1541 2124	1.6E 1.5F 1.6E 1.6F	**5 Tu**	0505 1048 1723 2311	0254 0822 1506 2038	1.3E 1.3F 1.3E 1.4F	**20 W** ○	0524 1114 1745 2340	0301 0842 1523 2104	1.6E 1.5F 1.6E 1.6F

Figure 160   Typical Page from a Current Table for the Reference Station at Boston Harbor

22 As an example: at the Boston Harbor reference station on Thursday 18 January 1996, slack current would occur at 0230, 0819, 1504, 2052. Maximum currents would be 1.3 knots on the midnight ebb, 1.4 knots on the a.m. flood, 1.5 knots on the a.m. ebb, and 1.4 knots on the p.m. flood.

23 If you were at a location other than Boston, you would consult the Current Differences table in the tidal current tables book and apply the differences shown for your location to the above information.

24 **Seek Local Knowledge.** The best computer tables do not compare with local knowledge from experienced boaters in a locale. Be sure to seek advice on tides, currents, shoals, or peculiar conditions along your course when you are in unfamiliar waters.

U.S. Coast Pilots

25 The National Ocean Service publishes nine *United States Coast Pilots* for coastal areas of various parts of the country. They provide detailed information to supplement nautical charts.

26 They include such information as channel descriptions, anchorages, location of fuel piers, location of haul-out and repair facilities, bridge and cable clearances, hours of drawbridge operation, tide and tidal current information, local weather conditions, navigational hazards, prominent features, small-craft facilities, and federal regulations applying to the areas.

27 These publications are listed in Appendix D, together with information as to how to obtain them.

Inlets

28 The entrances to sounds, bays, rivers, and waterways are frequently narrow inlets. Shoaling can be a constant problem, often making it difficult to define the limits of the navigable channel.

29 Breaking waves indicate shoaling. If there are breaking waves across the full width of an inlet, try to run the inlet at full high tide for the best chance of clearing the bottom.

Currents

30 Currents can be fast and turbulent in narrow inlets. They may be so fast that passage is impossible for boats with limited power. Expect strong currents where two bodies of water meet, for the times of tides, tidal ranges, and velocities and directions of currents can be different for each body of water. Currents in New York's East River and San Francisco's Golden Gate can exceed five knots.

31 Tidal Rips with steep short waves that are difficult to navigate occur where a fast current passes over an irregular bottom, or where there are sudden changes in depth. These are often found at the inlets to rivers and bays and near sharp points of land that protrude out into the ocean. Tidal rips are particularly dangerous when the direction of the wind is opposite the direction of the current.

32 Plan Ahead for running an unfamiliar inlet. Use charts, coast pilots, tide tables, current tables, and cruising guides to gather information about its buoys, beacons, ranges, currents, tidal rips, and shoals. If you need additional information, contact the Coast Guard on VHF Radio and ask their advice. Area marinas and dockmasters may also help you. If you call nearby vessels on the calling channel, a knowledgeable skipper may return your call. You may be able to follow an experienced local captain through the inlet.

33 Breaking waves are not always apparent from the windward or seaward side of an inlet. When approaching from sea, stand back and observe other boats as they move through the inlet. The real key to running an inlet safely is to obtain local knowledge.

34 **Running an Inlet Before a Sea.** When running before the waves in a planing boat, keep the stern of your boat square to the waves and run in on the back of a single wave. Use engine power to maintain a position about a third of the way back from the wave's crest. Be ready to adjust speed quickly; faster or slower to maintain steerage and control.

35 In a displacement vessel, you may not be able to keep up with a single wave. Concentrate on keeping the boat centered in the channel with its stern square to the waves coming up behind you, allowing successive waves to pass under your keel.

36 **Experience Is the Best Teacher.** It is impossible to learn to run a narrow or breaking inlet in the classroom. If you boat in an area with inlets, make practice runs on relatively calm days so that you can develop a "feel" for the way your boat operates under various circumstances.

Modern Tide and Current Tables

37 Several companies provide various modern computer versions of the typical tide and current tables shown in Figures 161 and 162. The following examples were provided by Nautical Software, 14657 SW Teal Boulevard, Suite 132, Beaverton, Oregon, 97007-6194, 503-579-1414.

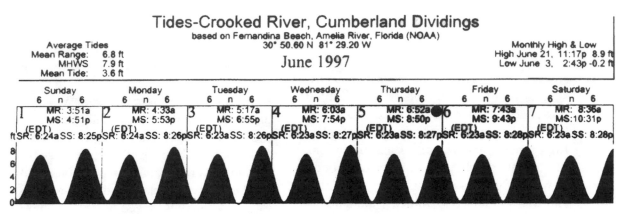

Figure 161   Typical Computer Tide Table

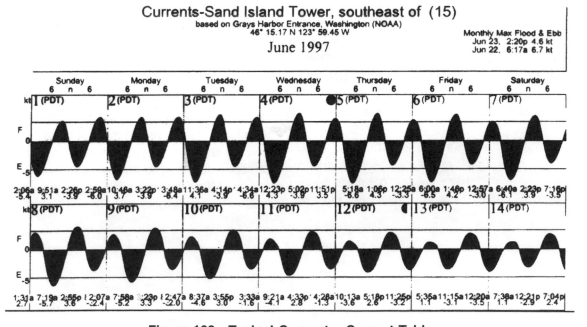

Figure 162   Typical Computer Current Table

C

Inland Boating

1 The continental United States has over 30,000 miles of improved waterways. Combine that with additional thousands of miles of lake shorelines and you have some of the finest boating to be found anywhere.

2 The original channels of many waterways have been widened, rerouted, deepened, and dammed to form huge, quiet pools. You will find facilities that make it easy to launch boats from trailers and marinas that provide slips, food, water, electricity, and other accommodations. A large number of recreational boaters use these great cruising areas.

Plan Ahead

3 Know the area where you will be boating. Obtain charts before you go. Such things as depth of water and clearances of highway and railroad bridges can affect your cruise plans. Marinas and fuel docks may be few and far between. Wise fuel planning is a necessity on inland rivers.

4 Emergency response may be very slow. Know how to contact emergency services before you go. On landlocked lakes, contact state park rangers in an emergency. Find out if they monitor VHF radio. You may find dead spots where VHF reception is poor. A cellular telephone might be helpful.

Charts

5 There are charts for many rivers and lakes, but there may be areas where you have to use road maps.

6 **River Charts** are similar to small-craft charts. North may not be at the top of the chart. They usually show channel lines, navigational aids, overhead cable crossings, piers, dams, bridges, safety harbors, and information on public facilities. River charts are often in book form with each page covering a short stretch of river. The course of the river is blue with a broken red line indicating the center of the channel.

7 Since river water depths vary greatly from time to time, river charts often do not show them. Also missing are prominent landmarks and the names of towns, cities, and other areas along the river banks. Road maps will be useful.

8 Chart symbols are sometimes different from those used on coastal charts. Look for a key to chart symbols on the front page of each chart.

9 The position of buoys on river charts will be only approximate. Buoys are moved frequently due to changing channels and depths of water.

10 Channel lines are usually labeled with mile markers. These mileage distances (in statute miles) usually start at the mouth of a river and run to its origin point.

11 Federal, state, and local boating agencies are good sources of maps and up-to-date information.

12 **The U.S. Army Corps of Engineers** charts inland non-tidal rivers, lakes, reservoirs, and canal systems. The Ohio, Mississippi, Missouri, and Alabama Rivers are examples. The Corps of Engineers makes their charts available through their various offices.

13 **The Tennessee Valley Authority** produces charts for its reservoirs, the Tennessee River, and its tributaries. See Appendix D for the address of the TVA map section.

14 **The Canadian Hydrographic Service** charts all but the smallest Canadian lakes and rivers. See Appendix D.

15 **The U.S. Geological Survey** publishes a series of brochures that include maps and items of interest on major rivers.

16 **The U.S. National Park Service** provides information on many U.S. lakes and rivers.

Piloting Equipment

17 It is seldom necessary to plot a dead reckoning course on a river. Mile markers and your chart will tell you where you are. You will need a good pair of binoculars to locate aids to navigation.

Aids to Navigation

18 Most aids to navigation on inland waters resemble those in coastal waters. In fact, many inland waters are navigable waterways controlled by the federal government. (Navigable waterways are waters that provide a means of transportation between two states or to the sea.) However, there are aids to navigation in the Western River and Uniform State Waterway Marking systems not seen in coastal waters.

Western River Aids to Navigation System

19 The U.S. Coast Guard maintains the Western River System which is found on the Mississippi River and its tributaries.

20 **Right and Left Bank** are designations used in the Western River system to refer to almost all land objects. When you travel downstream in this system, you are traveling seaward with the flow of the river. (Downstream is also called descending.)

21 When traveling downstream:
     the *right bank* is on your right
     the *left bank* is on your left

22 **Buoys and Beacons.** When traveling downstream, always keep green marks to starboard and red marks to port. See Chapter 6, page 60, color plate 4, U.S. Aids to Navigation, Western River System.

23 Barge traffic and flood waters often displace river buoys. So, use common sense and do not steer for a buoy marooned on a bank. Many buoys do not appear on navigational charts because they are constantly being shifted by the Coast Guard as water levels change.

24 River marks often do not have letters or numbers. Numbers that you see on aids may indicate mileage from a fixed point. However, their shapes, colors, and meanings are the same as in the coastal system.

25 **Daymarks** attached to daybeacons offer valuable assistance. Two special kinds of daymarks show river banks and identify changes in the direction of the channel: passing daymarks and crossing daymarks. See Color Plate 4 in Chapter 6, Aids to Navigation, page 60.

26 *Passing Daymarks* are red triangles or green squares that tell you the location of the

channel. A passing daymark on a bank tells you that the channel is on that side.

27 *Crossing Daymarks* are diamond-shaped and tell you when the channel changes from one side of the river to the other. (Always *head for the diamonds.*) You will find red diamonds on the left bank; green diamonds on the right bank. Channel crossings appear on most charts. Watch for them carefully for it is important to know when the channel changes direction.

28 Crossing Daymarks on opposite sides of a winding river help you line up the channel as it crosses from one side of the river to the other. Chapter 6, Aids to Navigation, describes ranges in detail.

29 Lighted daymarks (minor lights) make it possible to remain in the channel at night by steering from one white light to another.

30 **Mile Markers** of the Western Rivers System are among the most useful navigation aids on a river. As previously mentioned, they refer to the number of statute miles to the river's mouth. You will find them on daybeacons and in other prominent places. You can fix your position by comparing them with a chart. Note the mileage markers in Figure 164, page 230.

Uniform State Waterway Marking System

31 You will find this system described in Chapter 6, Aids to Navigation, and on Color Plate 4 of that chapter. States use this system to mark their waters.

River Boating

32 The greatest difference between coastal boating and river boating is the constantly changing nature of inland waters. Water depths never stay the same. Currents vary from fast to none at all. Channels move constantly with shifting sand, silt, and mud. Navigational aids move around regularly.

River Currents

33 Most rivers have strong currents that can create problems for both commercial and recreational boats. Currents in the Mississippi and other rivers can reach 8 to 10 miles per hour. (River distance is in statute miles and speed in miles per hour.) Some low powered boats may not be able to make it upstream.

34 After heavy rains, rough water conditions that are dangerous to small boats can occur in rivers and canals. It takes effort and practice to handle a boat in strong currents. Going downstream, a skipper can partially lose control of his boat and be at the mercy of the current. For this reason the Navigation Rules give the right-of-way to vessels traveling downstream.

35 The deepest water and strongest current on most rivers are on the outside of bends. You may use this information to advantage; move to the inside of a bend or get close to the inside shore where current is less.

36 However eddies and shoals may form on the inside of turns. (An *eddy* is a current that moves in the opposite direction to the regular current, often in a circular motion.)

Water Depths

37 Water depths in rivers vary depending on the amount of water coming from upstream. In droughts the water may fall too low to be navigable; in floods it may run high and strong and be littered with trees, logs, and debris. Damming and dredging help to keep a minimum depth of river channels, e.g., 10

feet. Many rivers have depth gauges posted at important points such as bridges and locks.

38 Detailed river charts are available from the Army Corps of Engineers. They are an indispensable tool for safe river boating. Check with the nearest Army Corps of Engineers office for availability of charts of area in which you boat. River charts show depths differently than coastal charts. Check your chart title block to see how depths are indicated.

39 The charts define safe channels with colored and shaded contour lines. Shoal depths beginning nine feet below low water (pool) are shown. (A *pool* is a river level in any given location created by a dam.)

40 Determine water depths by referring to daily river level information given on some weather forecasts and published in local newspapers.

41 Unless you are certain about the depth of the water and the draft of your boat, stay within marked channels. Avoid the temptation to take the shortest route between two points.

42 When the river is flooding, it can extend for miles beyond its normal banks. Because of the widened river it may be difficult or impossible to find the normal channels. This is especially true where channels move from bank to bank. Use common sense, careful boat handling, and make good use of charts and aids to navigation.

River Debris

43 The draining of the surrounding countryside carries much debris into rivers. Logs sometimes float just under the surface; at other times they stand on end and float upright. Keep a lookout for this type of debris. The part you do not see is often larger than that which is visible!

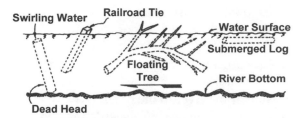

Figure 163   Floating Debris

44 Heavy damage from debris frequently occurs to propellers, shafts, lower unit casings, and hulls. If you hear or feel a thump, stop and check for damage. If you feel an unusual vibration, operate your boat at slow speed until you determine its source.

Reading the River

45 The river bank gives a clue as to the depth of the water. Along a steep bank you can expect relatively deep water up to the shoreline. A gently sloping beach running back a long way from the edge of the water usually means that the water is shallow a long way out from shore.

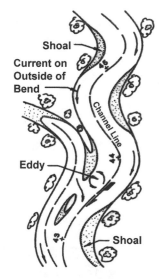

46 You can often tell shallow water by a difference in the color of the water, by ripples when the water is calm, or where there is a patch of quieter water in the midst of choppy water. If you suspect shallow water, slow down to bare steerageway. Engage the propeller only as needed to maintain headway. You may be able to partially raise the propeller on an outboard motor or stern drive.

Figure 164   Typical River Channel

47 Check your wake to see if you are stirring up mud or sand. Place a lookout at the bow to measure the depth of water with a boat hook or weighted line.

Mooring and Anchoring

48 Many rivers have hazardous shorelines which make it difficult to anchor along the shore. Riprap (broken stones), shallow water, and other dangers do not allow safe anchorage. *Safety harbors* in small protected deep-water coves appear on charts and are marked with symbols.

49 Always tie up at the downstream end of an island, especially if you plan to spend the night. If you anchor at the upstream end you could find your boat driven aground in the morning. Always make sure to anchor outside the channel.

50 When you moor alongside a bank, you must find a way to keep your boat off the bank. Setting anchors fore and aft will keep your boat in line with the bank. See Chapter 8, Boat Handling.

Bridges

51 Always approach a bridge slowly and cautiously. Make sure your wake does not create problems for other boats.

52 On many inland lakes and rivers there is no required minimum height for bridges. Maps and charts will show the center of the channel span and its horizontal and vertical clearances. In many cases, there will be enough clearance if you can see the furthermost girder of the bridge from the highest point of your boat. If you have any question about the clearances of a drawbridge, try to contact the bridge tender on VHF Channels 9, 12, 13, or 16.

53 Never ask for a bridge opening if your boat will fit under a closed bridge. You are required to lower radio antennas or moveable masts if necessary.

54 At night, a green light will mark the center of the channel under the bridge, and red lights will mark supporting piers. Stay away from bridge piers. You may not see protective framework until you are close aboard. Strong currents, exposed rocks, and trapped debris may also be present.

55 The signal for requesting a draw bridge opening is one prolonged (4–6 second) blast followed by one short (1 second) blast. If the bridge tender can open the bridge immediately he will return the same signal. If he cannot, or if the bridge is closing, he will sound the danger signal—five short blasts. If you are able to talk with a bridge tender on VHF radio, it is not necessary to sound whistle signals.

Dams and Locks

56 A *dam* is a barrier constructed across a waterway to control the level of water during flooding and droughts.

57 Red lights, *Keep Out, Danger—Dam,* or *Keep Away* signs usually warn boaters of the presence of dams. Water flowing over dams is always dangerous, especially after heavy rains.

58 Under such conditions it is easy for a boat to be carried over the dam. A boat venturing too close to a dam on the downside can be drawn in by water suction and become swamped. It is almost impossible to rescue a boater in a situation such as this. Low dams are extremely dangerous to boat traffic, for they are frequently under water.

59 Locks keep many rivers navigable by allowing boats to get around dams. A lock is a

chamber that is built in or around a dam. It has gates at both ends. A lockmaster controls the valves that fill and empty the lock.

60 Craft of any size may lock through providing they fit in the lock. Lockmasters have authority over all boats entering a lock and you must obey their instructions. A lockmaster may refuse lockage if he considers a vessel to be in an unsafe condition. Some vessels, such as commercial and government boats, have priority in entering a lock. Recreational and noncommercial boats have the lowest priority.

61 You cannot tie up near a lock. You must be prepared to enter when the lockmaster is ready for you. Fishing is not allowed. Horns or sirens will often warn of the opening of lock gates.

62 **Communicate With Lockmasters.** You may contact most lockmasters on VHF radio channels 13 or 16. When the lockmaster answers, identify your boat, request lockage, and give your estimated time of arrival.

63 The sound signals to request a lock opening is the same as for bridges one long and one short. You may find a rope attached to a sound signal to alert the lockmaster. After sounding the signal, move out of the approach area and await instructions.

64 **Locking Through** requires preparation. Place fenders on both sides of your boat. They should be large enough to prevent your boat from rubbing on the lock walls. Lock walls are usually rough and very dirty and can do a lot of damage to a fiberglass boat. You may want to reserve a pair of old fenders and lines for use in locks.

65 Locking lines should be $3/8$ or $1/2$ inch in diameter and at least 75 feet long. In large locks you may need even longer lines. A good rule is that a locking line should be twice the height of the lock. A boat hook is useful.

Make sure that crew members are wearing life preservers and non-slip shoes.

66 Most locks have signal lights similar to highway traffic signals:
   A steady red light—the lockmaster has not seen you
   A flashing red light—the lockmaster has seen you and is asking you to keep clear
   A flashing yellow light—approach the lock slowly
   A flashing green light—enter the lock

67 When directed, approach the lock slowly, with no wake. Watch carefully for exiting boats.

68 **Tying Up in a Lock.** The lockmaster tells you where to tie your boat. In many locks you will make fast to bollards (thick posts) on the side of the lock.

69 Get ready by tying a locking line to one end of your boat. Then come alongside the bollard and loop your line over it. Make a loose turn around a cleat at the other end of your boat with the free end of the line. Hold this free end in your hand—never fasten it permanently to the boat. This way you can always quickly and easily adjust it.

70 If your boat is large, you may need two locking lines: one at the bow and one at the stern, each manned by a crew member. Fasten the end of each line to the boat; one line to the bow, the other to the stern. Each line can then be looped over a bollard and its free end held by a crew member.

Figure 165   Making Fast in a Lock with One Line

71 Never *permanently* tie your boat to the side of a lock! Lines must be free for easy adjustment under any condition.

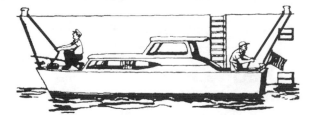

Figure 166   Making Fast in a Lock with Two Lines

72 On occasion you may have to "walk" your lock lines up or down the rungs of a lock ladder, changing from one rung to the next as the boat moves up or down. Be careful to keep hands, fingers, and feet out of harm's way. When in position with locking lines engaged, shut off your engine and stand by to fend off other boats that may come alongside to raft up with your boat.

73 As the water level changes, pay close attention to your lines. Adjust them so that your boat will not drift away from the lock wall. You may have to adjust fenders to protect your boat. Remain in your boat; never climb lock ladders. Be especially alert when the lower gates open. Discharge water on the down-side of a lock may create considerable turbulence.

74 **Leaving a Lock.** Wait for the lockmaster to sound the all-clear signal before starting your boat. Never start your engine until you are sure your bilge is free of all fumes—use your nose! Leave at idle speed, following the instructions of the lockmaster, keeping an eye for boats waiting to enter the lock.

Jetties and Dikes

75 A jetty, sometimes called a dike, is a structure projecting out into the water that directs the flow of water, or protects the shoreline

from erosion. They are usually made of stone riprap or rows of pilings extending from shore. Approach jetties with caution. Many are under the water and not easily seen. Always look for them on your charts.

76 Jetties help to speed up current in a channel. The fast current cleans the channel of silt and sand and helps maintain its depth. Eddies often form downstream of jetties, building up sand bars and mud flats.

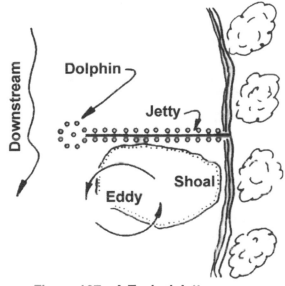

Figure 167   A Typical Jetty

Commercial Vessels

77 Keep well clear of barges whether moored or underway. Mooring lines just below the surface can be invisible. Towboats may pull barges from ahead, or push them from the side or stern. Towboats cannot stop, turn, or maneuver easily.

78 There is poor visibility from the pilot house of a towboat pushing a string of barges. A blind spot of 600 feet to 1300 feet is not unusual, especially if the barges are empty and riding high in the water.

79 Running close alongside or behind a tow-boat is dangerous. The suction from its propellers can pull small boats against its hull. The huge amount of water pushed out to the rear sometimes forms whirlpools a half-mile behind. These can create maneuvering problems for even large boats. Towboat wake also dislodges sunken logs, branches, mud, and debris.

80 Use sound signals required by the Inland Navigation Rules whenever you meet commercial vessels. (See Chapter 12, Navigation Rules). If you have a VHF radio, talk directly with their operators on Channel 13 or 16.

81 Large commercial vessels going downstream usually take outside river bends. Going upstream they may take advantage of lesser currents on inside bends. If you round a bend that obscures your view, sound the warning signal—one prolonged (4–6 second) blast on your whistle. Another vessel entering the bend from the opposite direction should return your signal.

82 Pass towboats on the inside of a bend. If you find yourself in a narrow channel with a tow, always move to the edge of the channel. If there is no room for the tow to pass, try to move outside the channel. If the water is not deep enough, turn around and retreat to a safe position. For all practical purposes, the responsibility for avoiding collision is yours.

83 Most commercial boats have radar. Install a radar reflector on your boat to help the operators of these large vessels see you.

84 Chapter 12, Navigation Rules, describes the navigation lights of commercial vessels. Note that on most western rivers, a vessel pushing does not display the regular two white masthead lights.

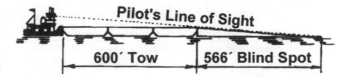

Figure 168   Restricted Visibility From a Towboat

Dredges

85 Dredges can pose problems for boaters. They pump large amounts of water, sand, and silt through long pipes and deposit it ashore or into a barge. In daytime it is easy to see dredges and their pipelines. They show three black day shapes in their rigging—a ball over a diamond over a ball. Pass on the side marked with two black diamonds.

86 At night, dredges show three all-round lights in a vertical line on its mast: red–over–white–over–red. Their pipelines have a row of rapidly flashing yellow lights with two red lights at each end. Pass the dredge on the side showing two green lights.

Lake Boating

87 Much of the above description of river boating also applies to lake boating. Water levels on lakes depend on the amount of rain, and may also change from controlled openings and closings of dam gates. The control of water levels relates to water needs for electrical power, irrigation, and community water supplies.

88 Even on relatively small lakes, water levels can vary greatly. You can anchor in a small cove at night and find yourself aground in the morning. You can also pull your boat up on shore at night and find it out in the lake in the morning. Keep these possibilities in mind when mooring.

Lake Bottoms

89 Often, the only trees cut down in the process of constructing man-made lakes and river pools are those necessary to provide clear areas near shore. Deeper parts of the lake may have standing trees and hedgerows for years to come. Imagine trying to recover your anchor from the top of a tall pine tree in 100 feet of water!

90 In addition, overhead power lines, submerged fences, roots, boulders, sunken barrels, and other debris may come as an unwelcome surprise. Use an anchor trip line.

Storms

91 Storms can develop suddenly over lakes. Hills often block the horizon and you do not notice approaching storms until they are suddenly on you. The same hills tend to channel wind down onto the lakes. Wind can create high waves and water turbulence on lakes just as on coastal waters.

Inland Navigation Rules

92 The Inland Navigation Rules govern the navigable waterways; waters that provide a means of transportation between two states or to the sea. Local regulations may be in effect on all other waters.

93 Follow the Navigation Rules and local regulations wherever you are boating. You need a lookout on a small river just as much as on a large sound. Meeting, passing, and crossing situations occur on lakes as well as rivers and coastal waters. You need navigation lights at night. Be familiar with all of the rules and observe them. See Chapter 12, Navigation Rules.

D

Sources of Charts and Related Publications

The National Ocean Service

1 National Oceanic and Atmospheric Administration, Department of Commerce
Distribution Branch, (N/CG33)
Riverdale MD 20737-1199
Tel. 301-436-6990; FAX 301-436-6829
www://oceanservice.noaa.gov

2 NOS issues charts used by most boaters, including coastal, river, harbor and Great Lakes charts. There are five free Catalogs of Charts, each covering a specific region, showing charts that are available.

3 NOS also prints nine regional Coast Pilots that provide detailed information to supplement NOS nautical charts. Examples are anchorages, channel descriptions, location of fuel piers and haul-out and repair facilities, bridge and cable clearances, hours of drawbridge operation, tide and tidal current information, local weather conditions, navigational hazards, small craft facilities, prominent features, and federal regulations applying to the areas.

- No. 1 Eastport, ME, to Cape Cod, MA
- No. 2 Cape Cod, MA, to Sandy Hook, NJ

- No. 3 Sandy Hook, NJ, to Cape Henry, VA
- No. 4 Cape Henry, VA, to Key West, FL
- No. 5 Gulf of Mexico, Puerto Rico, Virgin Islands
- No. 6 The Great Lakes and the St. Lawrence River
- California, Oregon, Washington, Hawaii
- No.8 Alaska, Dixon Entrance to Cape Spencer
- No.9 Alaska, Cape Spencer to Beaufort Sea

4 NOS also distributes some of the unclassified charts and publications of high seas and foreign waters published by the National Imaging & Mapping Agency. (NIMA is the former Defense Mapping Hydrographic Topographic Center/Defense Mapping Agency). NIMA no longer provides charts to the general public.

5 NOS charts and publications are sold by various authorized sales agents throughout the country, such as marinas and yacht clubs. If you know the chart number, you may purchase charts directly from NOS with a credit card by mail, telephone, or FAX.

Superintendent of Documents

United States Government Printing Office
Washington DC 20402
http://www.gpoaccess.gov/index.html

6   The U.S. Government Printing Office pro-
vides publications such as the U.S. Coast
Guard Light Lists and the U.S. Coast Guard
Navigation Rules.

Tennessee Valley Authority

Maps and Engineering Section
416 Union Avenue
Knoxville TN 37902-2111
615-632-2921
http://www.tva.gov/

7   The Authority produces charts for its reservoirs, and the Tennessee River and its tributaries.

The Great Lakes Cruising Club

20 North Wacker Drive
Chicago IL 60606-2806, Suite 1540
312-372-2344
http://www.glcclub.com/index.htm

U.S. Army Corps of Engineers

8   The U.S. Army Corps of Engineers charts
major inland non-tidal rivers, lakes, reservoirs, and canal systems including the Ohio,
Mississippi, Missouri, and Alabama Rivers.
Charts for these waters are available from
some of their district offices.
http://www.usace.army.mil/

U. S. Army Engineer District, New Orleans

PO Box 60267
New Orleans LA 70160-0267
504-862-2201
Charts of Mississippi and Atchafalaya
Rivers

U. S. Army Engineer District, Vicksburg

4155 Clay St.
Vicksburg MS 39180-3435
601-631-5052
Charts of waters in Mississippi, Arkansas,
and Louisiana

U. S. Army Engineer District, Rock Island

PO Box 2004
Rock Island IL 61204-2004
309-794-5338
Charts of Upper Mississippi River (St. Paul
to the Ohio River) and Illinois River (Chicago to the Mississippi)

Charts of the Lower Mississippi (mouth of
the Ohio River to the Gulf of Mexico)
901-544-3351
Also 800-537-7962

U. S. Army Engineer District, Tulsa

1645 S. 101st East Avenue
Tulsa OK 74128-4629
Public Affairs: 918-669-7366
Charts of McClellan-Kerr Arkansas River
system

U. S. Army Engineer District, Nashville

PO Box 1070
Nashville TN 37202-1070
615-736-7864
Charts of Cumberland and Tennessee Rivers

U. S. Army Engineer District, Little Rock

PO Box 867
Little Rock AR 72203-0867
Public Affairs: 501-324-5551
Charts of McClellan-Kerr
Arkansas River system

Canadian Hydrographic Service—East Coast

Department of Fisheries and Oceans
Chart Distribution Office
PO Box 8080, 1675 Russell Road
Ottawa, Ontario KIG 3H6, Canada
613-998-4931
Fax: 618-998-1217
http://www.chs-shc.dfo-mpo.gc.ca/chs/
The Service provides charts of Canadian coastal and Great Lakes waters and of all but the smallest Canadian lakes and rivers.

Canadian Hydrographic Service—West Coast

Department of Fisheries and Oceans
Chart Distribution Office
PO Box 6000
Sidney, B.C. V8L4B2, Canada
250-363-6358
Fax: 250-363-6841
http://www.chs-shc.dfo-mpo.gc.ca/chs/
Charts of Canadian west coast and western Arctic waters.

Private Publishers

9   Private publishers also reproduce nautical charts, many in chart kit form. Many charts for an area are bound into one chart book.

E

State Boating Law Agencies

1 This is a list of agencies where you can obtain material regarding the boating laws for your area. In many states, this document is free. There may be a local source for this information: County Sheriff's Office, Marine Laws Enforcement Office, or Natural Resources Office.

2 The list includes websites which are frequently subject to change.

Alabama (AL)
Dept. of Conservation & Natural Res.,
Marine Police Div.
64 N. Union St., Rm. 468
Montgomery, AL 36130-3020
Tel.: 334-242-3673
Web: www.dcnr.state.al.us

Alaska (AK)
Dept. of Natural Resources,
Div. Parks and Outdoor Recreation
Office of Boating Safety
550 W. 7th St., Ste. 1370
Anchorage, AK 99501-3561
Tel.: 907-269-8705
Web: www.alaskaboatingsafety.org

Arizona (AZ)
Arizona Game & Fish Dept.
Law Enforcement
2221 W. Greenway Rd.
Phoenix, AZ 85023-4399
Tel.: 602-942-3000
Web: www.azgfd.com

Arkansas (AR)
Arkansas Game & Fish Comm.
Boating Administration
#2 Natural Resources Dr.
Little Rock, AR 72205
Tel.: 501-223-6300
Web: www.agfc.state.ar.us

California (CA)
Dept. of Boating & Waterways
2000 Evergreen St.
Sacramento, CA 95815-3888
Tel.: 916-263-1331
Web: www.dbw.ca.gov

Colorado (CO)
Dept. of Natural Resources
Div. Parks & Outdoor Rec.
13787 S. Hwy. 85
Littleton, CO 80125
Phone: 888-593-BOAT
Web: http://parks.state.co.us/boating

Connecticut (CT)
Dept. of Environmental Protection
Boating Div.
333 Ferry Rd., PO Box 280
Old Lyme, CT 06371-0280
Phone: 860-434-8638
Web: www.dep.state.ct.us

Delaware (DE)
Dept. of Natural Resources &
Environmental Control
Div. Fish & Wildlife Enforcement
89 Kings Hwy.
Dover, DE 19901
Tel.: 302-739-3440
Web: www.dnrec.state.de.us/dnrec2000/
Boating.asp

District of Columbia (DC)
Metro Police Dept.
Harbor Patrol Sect.
550 Water Street, SW
Washington, DC 20024
Tel.: 202-727-4582
Web: www.mpdc.dc.gov

Florida (FL)
Fish & Wildlife Conservation Comm.
620 S. Meridian St.
Tallahassee, FL 32399-1600
Tel.: 850-488-4676
Web: www.floridaconservation.org

Georgia (GA)
Dept. of Natural Resources
Wildlife Resources Div.
Law Enforcement Section
2070 US Hwy. 278, SE
Social Circle, GA 30025
Tel.: 770-918-6408
Web: http://www.gadnr.org

Hawaii (HI)
Dept. of Land & Natural Resources
Div. Boating & Ocean Recreation
333 Queen St., Ste. 300
Honolulu, HI 96813
Tel.: 808-587-1966
Web: www.state.hi.us/dlnr/dbor/dbor

Idaho (ID)
Dept. of Parks & Recreation
Boating Program
PO Box 83720
Boise, ID 83720-0065
Tel.: 208-334-4199
Web: www.idahoparks.org

Illinois (IL)
Dept. of Natural Resources
Ofc. Law Enforcement
One Natural Resources Way
Springfield, IL 62702-1271
Tel.: 217-782-6431
Web: www.dnr.state.il.us

Indiana (IN)
Dept. of Natural Resources
Law Enforcement Div.
402 W. Washington St., Rm. W255-D
Indianapolis, IN 46204
Tel.: 317-232-4010
Web: www.state.in.us/dnr

Iowa (IA)
Dept. of Natural Resources
Conservation and Recreation Div.
Wallace State Ofc. Bldg.
East Ninth & Grand Ave.
Des Moines, IA 50319-0034
Tel.: 515-281-5918
Web: www.iowadnr.com

Kansas (KS)
Dept. of Wildlife & Parks
1020 S. Kansas Ave., Rm. 200
Topeka, KS 66612
Tel.: 785-296-2281
Web: www.kdwp.state.ks.us

Kentucky (KY)
Div. Of Law Enforcement
Dept. of Fish & Wildlife
Tourism Cabinet
#1 Game Farm Road
Frankfort, KY 40601
Tel.: 800-858-1549
Web: www.kdfwr.state.ky.us

Louisiana (LA)
Dept. of Wildlife & Fisheries
Enforcement Div.
PO Box 98000
Baton Rouge, LA 70898-9000
Tel.: 225-765-2999
Web: www.wlf.state.la.us

Maine (Inland) (ME)
Dept. of Inland Fisheries & Wildlife
284 State St.
Augusta, ME 04333
Tel.: 207-287-5220
Web: www.mefishwildlife.com

Maine (Marine) (ME)
Dept. of Marine Resources
State House Sta. #21
Augusta, ME 04333-0021
Tel.: 207-624-6550
Web: www.maine.gov/dmr

Maryland (MD)
Dept. of Natural Resources
Natural Resources Police
Tawes State Office Bldg. E-3
580 Taylor Ave.
Annapolis, MD 21401
Tel.: 410-260-3280
Web: www.dnr.state.md.us

Massachusetts
Dept. of Fisheries, Wildlife &
Environmental Law Enforcement
Div. Law Enforcement
251 Causeway St., Ste. 400
Boston, MA 02114
Tel.: 800-632-8075
Web: www.mass.gov/dfwelc/dle

Michigan (MI)
Dept. of Natural Resources
Law Enforcement Div.
PO Box 30257
Lansing, MI 48909
Tel.: 517-373-9900
Web: www.michigan.gov/dnr

Minnesota (MN)
Dept. of Natural Resources
500 Lafayette Rd.
St. Paul, MN 55155-4046
Tel.: 651-296-6157
Web: www.dnr.state.mn.us

Mississippi (MS)
Dept. of Wildlife, Fisheries & Parks
Law Enforcement Div.
1505 Eastover Drive
Jackson, MS 39211
Tel.: 601-432-2400
Web: www.mdwfp.com

Missouri (MO)
Dept. of Public Safety
Missouri State Water Patrol
PO Box 1368
Jefferson City, MO 65102-1368
Tel.: 573-751-3333
Web: www.mswp.state.mo.us

Montana (MT)
Montana Fish, Wildlife & Parks
Law Enforcement Div.
1420 E. Sixth Ave.
Helena, MT 59620-0701
Tel.: 406-444-2535
Web: www.fwp.state.mt.us

Nebraska (NE)
Nebraska Game & Parks Comm.
Outdoor Education Div.
2200 N. 33rd St.
Lincoln, NE 68503-0370
Tel.: 402-471-0641
Web: www.ngpc.state.ne.us/boating

Nevada (NV)
Div. Of Wildlife
Law Enforcement Bureau
1100 Valley Rd.
Reno, NV 89512-2817
Tel.: 775-688-1500
Web: http://ndow.org

New Hampshire (NH)
NH Deptartment of Safety
Div. Safety Services
31 Dock Rd
Gilford, NH 03246-7627
Tel.: 888-254-2125
Web: www.state.nh.us/safety/ss/

New Jersey (NJ)
New Jersey State Police
Marine Services Unit
PO Box 7068
West Trenton, NJ 08628-0068
Tel.: 609-882-2000, Ext. 6173
Web: www.state.nj.us/njsp.org

New Mexico (NM)
Energy, Minerals & Natural Resources
Dept.
State Parks Div.
Boating Safety Sect.
PO Box 1147
Sante Fe, NM 87505
Tel.: 1-888-NMPARKS
Web:www.emnrd.state.nm.us/nmparks

New York (NY)
Ofc. Parks, Rec. & Historic Pres.
Bureau Marine & Rec. Vehicles
Agency Bldg #1, 13th Floor
Empire State Plaza
Albany, NY 12238-0001
Tel.: 518-474-0445
Web: www.nysparks.com/boats

North Carolina (NC)
Wildlife Resources Comm.
Div. of Enforcement
1717 Mail Service Center
Raleigh, NC 27699-1717
Tel.: 1-800-628-3773
Web: www.ncwildlife.org

North Dakota (ND)
Game & Fish Dept.
Conserv. & Comm. Div.
100 N. Bismarck Expy.
Bismarck, ND 58501-5095
Tel.: 701-328-6352
Web: www.state.nd.us/gnf

Ohio (OH)
Dept. of Natural Resources
Div. of Watercraft
4435 Fountain Sq. Dr., Bldg. A
Columbus, OH 43224-1362
Tel.: 614-265-6480; 1-877-4BOATER
Web:www.dnr.state.oh.us/odnr/watercraft

Oklahoma (OK)
Oklahoma Highway Patrol
Lake Patrol Sect.
PO Box 11415
Oklahoma City, OK 73136-0415
Tel.: 405-341-5067
Web: www.dps.state.ok.us

Oregon (OR)
Oregon State Marine Board
435 Commercial St. NE, #400
PO Box 14145
Salem, OR 97309-5065
Tel.: 503-378-8587
Web: www.boatoregon.com

Pennsylvania (PA)
Pennsylvania Fish & Boat Comm.
PO Box 67000
Harrisburg, PA 17106-7000
Tel.: 717-705-7800
Web: www.fish.state.pa.us

Puerto Rico (PR)
Dept. of Env. & Nat. Resources
Commissioner of Navigation
PO Box 9066600
Plaza De Tierra Station
San Juan, PR 00906-6600
Tel.: 787-724-2340

Rhode Island (RI)
Dept. of Environmental Management
235 Promenade St.
Providence, RI 02908
Tel.: 401-222-4462
Web: www.state.ri.us/dem.htm

South Carolina (SC)
Dept. of Natural Resources
Boating Education Office
1000 Assembly St.
Columbia, SC 29201
Tel.: 1-800-277-4301
Web: www.dnr.state.sc.us

South Dakota (SD)
Dept. of Game, Fish & Parks
Div. Of Wildlife
523 E. Capital
Pierre, SD 57501-3182
Tel.: 605-773-3381
Web: www.state.sd.us/gfp

Tennessee (TN)
Tennessee Wildlife Resources Agcy.
Boating Div.
PO Box 40747
Nashville, TN 37204
Tel.: 615-781-6682
Web: www.state.tn.us/twra

Texas (TX)
Parks & Wildlife Dept.
Law Enforcement Div.
4200 Smith School Road
Austin, TX 78744
Tel.: 512-389-4800
Web: www.tpwd.state.tx.us

Utah (UT)
Division of Parks & Wildlife
1594 W. N. Temple, Ste. 116
Salt Lake City, UT 84114-6001
Tel.: 801-538-7220
Web: www.stateparks.utah.gov

Vermont (VT)
State Police
Recreational Enf. & Educ. Unit
2777 St. George Road
Williston, VT 05495-7429
Tel.: 802-878-7854
Web: www.dps.state.vt.us

U.S. Virgin Islands (VI)
Dept. of Planning & Natural Resources—
Enforcement
Cyril E. King Airport, 2nd Flr.
St. Thomas, VI 00802
Tel.: 340-774-3320, Ext 5186

Virginia (VA)
Dept. of Game & Inland Fisheries
4010 W. Broad St.
PO Box 11104
Richmond, VA 23230-1104
Tel.: 804-367-1000
Web: www.dgif.state.va.us

Washington (WA)
Washington State Parks & Recreation
Commission
Boating Programs
7150 Cleanwater Lane, Bldg. 17
PO Box 42650
Olympia, WA 98504-2650
Tel.: 360-586-6590
Web: www.parks.wa.gov

West Virginia (WV)
Div. Natural Resources
Law Enforcement Sect.
Capitol Complex, Bldg. 3
Charleston, WV 25305
Tel.: 304-558-2784
Web: www.wvdnr.gov

Wisconsin (WI)
Dept. of Natural Resources
Bureau of Law Enforcement
101 S. Webster St
PO Box 7291
Madison, WI 53707-7291
Tel.: 608-266-2621
Web: www.dnr.state.wi.us

Wyoming (WY)
Wyoming Game & Fish Dept.
5400 Bishop Blvd.
Cheyenne, WY 82006
Tel.: 307-777-4600
Web: http://gf.state.wy.us

F

Coast Guard District Offices

These are the United States Coast Guard District Offices and the contacts for boating safety at those offices for the various United States, Territories, and Possessions.

1st Coast Guard District
Office of Search and Rescue
408 Atlantic Ave.
Boston, MA 02110-3350
Phone: 617-223-8464
Web: www.uscg.mil/d1
Connecticut, Maine, Massachusetts, New Hampshire, New York, Rhode Island, Vermont

5th Coast Guard District
Chief of Operations
431 Crawford St.
Portsmouth, VA 23704-5004
Phone: 757-398-6204
Web. www.uscg.mil/d5
Delaware, District of Columbia, Maryland, New Jersey, North Carolina, Pennsylvania, Virginia

7th Coast Guard District
Chief of Operations
909 SE First Ave.
Miami, FL 33131-3050
Phone: 305-415-7057
Web: www.uscg.mil/d7
Florida, Georgia, Puerto Rico, South Carolina, U.S. Virgin Islands

8th Coast Guard District
Chief, Recreational Boating Safety
501 Magazine St.
New Orleans, LA 70130-3396
Phone: 504-589-6770
Web: www.uscg.mil/d8
Alabama, Arkansas, Colorado, Illinois, Indiana, Iowa, Kansas, Kentucky, Louisiana, Mississippi, Missouri, Nebraska, New Mexico, North Dakota, Oklahoma, South Dakota, Tennessee, Texas, West Virginia, Wyoming

9th Coast Guard District
Office of Law Enforcement
1240 E. 9th St.
Cleveland, OH 44199-2060
Phone: 216-902-6094
Web: www.uscg.mil/d9/d9boating/boatingsafety.html
Michigan, Minnesota, Ohio, Wisconsin

11th Coast Guard District
Chief of Operations
Building 51-1, Coast Guard Island
Alameda, CA 94501-5100
Phone: 510-437-5364
Web: www.uscg.mil/d11
Arizona, California, Nevada, Utah

13th Coast Guard District
Chief of Search & Rescue
915 Second Ave.
Seattle, WA 98174-1067
Phone: 206-220-7257
Web: www.uscg.mil/d13
Idaho, Montana, Oregon, Washington

14th Coast Guard District
Chief of Operations
300 Ala Moana Blvd., Rm. 9-236
Honolulu, HI 96850
Phone: 800-818-8725, Option #5, or 808-541-2161
Web: www.uscg.mil/d14
Hawaii, Guam, American Samoa, Northern Mariana Islands

17th Coast Guard District
Chief Maritime Operations
P.O. Box 25517
Juneau, AK 99802-5517
Phone: 907-463-2297
Web: www.uscg.mil/d17
Alaska

G

Navigation Light Supplement

Navigation Light Requirements
Powerboats Underway

1 Light requirements on power-driven vessels depend upon the length of the vessel, with some permissible options:

Vessel Length	White Masthead Light Forward	Sidelights Red & Green	White Sternlight	Options
Less than 39.4 ft (12m)	Required (2nd optional)	Required	Required	Required Options 1–2–3 Below
Greater than 39.4 ft, but less than 65.6 ft (20m)	Required (2nd optional)	Required	Required	Required Option 1 Below
Greater than 65.6 ft, but less than 164 ft (50m)	Required (2nd optional)	Required	Required	Required
Greater than 164 ft (50m)	2 required, 1 aft of and higher than the forward	Required	Required	Required

Table 32   Power-Driven Boat Light Requirements

2 **Option 1.** Under International and Inland Rules, the sidelights of a vessel under 65.6 ft (20m) long may be combined into one lantern carried on the fore and aft centerline of the vessel.

3 **Option 2.** Both Inland and International Rules allow a power-driven vessel less than 39.4 feet (12 m) to exhibit an all-round white light and sidelights, in place of masthead light, stern light, and sidelights.

4 **Option 3.** Under International Rules only, a vessel less than 2 3 feet (7 m) with a maximum speed of less than 7 knots, may exhibit an all-round white light in place of masthead and sternlights. It should display sidelights, if practicable.

Navigation Light Requirements
Sailboats Under Both Sail and Power

5 Sailboats under both sail and power must exhibit the lights of a power driven vessel, as described above. However, during daylight hours, International Rules require a sailboat under both sail and power to display a black conical day shape, pointed end down.

6 This is not required under Inland Rules, if the boat is less than 39.4 feet (12m), although the shape may be used.

Navigation Light Requirements
Sailing Vessels Underway

Vessel Length	Sidelights Red & Green	White Sternlight	Options
Less than 23 ft (7m)	Required	Required	Options 1–2–3–4 Below
Greater than 23 ft, but less than 65.6 ft (20m)	Required	Required	Options 1–2–3 Below
Greater than 65.6 ft, but less than 164 ft (50m)	Required	Required	Option 3 Below

Table 33   Sailboat Light Requirements

7 Light requirements for sailing vessels not under auxiliary power depend upon the length of the vessel.

8 They do not display a masthead light. Their sidelight and sternlight requirements are the same as for a powerboat of the same size.

9 **Option 1.** The sidelights of a vessel under 65.6 ft (20m) in length may be combined into 1 lantern carried on the fore and aft centerline of the vessel.

10 **Option 2.** A sailing vessel under 65.6 feet (20 m) may combine sidelights and sternlight into 1 lantern carried near or at the top of the mast. This tri-color light is recommended

for vessels sailed offshore, because it will be more easily seen. It must not be used when under power.

11 **Option 3.** A sailing vessel underway, in addition to sidelights and sternlight, may exhibit at or near the top of the mast, an all-round red light over an all-round green light. (These lights may not be used with the combination lantern option.)

12 **Option 4.** If it is not practicable for sailing vessels under 23 feet (7 m) to exhibit sidelights and sternlights, they may carry an electric torch or lantern showing a white light to be displayed in sufficient time to prevent collision.

Navigation Light Visibility Requirements

13 The required visibility of vessel lights depends on the length of the vessel.

14 Larger vessels have different requirements than those shown.

Navigation Light Visibility Requirements

Light	Vessel Length	
	Less than 34 Feet	Greater than 39.4 feet, but less than 65.6 feet (20 meters)
White Masthead Light	2 miles	3 miles
Green & Red Sidelights	1 mile	2 miles
White Sternlight	2 miles	2 miles
All-Around Lights	2 miles	2 miles

Table 34   Light Visibility Requirements

Complete this form before going boating and *leave it with a reliable person* who can be depended upon to notify the Coast Guard of other rescue organization in case you do not return as scheduled. **Do not file this form with the Coast Guard.**

A word of Caution: If you are delayed by other than an emergency, inform the holder of your float plan, the local authority, and/or the Coast Guard of your delay to prevent an unnecessary search for you!

FLOAT PLAN

A float plan template for on-line completion and printing may be found in the safety pages at http://usps.org/

NAME OF PERSON FILING THIS PLAN	PHONE NUMBER

DESCRIPTION OF BOAT

TYPE		COLOR	LENGTH	TRIM
REGISTRATION NUMBER	MAKE	NAME		

PERSONS ABOARD

NAME	AGE	ADDRESS	PHONE NUMBER

ENGINES

TYPE	HOW MANY?	HORSEPOWER	FUEL CAPACITY

SURVIVAL EQUIPMENT (*Check as appropriate*)

☐ LIFE PRESERVERS   ☐ FLARES   ☐ SIGNAL MIRROR   ☐ HORN   ☐ SMOKE SIGNALS   ☐ FLASHLIGHT

☐ RAFT OR DINGHY   ☐ EPRIB   ☐ PADDLES   ☐ FOOD   ☐ WATER   ☐ ANCHOR(S)

RADIO   ☐ YES   ☐ NO

TYPE	FREQUENCIES	CALL SIGN

TRIP EXPECTATIONS

LEAVING FROM:	DATE	TIME AM / PM
GOING TO:	RETURN BY:	TIME AM / PM
BUT IN NO EVENT LATER THAN:	DATE	TIME AM / PM

OTHER PERTINENT INFORMATION

AUTOMOBILE/TRAILER

MAKE	COLOR	LICENSE NUMBER
TRAILER LICENSE NUMBER	WHERE PARKED	

IF NOT RETURNED BY ABOVE DATE, CALL:

US Coast Guard:	PHONE NUMBER	
Local Authority:	PHONE NUMBER	NAME

Distress Communications Form

Complete this form now (except for items 6 through 9) and post it near your radiotelephone

Speak: SLOWLY—CLEARLY—CALMLY

1. Make sure the radiotelephone is turned "On."
2. Select either *VHF Channel 16 (156.8 MHz) or 2182 kHz.*
3. Press the microphone button, hold it close to your lips without touching them and say:
   "MAYDAY—MAYDAY—MAYDAY"
4. Say:
   "THIS IS _____, _____, _____**."**
             your boat's name   your boat's name   your boat's name
5. Say:
   "MAYDAY, _____
              your boat's name
6. Tell where you are. (What navigational aids or landmarks are near?)
7. State the nature of your emergency.
8. Give the number of adults and children aboard and the condition of any who may be injured.
9. Estimate the present seaworthiness of the boat.
10. Briefly describe the boat.
    "_____" State Registration Number.
    "_____" Length of the boat. "_____" Draft of the boat
    "_____" Type of boat. "_____" Hull color. "_____" Trim color
    "_____" Masts. "_____" Power. "_____" Construction
    Say anything else you think will help someone find you.
11. Say:
    "I WILL BE LISTENING ON CHANNEL 16 (2182)."
12. Say:
    "THIS IS _____**, OVER."**
               your boat's name
13. Now, release the microphone button and listen.
    Make sure the volume control is about halfway to maximum and the "Squelch" control is
    all the way to minimum.
    Someone should answer immediately. If not, go back to step 3 and repeat the call.
    If there is still no answer and you hear a "hissing" sound when you release the
    microphone button, make sure the "Power" or "Level" or "H/L" control is in the
    high power "H" or "25 Watt" position. There may also be a "CH16" button to push.
    Do not panic. Stay calm and make sure the radiotelephone is working. When you press
    the microphone button a red (green) light should illuminate on the controls.

Boating Accident Report

Complete all Blocks
(Not Applicable, Mark "NA")

Operators and owners of recreational boats must file a written report if an accident results in: (a) loss of life or disappearance from a vessel (report within 48 hours); (b) an injury requiring medical treatment beyond first aid (report within 10 days); or (c) complete loss of the boat or property damage in excess of $500 (report within 10 days). Submit your report to the authorities in the state where the accident occurred. This form is provided to help you if you must file a written report.

Accident Data

Date of Accident	Time ☐ AM ☐ PM	Name of Body of Water	Location (give location precisely)

Number of Vessels Involved	Nearest City of Town	County	State	ZIP Code

Weather
(Check all that apply)
☐ Clear   ☐ Rain
☐ Cloudy ☐ Snow
☐ Fog   ☐ Hazy

Water Conditions
☐ Calm (Waves Less than 6')
☐ Choppy (Waves 6" to 2')
☐ Rough (Waves 2' to 6')
☐ Very Rough (Greater than 6')
☐ Strong Current

Temperature
(Estimated)
Air _____ °F
Water_____ °F

Wind
☐ None
☐ Light (0–6)
☐ Moderate (7–14)
☐ Strong (15–25)
☐ Storm (over 25)

Visibility
Day   Night
☐ Good ☐
☐ Fair ☐
☐ Poor ☐

Name of Operator	Operator's Address

Operator's Phone Number

Operator's Gender
☐ Male   ☐ Female

Date of Birth
Month _____
Day _____
Year _____

Operator's Experience
☐ None
☐ Under 100 Hours
☐ ≥ Hours

Boating Safety Instruction
☐ USPS Course
☐ USCG Auxiliary Course
☐ State Course
☐ American Red Cross
☐ None

Name of Owner	Owner's Address

Owner's Phone Number	Number of People Aboard	Number of People Being Towed	Rented Boat? ☐ Yes ☐ No

Boat No. 1 (Your Boat)

Boat Registration or Documentation Number	State	Hull Identification Number	Boat Name

Boat Manufacturer	Length	Model	Year Built

Type of Boat
☐ Open Motorboat
☐ Cabin Motorboat
☐ Auxiliary Sail
☐ Sail (only)
☐ Rowboat
☐ Pontoon Boat
☐ Houseboat

Hull Material
☐ Wood
☐ Aluminum
☐ Steel
☐ Fiberglass
☐ Rubber/Vinyl/Canvas
☐ Other (specify)

Engine
☐ Outboard
☐ Inboard
☐ Inboard/Outboard (I/O)
☐ Airboat
☐ Diesel
☐ Electric
Total Horsepower
_____

Propulsion
☐ Propeller
☐ Water Jet
☐ Air Thrust
☐ Manual
☐ Sail
☐ No. of Engines _____

Personal Flotation Devices
(PFDs): Was boat adequately equipped with Coast Guard Approved PFDs?
☐ Yes   ☐ No
Were PFDs Accessible?
☐ Yes   ☐ No
Fire Extinguisher On Board?
☐ Yes   ☐ No
Fire Extinguisher Used?
☐ Yes   ☐ No

Information At Time of Accident

Operation
(Check all applicable)
☐ Cruising
☐ Changing Direction
☐ Changing Speed
☐ Drifting
☐ Towing
☐ Being Towed
☐ Rowing/Paddling
☐ Sailing
☐ Launching
☐ Docking/Undocking
☐ At Anchor
☐ Tied To Dock/Moored
☐ Other (Specify)

Activity
(Check all applicable)
☐ Fishing
☐ Tournament
☐ Hunting
☐ Swimming/Diving
☐ Making Repairs
☐ Waterskiing/Tubing/etc.
☐ Racing
☐ Whitewater Sports
☐ Fueling
☐ Starting Engine
☐ Non-Recreational
☐ Other (Specify)

Estimated Speed (MPH)
None
☐   <10
☐   10–20
☐   21–40
☐   > 40

Type
☐ Grounding
☐ Capsizing
☐ Flooding/Swamping
☐ Sinking
☐ Fire Or Explosion (Fuel)
☐ Fire Or Explosion (Other)
☐ Skier Mishap
☐ Collision With Vessel
☐ Collision With Fixed Object
☐ Collision With Floating Object
☐ Fell Overboard
☐ Fall In Boat
☐ Struck By Boat
☐ Struck By Motor/Propeller
☐ Struck Submerged Object
☐ Hit And Run
☐ Other (Specify)

Contributing Factors?
(Check all applicable)
☐ Weather
☐ Excessive Speed
☐ Improper Lookout
☐ Restricted Vision
☐ Overloading
☐ Improper Loading
☐ Hazardous Waters
☐ Alcohol Use
☐ Drug Use
☐ Hull Failure
☐ Machinery Failure
☐ Equipment Failure
☐ Operator Inexperience
☐ Operator Inattention
☐ Congested Waters
☐ Passenger/Skier Behavior
☐ Dam/Lock
☐ Other (Specify)

Injury (If more than two injuries, attach additional forms)

Name of Victim #1	Address of Victim

Date of Birth	Medical Aid Beyond First Aid? ☐ Yes ☐ No Admitted to Hospital? ☐ Yes ☐ No	Describe Injury

Was PFD Worn? ☐ Yes ☐ No **Prior to Accident?** ☐ Yes ☐ No **If No, Was it Put On As a Result of the Accident?** ☐ Yes ☐ No
Was it Inflatable? ☐ Yes ☐ No

Name of Victim #2	Address of Victim

Date of Birth	Medical Aid Beyond First Aid? ☐ Yes ☐ No Admitted to Hospital? ☐ Yes ☐ No	Describe Injury

Was PFD Worn? ☐ Yes ☐ No **Prior to Accident?** ☐ Yes ☐ No **If No, Was it Put On As a Result of the Accident?** ☐ Yes ☐ No
Was it Inflatable? ☐ Yes ☐ No

Death (If more than two fatalities, attach additional forms)

Name of Victim	Address of Victim	Was PFD Worn? Yes No
Date of Birth Male Female	Death Caused by ☐ Drowning ☐ Other ☐ Disappearance	
Name of Victim	Address of Victim	Was PFD Worn? Yes No
Date of Birth Male Female	Death Caused by ☐ Drowning ☐ Other ☐ Disappearance	

Other People Aboard your Boat (If more than two people, attach additional forms)

Name	Address

Date of Birth	Was PFD Worn? ☐ Yes ☐ No If No, As a Result of Accident? ☐ Yes ☐ No	Prior to Accident? ☐ Yes ☐ No Was it Inflatable? ☐ Yes ☐ No

Name	Address

Date of Birth	Was PFD Worn? ☐ Yes ☐ No If No, As a Result of Accident? ☐ Yes ☐ No	Prior to Accident? ☐ Yes ☐ No Was it Inflatable? ☐ Yes ☐ No

Boat No. 2 (If more than two vessels, attach additional forms)

Name of Operator	Operator Address
Operator Phone Number	Boat Registration or Documentation Number State
Name of Owner	Owner Address
Owner Phone Number	

Property Damage

Estimated Amount $	Your Boat and Contents $	Other Boat(s) and Contents $	Other Property $
Describe Property Damaged			

Witnesses Not On Your Boat

Name	Address	Phone Number
Name	Address	Phone Number

Person Completing Report

Name	Address	Phone Number
Signature	Qualification ☐ Operator ☐ Owner ☐ Investigator ☐ Other	Date

Accident Description (Use Separate Sheet of Paper)
Describe what happened (sequence of events). Include failure of equipment. Include a diagram if needed. Continue on additional sheets if necessary. Include any information regarding the involvement of alcohol and/or drugs in causing or contributing to the accident. Include any descriptive information about the use of PFDs. (Use additional sheets of paper as necessary.)

I

Glossary

A

abaft
Behind, aft of.

abeam
Off the boat at right angles to centerline.

adrift
Unattached to shore or bottom, floating out of control.

aft, after
At, near, or toward the stern.

aground
Touching or stuck on the bottom.

ahead
1. The direction toward the bow of a boat (relative to the position of the observer). 2. In front of a boat. 3. Moving in a forward direction. Compare astern.

aids to navigation
Charted objects available to assist in determination of position or safe course or to warn of danger (e.g., buoys, beacons, fog signals, lights, radio beacons, range marks). Also, any electronic device used for navigation.

amidships
In or near the middle of the boat.

anchor
Device used to secure boat to bottom of body of water.

anchorage
Suitable or designated place where boats anchor.

astern
1. The direction toward the stern of the boat (relative to the position of the observer). 2. In back of or behind a boat. 3. Moving in reverse (backwards). Compare ahead.

athwartship
Direction at right angles to the centerline of a boat.

atmosphere
The envelope of air surrounding the earth.

B

backstay
Part of standing rigging, usually cable, that supports a mast from aft.

bail
To remove water by scooping it out with a bucket.

beacon
Anything that serves as a signal or indication for guidance or warning. A fixed (non-floating) aid to navigation.

beam
1. Maximum width of a boat. 2. A horizontal athwartship support for the deck.

beam sea
Sea that is abeam.

bearing
1. Horizontal direction of an object from an observer, expressed as an angle from a reference direction, e.g., compass bearing, true bearing, relative bearing. 2. A device for supporting a rotating shaft with minimum friction. May take the form of a metal sleeve (a bushing), a set of balls (a ball bearing), or a set of pins around a shaft (a roller or needle bearing).

below
Beneath the deck.

bend
1. To make fast a sail to a spar or stay. 2. A knot to secure a line to another line or object.

bilge
Lowest part of a boat's interior.

bitt
A perpendicular post through the deck used for securing lines and cables.

bitter end
The inboard end of a line, chain, or cable; the end made fast to the vessel, as opposed to the working end, which may be attached to an anchor, cleat, or other vessel.

bollard
Stout post on a deck, wharf, or pier for securing mooring lines.

boot top
Distinctive stripe on exterior of hull just above the waterline.

bow
Forward end of a boat.

bow chocks
Fittings (usually metal) on deck at the bow, through which mooring and anchor lines are led.

bow line
A line used at the bow of a vessel.

bowline
Knot used to form an eye or loop in the end of a line. (Pronounced "bo-lin".)

bridle
A length of line or wire rope with both ends secure (or a secured loop) to the middle of which another line is attached.

broach
Turn a boat broadside to wind or waves, subjecting it to possible capsizing.

bulkhead
Vertical partition separating compartments in a boat.

bulwark
Portion of hull extending above the deck.

buoy
Anchored floating device used as an aid to navigation. May carry a light, horn, whistle, bell, gong, or combination for identification. Also, may be used to mark a mooring (i.e. anchor buoy).

buoyancy
The upward force exerted by a fluid on a body or object in that fluid. The upward force that keeps a boat floating.

C

cabin
The enclosed or decked-over living space of a boat.

capsize
To turn over, upset.

cast off
To let go a line; to set loose, unfasten; to undo all mooring lines in preparation for departure.

catamaran
Boat with twin, narrow hulls connected by a deck or crossbeams resulting in a wide beam and good stability.

catboat
Sailboat with a mast stepped near the bow, and no jib.

centerboard
A pivoted board that can be lowered through a slot in the keel to reduce leeway.

centerline
Fore-and-aft line that runs along the exact center of a boat.

chafing gear
Sacrificial wrapping around lines, rigging or spars to prevent wear.

chock
1. Fitting to guide a line or cable. 2. Wedge or block to keep an object from moving.

cleat
Fitting, usually with two projecting horns, to which lines are made fast.

clove hitch
A knot used to secure a line temporarily to a bitt, spar, or rope.

coaming
Vertical structure around a hatch, cockpit or skylight to repel water.

cockpit
Well or sunken space in the deck.

coil
To arrange a line in loops.

compass course
The course by boat's compass. The angle between the boat's keel and the north point of the compass card when the boat is on course.

compass error
Combined effect of variation and deviation.

cordage
A general term for all types of rope.

course (C)
The direction in which a boat is steered through the water.

course over ground
Actual direction of travel of a boat over the bottom. (This is a term in common usage, although *course* is a misnomer. The path of a boat with respect to the bottom is *track*.)

course steered
The direction in which the bow of the boat is pointed when underway.

crown
The point on an anchor where the shank joins the arms.

cuddy
A shelter cabin in a small boat.

current
1. The horizontal movement of water. 2. The movement of electrons through a conductor.

cutter
A single-masted boat with mainsail and usually two headsails, with the mast stepped close to amidships (from 40% to 50% aft of the bow, versus 33% for a sloop).

D

daggerboard
A sliding board that can be lowered through the keel to reduce leeway.

Danforth® anchor
An anchor with long, pointed, hinged flukes with great holding power. (Fortress®, West Marine®, Hooker®, and Suncor® are other examples of this type of anchor.)

datum
The reference plane from which depths of water are measured and recorded on charts (as "charted depths" or "soundings") and, in coastal waters, to which height of tide is added algebraically to determine depth of the water.

daybeacon, daymark
Unlighted fixed aid to navigation.

dead reckoning (DR)
Calculating a boat's position based on its course, speed, and time run from a previous position.

decibel (db)
The standard unit for measuring relative power levels. It is also used to indicate power levels above or below a standard reference level.

deck
The portion of the boat that covers the hull.

deck log
Journal kept on board to record all information pertaining to boat movement, position, and important events.

deviation
Disturbing effect of boat's magnetic field upon its compass.

dinghy
Small open boat used as a tender or lifeboat.

displacement
The weight of water displaced by a floating vessel; hence, the weight of the vessel itself.

displacement hull
A hull that maintains its full displacement of water whether at rest or moving at various speeds (as opposed to a planing hull that generally decreases its displacement with increased speed).

distress call
See Mayday.

dock
1. An area of water, within which a vessel can be made fast, between two landing piers or wharves. 2. To guide a vessel alongside a float, pier, or wharf.

DR position
The presumed position of a vessel on a DR track. See dead reckoning.

draft
1. Depth of water needed to float a boat. 2. The fullness or "belly" of a sail.

E

ease
To let out a line gradually.

ebb current
A tidal current in which the flow of water is generally away from the major land mass and towards the open sea. (Often incorrectly termed "ebb tide.")

eddy
A small whirl or circling movement of a fluid, such as air or water, embedded within a larger current.

even keel
A boat is on an even keel when it is floating level.

eye splice
A permanent loop in the end of a rope.

F

fast
Secure: to make something fast is to secure it.

fastenings
Screws or nails used to hold parts of a boat together.

fathom
Nautical linear measurement equal to 6 feet.

fender
Protective device between a boat and another object.

fid
Tapered tool used in splicing. See marlinespike.

figure-eight knot
A stopper knot; used to keep the bitter end of a line from running through a block.

fix
Relatively accurate position determined without reference to any former position. Usually determined by nearness to a known charted object or by crossed (intersecting) lines of position

flood current
A tidal current in which the flow of water is generally towards the major land mass from the open sea; (often incorrectly termed flood tide).

fluke
Flattened end of an anchor arm which bites into the ground.

fog
Minute water droplets suspended in the atmosphere. Differs from a cloud only in that it is at the surface instead of aloft.

fore-and-aft
Parallel to the centerline or keel.

foresail
The sail set from a schooner's foremast.

forestay
A stay below and aft of the headstay on a yacht carrying two headsails. Also used as the term for headstay.

forward
Toward the bow.

foul
Jammed, entangled; not clear; being hindered or impeded.

foul ground
Bottom that is unsuitable as an anchorage because holding qualities of an anchor are poor or obstructions exist.

frame
Athwartship structural member (rib) which gives shape and stiffening to the hull and to which planking is attached.

freeboard
Vertical distance from the water surface to the lowest point where unwanted water could come aboard.

frequency modulation
Transmission of intelligence by varying a radio frequency about its center frequency or "carrier."

G

galley
Area where food is stored and cooked; nautical kitchen.

gear
General name for all non-permanent nautical equipment, including crew's clothing and personal effects.

give-way vessel
A term, from the Navigation Rules, used to describe the vessel that must yield in meeting, crossing, or overtaking situations. Compare stand-on vessel.

ground tackle
Anchor with rode and related gear.

grounding
A slang term, sometimes used for "having run aground."

gunwale
Upper edge or rail of a boat. (Pronounced "gun'el".)

gust
A sudden, brief increase in wind speed.

H

halyard
Line for hoisting sails or flags.

hatch
Closable opening in the deck.

haze
Fine salt, dust, or other particles in the air, too small to be seen individually, reducing visibility slightly or moderately but seldom below 3/4 mile.

head
1. Marine toilet and its compartment. 2. Upper corner of a triangular sail or upper edge of a four-sided sail. 3. Upper end of the mast, masthead. 4. Foremost part of a boat, bow

heading
Direction in which a boat is pointing at a given moment.

headway
Boat's forward momentum.

heave to
To bring a boat into a position where there is little or no headway, usually with the bow into the wind or current.

heel
Incline to one side due to force of wind or waves.

height of tide
The vertical distance between the surface of tidal water at a given moment and the datum (reference plane) from which depths are measured and recorded on charts of the area. Values may be + or − and are added algebraically to the charted depth to give the depth of water.

helm
The tiller or wheel and related steering gear.

helmsman
The one who steers the boat with the tiller or wheel.

hitch
A knot used to secure a rope fast to another rope or object.

hoist
To raise a sail or flag. Also, the length of a sail's luff.

hull
Basic structure and shell of a boat.

hurricane
A tropical cyclone with wind speeds of 73 miles per hour or greater or of 64 knots or greater.

I

impeller
A rotor or wheel with blades used to pump water or other fluids.

inboard
Toward the centerline of the boat; inside the boat.

inboard-outboard (I/O)
Propulsion system consisting of an inboard engine connected through the transom to an outboard drive unit.

internal combustion
Burning of fuel within an enclosed space.

international dateline (IDL)
The boundary between the - 12 and + 12 time zones, corresponding approximately with 180th meridian.

J

jib
Triangular sail set on a stay forward of the mast.

jib downhaul
A line from the head of a jib to block near the tack and then leading aft. Used to douse the jib without going forward.

jury rig
Makeshift repair or substitute.

K

kedge
1. Move boat by pulling it up to its anchor. 2. Type of anchor.

keel
Main centerline structural member (backbone) of a boat. Also, downward extension of hull to increase lateral resistance and stability.

ketch
A two-masted sailboat with the after mast stepped forward of the rudder post.

knot
1. General term for securing a line to an object, another line, or itself. 2. Unit of speed of one nautical mile per hour.

L

lanyard
Short line used as a handle or to secure an object.

lay
1. To lay a mark is to be able to reach it in a single tack, close-hauled. 2. The lay of a line is the direction in which its strands are twisted.

lay to
To lie without headway either to a sea anchor, to lines streamed over the side, or merely drifting (lying ahull).

lee (lee side)
Side away or opposite that from which the wind blows. Also, area sheltered from the wind.

lee shore
One onto which wind or current can force a boat; shore to leeward of boat.

leeway
1. Sideways movement of a boat through the water caused by wind. 2. The angular difference due to wind between the true course steered and the true course over ground.

lightning
A visible electrical discharge, generally produced during a thunderstorm.

line of position (LOP)
1. A line, usually plotted on a chart, along which the boat lies, as determined from a single observation. 2. A visual or electronic reference line from or about a known navigational aid.

line of sight
Line of direct visual observation from one point to another.

list
Inclination of a boat to one side due to weight distribution.

LOA
Length overall.

locker
A storage or stowage compartment.

log
1. Instrument to measure distance or speed through the water. 2. A book in which all matters pertaining to a vessel's navigation are recorded.

log book
See deck log and log.

loran
An electronic navigation system for establishing lines of position by using the time difference between the reception of signals from different terrestrial locations.

lubber's line
A compass reference oriented parallel to the fore-and-aft keel line of the vessel.

M

mainsail
Boat's principal sail, set aft of mainmast, (pronounced "mains'el").

marlinespike
A pointed steel tool used in splicing to open the strands of a rope or cable. See fid.

marlinespike seamanship
General knowledge of knots, bends, hitches, splices, and care of lines (rope).

mast
1. A vertical spar on a sailboat, on which sails may be set. 2. A vertical spar on a powerboat, from which may be flown a steadying sail or flags and burgees, and which can be used with a boom to lift gear.

masthead
The top of the mast.

Maximum Capacities Label
Required on boats less than 20 feet in length showing the number of people, total weight of those people; combined weight of persons, motor, and gear; the maximum horsepower of a motor that can be used on the boat.

Mayday
The term used to signify an urgent distress communication under international radiotelephone procedures; the highest priority transmission, indicating there is immediate danger to a vessel or to someone on board.

meridian
A great circle of the earth passing through both poles in the direction of true north or true south.

mooring
Permanent ground tackle to which a boat is attached or moored. A place where vessels are kept at anchor.

N

nautical mile
A unit of distance equal to one minute of latitude and equal to approximately 6,076 feet, or 1.15 statue miles.

O

offshore
A direction away from the shore, as offshore wind.

onshore
Towards the shore, from seaward, as onshore wind.

outboard
Toward the outside of a boat.

outboard motor
An engine with propeller attached, designed to be fastened to the transom of a boat.

P

painter
Line tied to the bow of a dinghy to tow or secure it.

Pan-Pan
The term used to signify an urgent communication under international radiotelephone procedures; the second highest priority transmission, indicating that the safety of the vessel or someone on board is involved, but the need for assistance is not immediate. (Pronounced *pahn-pahn*)

pay out
Slacken or let out a line gradually.

pendant
Short rope serving as an extension of a line, chain, or cable with descriptive name based on use; e. g., mooring pendant; (usually pronounced "pen'ant").

pennant
A tapering flag.

pier
Structure extending into the water from shoreline to provide dockage.

pile
A pole or post driven vertically into the bottom, usually to support a pier or float or to moor a boat.

piling
A structure of piles often used to protect wharves and piers.

pitchpole
Capsize end-over-end.

planing hull
A hull design to climb towards the surface of the water as sufficient power is applied and to skim along the water at a greatly reduced displacement attitude.

planking
Boards used for covering the bottom, sides and deck of a vessel.

plow anchor
An anchor shaped like a farmer's plow.

plug
A piece of wood fitted into a hole in a vessel, usually below the waterline.

port
1. Left side of a boat when facing the bow. 2. Toward the boat's left. 3. Opening in a boat's side, e. g., portlight. 4. Harbor.

precipitation
Forms of water particles, solid or liquid, that fall from the atmosphere and reach the ground; drizzle, rain, snow, sleet, or hail.

propeller
A multi-bladed, rotating wheel that furnishes propulsion.

propeller shaft
A rod that transmits power from engine and transmission to propeller.

Q

quarter
1. After part of a boat's side, e.g., port quarter. 2. Direction 45° abaft the beam.

R

radar
An electronic navigational system using reflected radio pulse signals to determine the relative bearing and distance of an object from the vessel.

rail
A boat's side above the deck line.

range
1. Two or more objects in line. 2. Maximum distance at which an object may be seen. 3. Distance between any two points, such as a radar range to a navigational aid. 4. Difference in elevation (height) between any successive pair of high and low tides.

reciprocal
In navigation, a bearing or direction 180° from another bearing or direction.

rode
Anchor line or chain.

rope
Cordage made of natural or synthetic fibers; can be made of steel wire.

round turn
A complete turn of line around a cleat, bitt, or post.

rudder
A flat board or plate hung on the aft end of a boat and used to steer the boat.

rudder post
The shaft to which a rudder blade is attached. The tiller or other steering apparatus is affixed to the other end.

S

schooner
A vessel with two or more masts rigged fore-and-aft, with the forward mast being shorter or equal in height to the aft mast.

scope
Ratio of the length of payed out anchor line (rode) to the height of the chock above the bottom of the body of water.

scupper
An opening in the rail or bulwark to permit water to drain overboard.

sea
A system of wind waves that are still being blown by the wind force that created them. Usually irregular and choppy, unlike swell.

seaworthy
Said of a boat that is in fit condition to put to sea.

secure
To cover openings and make movable objects fast.

Security
The term used to signify a message concerning the safety of navigation under international radiotelephone procedures; the third priority transmission, (pronounced "sea-cur-i-tay").

seize
1. To bind by many wrappings of small line. 2. To secure the pin of a shackle using non-corrosive wire.

shackle
A U-shaped metal device with removable pin used to connect a sail, line, or fitting.

shaft
A cylindrical rod. A rotating shaft is used to transmit power from the engine to the propeller.

skeg
An extension of the keel, or a keel-like projection at the aft end of the hull, for protection of propeller and rudder.

slack
1. Not carrying any load, loose. 2. To ease or pay out a line.

sloop
Single-masted sailboat with the mast stepped less than 40% of boat length aft of the bow and setting a mainsail and normally one triangular headsail.

small stuff
Light line, marline, waxed twine, etc. used for whipping, seizing and serving.

snub
To stop a line running out by taking a turn around a bitt or cleat.

sounding
A measured or charted depth of water, or the measurement of that depth.

speed
Rate of motion.

speed over the ground
Actual speed being achieved relative to the ground.

square knot
A knot used to join two lines of similar size; also called a reef knot.

stability
The ability of a boat to resist heeling and overturning.

staff
An upright pole to which a flag or light is fixed.

stanchion
A vertical post or column used to support a deck, cabin top, or lifelines.

standing part
The part of a rope that is made fast.

stand-on vessel
A term, from the Navigation Rules, used to describe the vessel that continues its course in the same direction at the same speed during a crossing or overtaking situation, unless a collision appears imminent. Compare give-way vessel.

starboard
Side of a boat, or direction, to the right when facing toward the bow.

steerageway
Enough speed to steer the boat.

stem
The upright structural member or post of the bow, attached to the foremost part of a vessel's keel.

stern
After end of a boat.

sternway
Movement stern first, as opposed to headway.

stock
The crossbar of an anchor. Also, a rudder shaft.

stow
To put something in its proper place.

strand
1. To drive a vessel ashore or aground. 2. One of the lays of a rope (the wound yarns or fibers that are woven with other strands to make a rope).

strut
A bracket which supports the propeller shaft; located outside of the hull.

swamp
To fill with water, but not to founder.

swell
A wave system that has outrun or is no longer being acted upon by the wind that created it. A swell is characterized by regular, smooth-crested wave forms, usually of long wave length.

T

tachometer
A device for measuring and indicating the rotational speed of an engine.

thimble
A grooved metal loop, around which a rope or wire rope may be spliced, thus making the spliced eye more resistant to chafing.

thunder
The sound emitted by rapidly expanding air along the channel of a lightning discharge.

thunderstorm
A storm produced by a cumulonimbus cloud. The thunderstorm is accompanied by lightning and thunder, usually with strong gusts, heavy rain, and sometimes hail.

tidal current
The horizontal movement of water caused by tidal action. See also ebb current and flood current.

tidal range
Difference in height of tide between any successive pair of high and low tides.

tide
The vertical rise and fall of ocean water (most noticeable in coastal regions) resulting mainly from the gravitational attraction of the moon and sun.

tiller
A lever attached to the upper end of a rudder stock, used by the helmsman to turn the rudder.

toe rail
A small raised section around the perimeter of the deck.

topside
On or above the weather deck (wholly exposed to the elements).

topsides
The sides of a vessel between the water line and the deck.

transceiver
A radio set which combines transmitting and receiving modes in one package. It may have circuits or components common to both.

transmitter
An electronic unit capable of generating a signal for propagation through a medium.

transom
The portion of the hull at the stern that is at right angles to the centerline of the boat.

trip line
1. A buoyed line attached to the crown of an anchor for the purpose of freeing it when fouled. 2. A line fastened to the small end of the cone of a sea anchor to collapse it, thus spilling the water from the cone.

tropical storm
A distinct rotary circulation; constant wind speed of 39 to 73 miles per hour (34 to 63 knots).

true course
The course as plotted on the chart, measured from true north.

turnbuckle
A tension-adjusting device for tightening wire rigging or cable, composed of threaded rods extending from within a threaded barrel.

typhoon
A severe tropical storm in the western Pacific or the China Sea; same as a hurricane except for location.

U

under power
A boat being propelled by an engine even though sail may be set.

underway
1. Making progress through the water. 2. Afloat, but not at anchor, aground, or made fast to the shore.

urgent call
See Pan-Pan.

V

variation
The angle between the geographic meridian and the magnetic meridian at a given locality. Variation is easterly or westerly, as the direction of the magnetic meridian is toward the east or west of geographic north.

visibility
The greatest distance at which one can see and recognize prominent objects.

W
wake
Water surface turbulence left by a moving boat.

warning
In weather advisories, a bulletin indicating that a hazardous condition, such as a tornado or flash flood, is in existence and may threaten some portion of the warning area.

watch
1. In weather advisories, a bulletin indicating that a hazardous condition, such as a tornado or flash flood, may develop. 2. A period of time during which a crew member is on duty.

wave
In water, a series of undulations that move along the surface.

way
Movement of a vessel through the water, such as headway, sternway, or leeway.

weather
1. The condition of the atmosphere at any given time and place. 2. The windward side.

winch
A geared drum turned by a handle and used to pull lines such as sheets and halyards.

wind
Horizontal motion of the air, reported in both speed and direction.

working end
The outboard or free end of a line, chain, or cable, used to make knots, bends, and splices and to attach to an anchor, cleat, other vessel, etc.